ELCOMED HOME ON THE CONCLUSION OF MY ENGLAND–NEW ZEALAND FLIC
OCTOBER 16, 1936

Photo "Auckland Star"

JEAN BATTEN : MY LIFE

New Zealand's greatest woman pilot

by

Jean Batten

Trotamundas Press

Trotamundas Press Ltd.
The Meridian, 4 Copthall House, Station Square, Coventry
CV1 2FL, UK

"Jean Batten : My Life " by Jean Batten

First published in 1938 by George G.Harrap &Co.Ltd

copyright © 2010 of this edition, Trotamundas Press Ltd.

ISBN: 978-1-906393-19-9

Trotamundas Press is an international publisher specializing in travel literature written by women travellers from different countries and cultures.

Our mission is to bring back into print great travel books written by women around the world which have been forgotten. We publish in several languages.

It is our privilege to rescue those travel stories which were widely acclaimed in the past and that are still relevant nowadays to help us understand better the diversity of the countries and the world.

The travel stories also make an enjoyable reading, full of adventure and the excitement of discovery.

We are proud to help preserving the memory of all those amazing women travellers which were unjustly forgotten and hope that you will enjoy reading about their interesting experiences as much as we have enjoyed researching them.

www.trotamundaspress.com

**Jean Batten
(1909-1982)**

Jean Batten was born on September 15, 1909 in Rotorua, a spa town on the North Island of New Zealand. Her father was a dentist and when Jean was four years old the family moved to Auckland, where she attended private schools. When her parents divorced in 1920, Jean stayed with her mother, while her two brothers lived with her father. Eventually the two sides of the family ceased all contact with one another.

Jean was a talented pianist but her destiny changed when her father took her in 1928 to an outing in Auckland where the star speaker was the aviator Charles Kingsford-Smith who was one of Australia's heroes of the era and had been the first pilot to fly from Australia to the United States by the challenging eastward route.

Despite her father's opposition, Jean's mother took her side and encouraged her daughter's dream to become a pilot. The two women moved to London, England where Jean's brother John had found some success as a film actor. Jean took flying lessons at the London Aero Club in Stag Lane and in December 1930 she qualified for her private pilot's license and within a year had received a commercial license as well. Jean took courses in plane mechanics and maintenance and was willing to get her hands dirty in the grittier side work that flying entailed.

Jean Batten's immediate goal was to break the solo flight record from England to Australia that Amy Johnson had established in early 1930. She needed a plane in order to fulfill her ambition and she sold her prized piano to raise some funds and secured the rest thanks to one of her admirers, an englishman called Victor Doree who helped her obtain her first plane, a bi-wing, de Havilland Gipsy Moth.

Jean took off in pursuit of Amy Johnson's 20 day England to Australia flight record in April 1933 but a sandstorm caused her engine to fail and she crashed in Karachi, Pakistan. Jean escaped serious injury but the plane was a wreck. After returning to England, the Castrol Oil Company bought her another Gipsy Moth.

Jean's second attempt at Johnson's record began on April 21, 1934 but she miscalculated fuel consumption and damaged her plane while making an emergency landing outside Rome. Her third attempt on May 8, 1934 was successful and after flying more than 10,500 miles she bettered Amy Johnson's record by more than six days. Jean Batten reached Darwin, Australia and became an international hero. She bought a new aircraft, a Percival Gull monoplane, which was perfectly suited for long distance record attempts. On November 11, 1935, Jean set off in pursuit of another record, the best time from England to South America. After flying to Dakar, Senegal, Jean began the most dangerous part of her journey, a 1,900 mile leg over the South Atlantic to Port Natal in Brazil. She used only a watch and a compass to guide her and made the transatlantic trip in 13 hours, 15 minutes. Jean Batten had become the first woman to pilot a plane across the South Atlantic.

One year later, on October 5, 1936 Jean set out to better the England to New Zealand record. She made it to Australia in six days and then after waiting a few days for better weather conditions over the Tasman Sea, she left for New Zealand. The total journey of 14,224 miles had taken 11 days, 45 minutes and set a record that would stand for another 44 years.

Soon after, Jean faced some personal hardships. During her hero's tour of New Zealand, she suffered a nervous breakdown and went into seclusion with her mother. After recuperating she travelled to Sydney in February 1937 to reunite with her fiancé, Beverly Shephard, but on the day she arrived, he died in a plane crash. He was the only man she truly loved and Jean sunk into a deep depression.

It took her another eight months to fly again.

In October 1937, Jean set another record, and her final one, by flying from Australia to England in five days,18 hours and 15 minutes. As a result, Jean Batten became the first person to simultaneously hold the solo flight records between England and Australia in both directions.

After this final record, Jean and her mother travelled the world unnoticed. Although Jean resurfaced for a while during World War II, she and her mother returned to seclusion after the war in the Spanish Island of Majorca. Her mother died in 1966 and after a short return to public life in 1969, Jean became a recluse again. On November 22, 1982 Jean died of an infection caused by a dog bite whish she had refused to have treated.

Because people in Majorca did not know who she was, she received a burial in an unmarked pauper's grave. Friends who corresponded with her began to worry when they had not heard from her in some time and a cursory inquiry was launched but soon dropped. Finally, a documentary filmmaker and writer, Ian Mackersey, went to Majorca in search of her and discovered that she had died five years earlier.

A plaque was put in her grave and eventually a street was named in her memory. Jean Batten's Percival Gull plane is preserved at Auckland Airport, where the international terminal is named after her. A bronze sculpture of Jean is now located in the main terminal of the Rotorua Airport and a small park in the middle of the city is also named after her.

CONTENTS

CHAPTER   PAGE

I. EARLY LIFE   15

II. ENGLAND CALLS   23

III. FLIGHT TO AUSTRALIA   32

IV. OVER ASIA   51

V. ARRIVAL IN SYDNEY   68

VI. INTERLUDE   82

VII. RETURN FLIGHT   95

VIII. SOUTH AMERICAN FLIGHT   104

IX. SAND AND SUN   119

X. SHOCKS AT THIES   133

XI. ACROSS THE SOUTH ATLANTIC   148

XII. RIO DE JANEIRO   162

XIII. BUENOS AIRES AND MONTEVIDEO   175

XIV. INVITATION TO PARIS   197

XV. AERIAL TOUR   203

XVI. SOLO TO NEW ZEALAND   220

XVII. SOUTHWARD FROM SINGAPORE   236

XVIII. ACROSS THE TASMAN SEA   247

XIX. AUSTRALIA   259

XX. FLIGHT TO ENGLAND   272

XXI. GUEST OF HONOUR   290

ILLUSTRATIONS

PAGE

WELCOMED HOME ON THE CONCLUSION OF MY
ENGLAND–NEW ZEALAND FLIGHT   *Frontispiece*

AT STAG LANE AERODROME   26

BEING GREETED BY COLONEL TEMPESTI AT ROME   27

SUPERVISING THE ENGINE WORK AT CALCUTTA   58

ACKNOWLEDGING THE WELCOME ON ARRIVAL AT SYDNEY   59

A MAORI GREETING   88

TAKING OFF FOR ENGLAND   89

THE PRESIDENT OF BRAZIL, DR VARGAS, CONFERS UPON
ME THE ORDER OF THE SOUTHERN CROSS   170

MY ARRIVAL AT BUENOS AIRES   171

BEING WELCOMED TO URUGUAY BY THE PRESIDENT'S
DAUGHTER   192

AT THE SORBONNE   193

WITH MY MOTHER AND OFFICERS OF THE SPANISH AIR
FORCE AT SEVILLE   210

RECEIVING THE CROSS OF THE LEGION OF HONOUR
FROM LIEUTENANT-COLONEL WATEAU   211

WITH THE GULL AT HATFIELD AERODROME   220

A FILM INTERVIEW BEFORE LEAVING FOR NEW
ZEALAND   221

THE GULL TAKES OFF INTO THE DAWN BOUND FOR
NEW ZEALAND   238

MOUNT EGMONT, NEW ZEALAND   239

FLYING OVER AUCKLAND   252

ARRIVING AT AUCKLAND   253

TROUT-FISHING AT LAKE WAKATIPU   260

SEARCHING FOR THE MISSING AIR LINER   261

MAGNETIC ANTHILLS NEAR DARWIN   268

CUSTOMS CLEARANCE DOCUMENT FROM PORT DARWIN   269

AT RAMBANG WITH THE DUTCH ADMINISTRATOR,
    M. BAKKER, AND HIS PARTY   282

THE AERODROME AT NICOSIA AFTER THE CLOUDBURST   283

THE WELCOME AT CROYDON   288

AT THE ROYAL AERO CLUB RECEPTION   289

BEING TELEVISED AT THE B.B.C. STUDIOS, ALEXANDRA
    PALACE   292

TEA AT THE MANSION HOUSE WITH THE LORD MAYOR
    AND LADY TWYFORD AND VISCOUNT WAKEFIELD   293

WITH " JEAN BATTEN " AT MADAME TUSSAUD'S   296

ARRIVAL AT STOCKHOLM   297

CHAPTER I: EARLY LIFE

I WAS BORN IN NEW ZEALAND ON SEPTEMBER 15, 1909, six weeks after Blériot's historic flight across the English Channel. At that time my father, a dental surgeon, practised in the town of Rotorua, in the heart of the thermal district. This region, abounding in geysers, mineral springs, pools of boiling mud, and every kind of thermal activity, is vastly different from any other in New Zealand and unique in the world. At an early age I took a great delight in the wonders of Nature amid which we lived. In the beautiful gardens in the centre of the town were mineral waters of every description where people from many parts of the world came to find health and put new life into their disabled or paralysed limbs. The people who visited New Zealand, whether they came to see the great snow-covered ranges and lovely lakes of the big South Island or the glorious scenery of the North, or to indulge in the winter sports or to catch the gigantic deep-sea fish or the lovely salmon trout, one and all visited Rotorua to see its wonders before returning to their own countries. So it was that a large part of the population of the town was composed of tourists, and my parents entertained an interesting variety of sportsmen and travelled people.

It was therefore not surprising that even at the early age of two years I had developed a great desire to roam. One afternoon the town was thrown into an upheaval at my disappearance. The house and garden were searched by my anxious mother, who only discovered that I had after much endeavour managed to negotiate the little gate on the wide veranda, and which for some time past had proved a barrier to the outside world, which I had on more than one occasion set off to explore. Eventually I was discovered contentedly playing on the floor of a stable among the horses, which had fortunately stood quiet. My mother used to ride a lovely milk-white mare, and to my great delight she would sometimes hold me on the front of the saddle and speed along like the wind.

I never ceased to wonder and marvel at the great bubbling mud pools, the streams where hot and cold water ran side by side, where the Maori women used to wash clothes and cook, and the warm pools invariably filled with chubby, laughing native children splashing about and playing. "Where does it come from?" I would ask my two brothers, clasping their hands tightly as we stared at crevices in the ground from which came blasts of steam while we listened to the thumping of little gas explosions under the ground. It was always great fun when the family went to see these thermal wonders and an outing of which we children never tired. My elder brother would sometimes 'make magic,' as he called it, and putting a copper in some dark wet sand would laugh at my amazement as the chemicals turned the penny silver. Then he would place a silver coin in a pool, where it was turned black. Gasps of admiration and delight used to accompany a display by one of the geysers sending a huge column of boiling water into the air, sometimes nearly a hundred feet high.

No two of the ever-fascinating wonders were quite alike. In some places pale pink and white bubbling mud made pretty flower patterns, while in others large pools of black mud splashed up like miniature volcanoes. There were also fairylike caves patterned with yellow sulphur crystals, silica deposits forming even little terraces; exquisite crystal-like waterfalls showered down over pure white rocks, and jet-like streams of water rose high into the sky.

It is not to be wondered at that when practically a baby I developed a vivid imagination and deep appreciation of beauty. My father was a very keen yachtsman, and we would often sail in his lovely yacht across the shimmering blue waters of the lakes near which we lived. Sometimes we would sail over Lake Taupo and set up camp on the far shore. This great freshwater lake is twenty-five miles across, and is set like a great sapphire amid magnificent scenery in the heart of the North Island. There were delicious pink trout to be caught in the lake, and my two brothers would climb the big cherry-trees planted by early missionaries and return with baskets laden with fruit. They were happy days, and I used to like gathering the lovely ferns and gorgeously coloured wild flowers in the bush and listening to the beautiful songs of the native birds.

The family moved to Auckland when I was only four years of age, and there my home has been ever since. Scarcely three months after we had settled in our new home Britain entered the World War. My father had long been interested in military matters, and held a commission in the Territorial Army. Immediately the news came through he enlisted in company with other officers. I was too young to realize the full significance of the event, and New Zealand too far away to feel the deadly effect of the War immediately. I could not understand what it all meant—only that the hundreds and hundreds of men in khaki who marched down the street to the stirring tunes of the bands boarded ships and sailed far away from our island to the other side of the world. It was not until, tightly clasping my mother's hand, I stood on the quay and watched the ship taking my father away that I began to realize what a wrench it was. My two brothers were twelve and fourteen years of age, and I was barely five, so that for the next two years the full responsibility of bringing up the family was to rest on my mother's shoulders. The ship with its khaki-clad figures became blurred as I strove to keep my tears back and my mother looked at me with her large dark eyes and reminded me that brave girls never cried.

There was always great excitement when the mail arrived, and we would gather round as my mother read passages from my father's letters, written " Somewhere in France." Sometimes letters came from London, and my brothers would open the atlas and trace a line right across the page to where they would triumphantly show me the position of the great city. "Look—all this way!" they would say "Right across the sea to Australia, and over the equator, and away up there," pointing to England or France. "That's where Dad is now." They were always pleased when I was suitably impressed, and laughed heartily when I once announced that some day I too would cross the sea to London.

One day a letter arrived which on being opened disclosed a bunch of violets specially for me. A note read that my father had gathered them in the woods of France. Looking at the little purple and white flowers, I was intrigued. "Were they really growing wild in the bush?" I asked my mother incredulously, thinking of the violets in our garden which she tended so carefully. I knew there were lovely native flowers growing in the bush among the ferns and tangled undergrowth—the brilliant rata, silvery clematis, and yellow kowhai—but anything so delicate as a wild violet seemed to my mind almost unthinkable. "We will go to England and France one day, won't we?" I had asked my mother. We experienced a vague idea, of the deadly effect of war when troopships brought hundreds of wounded, maimed, and blind men home in place of the happy, strong boys who had gone forth so eagerly to fight for their country.

After two years my father returned; also two of my mother's brothers, who fought at Gallipoli. When the interesting-looking military trunk belonging to my father was opened it disclosed all manner of wonderful things which gave pleasure to my brothers and me: plans, books, maps, and to my delight a small compass, which interested me more than anything else. " It's a bearing compass," my father had explained. " North, south, east, west," he added, showing me the cardinal points on the graduated dial. " Oh, can I have it? " I had pleaded. " No, not now," he had replied, adding, " I shall give it to you some day when you are a big girl."

The War had been a big blow to every one, and among others my father had to start in business all over again, for his practice had been closed while he had been away. At this time I was attending a preparatory school, and my two brothers were going to college. As we lived not far from the sea swimming was our favourite sport, and one at which my brothers excelled. I had always loved the sea, and even as a baby had clung to my mother as she swam with me on her back. At five years of age I had been able to swim, and as I grew older swimming remained the sport in which I delighted most.

In 1919 great interest was aroused in Australia and New Zealand when an air race from England to Australia was organized. A big prize of some thousands of pounds was offered to the winner, and almost one month after the commencement of the race the Vickers machine piloted by the two brothers Ross and Keith Smith (both afterwards knighted) landed on Australian soil, completing the first flight from England to that Dominion. With their crew the two brothers were fêted by their country, and even in New Zealand there was tremendous excitement at their arrival in Darwin, which was afterwards to witness the landings of other great pilots who strove as time went on to lessen the time between England and Australia. Although I was only ten years of age, this flight impressed me tremendously, for the same year we had heard of the great pioneer flight across the Atlantic from Newfoundland to Ireland by John Alcock and Arthur Whitten Brown.

When I grew older I was sent to board at a very beautiful college, which was designed on the lines of a small castle and situated amid wide lawns and lovely gardens. The headmistress was an Englishwoman, and with her daughters endeavoured to instil the English traditions into the pupils. The time I spent at the college was a happy one. My favourite subject was, I think, geography. I was very fond of art too, and had evinced a deep love of music. I passed several music examinations, and was very pleased on one occasion when an original design for a poster which I painted won a silver medal in an exhibition. All New Zealanders are fond of sport, and I was never happier than when indulging in one game or another or striving earnestly for my team in a basket-ball match or tennis tournament.

For many years books of travel and adventure had increased my enthusiasm and longing to travel abroad. One school vacation had been spent in Sydney, but this experience only made me want to see more of the world. In 1928 two events occurred which may have indirectly helped me to find the element for which I was evidently destined. The first solo flight from England to Australia was completed by Squadron-Leader Hinkler, who achieved the then astounding time of fifteen days for the flight. Shortly afterwards Charles Kingsford Smith, Charles Ulm, and their companions flew across the Pacific Ocean from America to Australia, thus linking the two countries by air for the first time. I was deeply interested in these two flights, and when later Charles Kingsford Smith flew over the Tasman Sea to New Zealand my enthusiasm for aviation increased and I decided to become a pilot.

CHAPTER II: ENGLAND CALLS

S EVERAL FLYING CLUBS WERE ALREADY IN existence in New Zealand, but my enthusiasm was frowned on by my father. "It's very dangerous," he had told me when I asked to join a club, "and very expensive," he added in a stern voice.

I had met Kingsford Smith during his tour of New Zealand, and when early the following year I again visited Australia he offered to take me for a flight. Cruising about high above the Blue Mountains I had felt completely at home in the air and decided that here indeed was my element. I was even more determined to fly myself, but as my father was opposed to any such idea there was the apparently insurmountable obstacle of finance. When I suggested selling my piano to help raise the amount necessary to learn to fly there was great consternation in my family.

My mother was going to visit England early in 1929, so I decided to accompany her. In England it seemed I should be in the centre of flying activity, and it would not be so difficult to make a start. It seemed that I was well and truly burning my bridges when very reluctantly I consulted an auctioneer and sold my beloved piano. Barely nineteen, I declared to my astonished father that I was old enough to make my own decisions and had decided to make a career for myself in aviation.

As we travelled to England a new world was opened up to me: crossing the line and seeing the North Star for the first time; meeting new people, forming new impressions; the quaint shops, rickshaws, temples, and gardens of Ceylon; crossing the Red Sea; the Suez Canal; the natives, coloured cloths, camels and sand of Port Said; then lovely Naples, at the base of mighty Vesuvius, the impressive rock of Gibraltar, and finally . . . England.

The immensity of London astounded me, and I marvelled at the smooth, efficient way in which the great city was run. The tremendous number of people was bewildering, for the total population of my own country was less than two millions. With the help of a guide-book and many maps we learned the names of the principal streets, and gradually began to find our way about with less difficulty. Happy days were spent exploring the wonderful sights of London and the historical buildings which for so many years had been merely names to me: Westminster Abbey, the Houses of Parliament, Big Ben, Whitehall, and Trafalgar Square; the Tower of London, the British Museum and various art galleries, Hyde Park, and even the Old Curiosity Shop, which we were thrilled to discover hidden among the high modern buildings. We were also deeply interested to watch the changing of the guard at Buckingham Palace, and visits to Windsor

Castle, Kew Gardens, Hampton Court, and Richmond were all crowded into those first few weeks in England, which were in the nature of a revelation to me.

A short time after our arrival I made inquiries about the different flying clubs. My mother, who already sympathized in my keen interest in flying, agreed to help me. We went together to the London Aeroplane Club, where I joined and commenced training.

Very soon I was being initiated into the art of flying an aeroplane straight and level; then followed hours of careful practice in turning, gliding, landing, etc. At that time the London Aeroplane Club, now at Hatfield, had its headquarters at Stag Lane Aerodrome, which has since been closed and built upon. Stag Lane Aerodrome takes a prominent place in aviation history, for it was there that Captain Geoffrey De Havilland designed and tested the first of the Moth aeroplanes, which became so universally popular. In addition, the London Aeroplane Club has the unique distinction of having trained or numbered among its members the majority of the famous and well-known women pilots. Among these were Lady Heath, the first airwoman to fly to South Africa; the Duchess of Bedford, who with a co-pilot made several flights to India and Africa; Lady Bailey, first airwoman to make a return flight to Cape Town; Miss Winifred Spooner, well known in international and competitive events; Miss Amy Johnson, famous for her many great flights; the Hon. Mrs Victor Bruce, who flew to Japan only a few months after taking her ticket; Miss Joy Muntz, afterwards test pilot for an aviation company; Miss Pauline Gower, who operated an aerial taxi service with Miss Dorothy Spicer, first airwoman to hold all aviation engineering licences; Miss Joan Meakin, well known in gliding circles in England and abroad. These are some of the airwomen who received their training at this club or were members of it, and whom I used frequently to meet during the happy years when I flew the familiar yellow Moths at Stag Lane.

When I had completed a few hours' flying and passed tests for the A licence I optimistically though vainly tried to obtain backing for a flight to Australia which I had contemplated even before leaving New Zealand. Thinking that it might not be so difficult to interest people in my own country and hoping that my father might help, I sailed home to New Zealand.

Although my father had not known I was learning to fly until I obtained my licence he was very pleased when he saw me give a display of aerobatics at the local club which I joined on arriving back in Auckland. He was, however, not at all enthusiastic about the prospect of his only daughter flying across the world alone. Considerable doubt was expressed, in view of the fact that I had only a few hours' solo flying to my credit, of the advisability of making such a long flight alone. None of my relatives or the people whom I interviewed would help in any way, and admitted that they did not wish to take the responsibility of financing such a flight.

The urge, however, was very strong within me, and I returned to England in June 1931 to study for the commercial or B licence, as I considered that the

AT STAG LANE AERODROME
Photo Barratt's Photo Press Ltd.

BEING GREETED BY COLONEL TEMPESTI AT ROME

Photo Agenzia Fotografica Italiana, Rome

[*See p.* 35]

possession of this ticket would give me a certain amount of prestige in further efforts to obtain finance for the flight. There was a great deal of study in connexion with the commercial licence, and examinations to be passed in navigation, air legislature, elementary meteorology, and inspection of aircraft and engines, etc. In addition to the general flying and cross-country tests there was also a solo night flight to be completed between Croydon and Lympne. It was necessary for a candidate to have completed a hundred hours' solo flying, and in view of the small allowance I received from home and the fact that to hire an aeroplane for one hour cost thirty shillings it was very difficult to make ends meet.

For some time I had been studying hard and saving up for the B licence examination. As I wished to increase my knowledge of engineering I took a course in general maintenance of aircraft and engines in the workshop of the London Aeroplane Club. In order to arrive punctually at 8 A.M. every morning I took lodgings near Stag Lane Aerodrome.

For several months the day used to be spent in the hangar, where attired in overalls I worked on the engines with the regular mechanics and in the evenings attended lectures and studied navigation. Rain, snow, or fine, I somehow managed to arrive punctually each morning, and the aeroplanes, carefully inspected, would be wheeled out of the big hangar, propellers swung, and engines warmed up. After being refuelled they were taxied round to the front of the club-house in readiness for the day's flying. Our chief engineer was very conscientious and thorough, and in the workshops I learned the importance of careful inspection of aircraft and engine before flight.

About this time a great depression was afflicting world commerce, and New Zealand, almost entirely dependent on primary produce, felt the trade slump very deeply. When I was half-way through the tests for my commercial licence my income was stopped. I had already made frequent trips to the pawnbroker in order to keep up my solo flying, so that when fate dealt me this dreadful blow I had no reserve to fall back on. Fortunately my mother saved the situation by providing the funds necessary to enable me to complete the tests and continue flying. In spite of this, however, I felt very worried when on a murky night in November I flew to Croydon to complete tests for my cross-country night flight. I knew that if I failed it would not be possible to sit again because of the expense involved.

Just as I was about to take off on the return flight from Lympne my instructor hurried across to the aeroplane and handed me a small torch, which proved of vital importance on that memorable night. Only about fifteen minutes after I had left the aerodrome the navigation lights failed owing to a loose terminal, and the machine was plunged into darkness. None of the instruments was luminous, and my predicament was an unenviable one as I sat in the dark cockpit flashing the torch on the instrument panel. The aeroplane was reported flying over Biggin Hill without lights, and when at last the red beacon at Croydon appeared ahead

I sighed with relief. Circling the aerodrome several times and flashing my torch I eventually saw the green rocket signal for me to land pierce the darkness beneath, and, shutting off the engine, glided down to a landing on the floodlit pathway. Although I arrived home in the early hours of the morning I returned to Croydon after breakfast to complete the final test, comprising a series of spins.

After gaining the commercial licence I felt very sorry for my relatives and friends who had tried to dissuade me from attempting to fly. My family, however, gave up all further attempts to put me off my plan, realizing that opposition only made me keener to attain the apparently unattainable. Once my mind was set on anything it was quite useless to attempt to swerve me from my purpose or dampen my enthusiasm in any way.

One day at the club I met a pilot who was interested in my plan for a solo flight to Australia and agreed to help finance the flight. I was to have a half-share in a second-hand Moth which was to be purchased. In return I signed an agreement to give the other pilot 50 per cent. of any proceeds ensuing from that flight and to tour Australia and New Zealand for twelve months afterwards giving passenger flights.

After months of preparation and organization I took off for Australia in April 1933. My first non-stop flight of almost a thousand miles to Rome caused considerable comment. All went well until I arrived in India, where a major engine-failure occurred in which a connecting-rod broke and went through the side of the crankcase when I was flying at an altitude of only 500 feet and nearing an aerodrome. I made a forced landing, fortunately without any personal injury. The engine trouble would never have occurred had the engine been of a later design or the connecting-rods modified before leaving England. I was far too proud to ask anyone for help, but actually everything I possessed had gone into the flight, and I was now considerably in debt and practically penniless. It was at this stage that I first experienced the kindness and generosity of Lord Wakefield, who has for many years been connected with the most successful events in the world of sport. He had been interested in my progress during the flight to India, and with his customary generosity arranged for me to travel back to England.

On my arrival in London it was to find that the part-owner of the machine was not interested in another projected flight to Australia, so the aeroplane was sold and afterwards reconditioned. Fortunately I was able to interest Lord Wakefield, who agreed to help me finance another flight.

In April 1934, after I had set off again, I had one of the most thrilling experiences of my career. Having battled with head winds on a flight from Marseilles to Rome, my aeroplane ran out of petrol at midnight in teeming rain and pitch darkness over the Italian capital. Gliding the silent machine to the outskirts of the city I managed to bring it safely down with very little damage in a small field surrounded by wireless masts. When I saw this field in daylight I was astounded at my miraculous escape. The masts between which I had glided were some hundreds of feet high; bordering the field were high-tension wires over which I had glided in the darkness, and only twenty-five yards in front of the spot where I landed was the high embankment of the river Tiber.

About a week afterwards I flew my aeroplane back to London to make a fresh start. My reason for returning to England instead of flying on was that I was reluctant to add the week spent in Rome on to my time, for I wished to make a reasonably fast flight through to Australia. It was my intention to establish at least a women's record for the journey, realizing that my aeroplane was not suitable for anything faster at this stage.

CHAPTER III: FLIGHT TO AUSTRALIA

ALTHOUGH I ONLY ARRIVED BACK IN England from Rome on May 6, 1934, I set off again at dawn on May 8, accompanied with the good luck that has flown with me ever since.

The aeroplane which I flew was by no means a modern one: in fact, it was fifth-hand and nearly five years old. I had bought it for the modest sum of £260, and after spending a considerable amount on having the engine overhauled and a number of modified and new parts fitted thought it capable of flying the 12,700 odd miles to Sydney without failing me. On looking through the log-books I had found that the history of the aeroplane was an extremely interesting one. The Gipsy I Moth had been purchased from the manufacturers in 1929 by a Flight-Lieutenant. He was stationed at Amman, in Transjordania, and flew the Moth across Holland, Germany, Austria, Hungary, Rumania, Bulgaria, Turkey, and Syria to his base. It was kept there for some time, and frequently visited Baghdad and Cyprus, and made various flights over the Holy Land. At one stage it was flown to Baghdad, where the wings were removed and transferred to an aeroplane that had crashed in Persia. It was afterwards sold and flown back to England by Flight-Lieutenant Atcherley, of Schneider Cup fame. In England the Moth changed hands again, being on this occasion bought by an aircraft firm, who in turn sold it to the French airwoman Madeleine Charnaux, who did a considerable amount of flying with the machine. Later the Moth was damaged at Marrakesh, in Morocco, and eventually found its way once again to England, where it was traded in to an aircraft firm as part payment for a new machine. The aeroplane was used for passenger flying and instructional purposes in Wales, where an accident befell it. When it was being reconditioned I heard of the machine, and, thinking the Moth the bargain it ultimately transpired to be, bought it with the limited funds at my disposal.

The cruising speed of this veteran was only 80 m.p.h. Therefore the schedule of fourteen days which I had set myself was a fairly ambitious one. The route I planned to follow differed from that taken on previous flights to Australia. Instead of calling at Aleppo, in French Syria, as I had done on my flight to India, I intended to fly along the Mediterranean to the eastern end and land on the island of Cyprus, then cross the Lebanon Mountains to Damascus and the Syrian Desert to Baghdad. From there I would fly along the usual route to Australia *via* Persia, India, Burma, Malaya, and the Dutch East Indies. This route was about five hundred miles farther than the route across Central Europe, and entailed the crossing of considerable stretches of water.

I looked forward to visiting Cyprus, and planned to make the first direct solo flight to that historic island from England.

Britain's only possession in the Levant, the island of Cyprus had always intrigued me, and as a child, reading of the Crusaders, I had looked at it on the map of the world, where it appears as a tiny red dot at the eastern end of the Mediterranean, and resolved to go there if ever I had the opportunity.

On the take-off from Lympne my heavily laden Moth climbed gallantly above the boundary of the aerodrome and over the misty Channel towards the coast of France. It was bitterly cold sitting in the open cockpit and exposed to the icy blast of the slipstream from the propeller. Despite the fact that I was wearing a leather helmet, goggles, a heavy lined flying-suit, and fur gloves, I felt the cold dreadfully. South of Paris I was obliged to fly at 7000 feet, owing to low clouds on the mountains, and very soon my hand gripping the control column became numb with the cold. After a cup of coffee from the thermos flask I felt better, and my spirits rose as I passed over Lyons and the sun came timidly from behind the clouds. Away to the east I could see the great snow-capped peaks of the Alps, and as I flew down the Rhône valley I began to enjoy the flight. Valence, Montélimar, and Avignon slipped beneath the wings of my Moth as I flew southward. At times I would almost lose sight of the Rhône as it made great sweeping curves, as if loath to leave any of the pasture-land ungraced by its beauty.

On arrival at Marseilles six and a half hours after

leaving England I cleared customs while the machine was being refuelled, and had a welcome cup of coffee with my friend M. Fournier, controller of the aerodrome. The weather report was fair, so within an hour I took off for Rome. My course lay over the Étoile Mountains to the French coast, thence over the Mediterranean and the island of Corsica to Italy. After I had left sunny St Tropez, on the Riviera, it seemed almost an eternity before the majestic snowy peaks of the mountains of Corsica came into view. Very soon I passed over the rugged coast and the little town of Bastia, with its white houses clustered together, then out over the sea again. Pianosa island lay ahead, and to the north I could see the island of Elba, and to the south the island of Monte Cristo. As I neared the coast of Italy I realized it was going to be a race against the sun if I were to arrive in Rome before dark.

The sun sank rapidly lower as I speeded towards the Italian capital. The little white villages over which I passed at intervals soon became enveloped in the purple shadows, and here and there a light gleamed through the misty veil which furtively spread itself over the countryside. At last. There were the lights of Rome ahead, and as I flew over the aerodrome I was relieved to find the landing lights already on for me. It was nearly 8 P.M., local time, as I landed and taxied up to the tarmac, where I found my Italian friends waiting for me. I had flown a thousand miles, for I had left Brooklands before clearing customs at Lympne, and had been in the air for thirteen and a half hours, so I enjoyed the luxury of the new aerodrome hotel, and fell asleep the moment my head touched the silken softness of the pillow.

The Littorio Aerodrome is large and beautifully appointed, but owing to its proximity to the river Tiber there is frequently an early morning mist covering its smooth surface. The air was quite clear next morning, however, and a clear sky gave promise of a fine day. The large hangars are raised above the level of the aerodrome and approached up a wide concrete ramp.

Although I had been at Littorio before, I always experienced a distinctly unpleasant sensation when I watched my aeroplane being wheeled from the hangar to the edge of the ramp. The two Italian mechanics pointed the nose of the Moth down the centre of the ramp, then gave the machine a push, whereupon it ran swiftly down the fairly steep incline and came to rest on the tarmac below. The mechanics laughed at my anxiety. " Why don't you sit in the machine? " I had asked one of them. " Oh, no," he answered, laughing, "it might run over the edge." This method of pushing the aeroplane down the ramp was the usual procedure at Littorio, and I have seen aeroplanes of all sizes run down the steep ramp unattended, and have never heard of one running over the side.

While the engine was warming up the customs officer arrived with my journey log-book, which he had retained overnight together with my Certificate of Airworthiness, registration papers, my passport and *carnet de passage*. I accompanied him over to the control office, where I paid the landing and hangar fees, signed the declaration forms, cleared customs for Greece, and obtained a weather report for Brindisi and Athens. This was the usual procedure with slight variations at each stopping-place on the way to Australia. Few people realize that flying an aeroplane to different countries is similar to sailing a ship to foreign ports, and at most places the same declaration forms and customs manifests stating the name of the captain of the vessel, passengers, crew, freight, destination, etc., are used for ship and aeroplane.

The weather report on this occasion was a very detailed one and written in Italian. After puzzling over it for a few minutes I grasped the main text: fair with low cloud on the Apennines and the wind N.N.W. at 15–20 m.p.h. Putting the report into my pocket, I decided to read it again on the flight to Naples. All these formalities took time, and were always most distasteful so early in the morning. However, I silently blessed the officials for arriving punctually at such an unearthly hour and completing them comparatively quickly. The Moth had been refuelled the previous night in accordance with my usual procedure, so there was only the engine to check and test before I took off. Bidding good-bye I was soon in the air, speeding on my way to Naples.

Rome looked very lovely in the early morning light, although the streets were still deserted owing to the earliness of the hour. I recognized parts of the city with which I was familiar. On a previous visit I had spent seven delightful days as guest of Mr Reason, secretary of the Air Attaché, and with Mrs Reason had visited most of the famous beauty-spots. Many unforgettable hours had been passed marvelling at the excavations and admiring the exquisite beauty of the gardens. It was most intriguing to walk through the streets of Rome and see the high rush screens which Signor Mussolini ordered should always be placed round an area where excavations were in progress until the work was finished and the beauty discovered revealed in full. In one of the main streets I had seen two large coloured panels depicting the maps of the Roman Empire as it was at the height of its power and as it is to-day. The contrast, of course, was very striking, and evidently intended to create a desire in the minds of young Italians to rebuild the Roman Empire. There was the place of St Peter with its fountains, the Colosseum, the Capitol, the ancient Forum, and the Arch of Constantine, under which Marshal Balbo and his companions had driven in triumph after their flight across the Atlantic. All these sights I was able to identify again as I flew over Rome towards the Pontine Marshes. As I flew southward I glimpsed the Appian Way, leading like a slender ribbon towards Naples. The sight brought back memories of a most enjoyable drive along that ancient highway. We had driven slowly over the strong white cobblestones and stopped occasionally to gaze in wonder at the ancient monuments and tombs which stand like sentinels on each side of the Appian Way. Some of the tombs, crumbling with age, had been built up with cement into which had been pressed fragments of pottery and exquisitely carved broken pieces of terra-cotta and marble. It seemed to be the general rule in Rome that any pieces of carving or pottery unearthed during excavations were to be preserved in this fashion on the site of their discovery. So it was that one would come upon new blocks of flats or houses with assorted fragments discovered during the building artistically decorating an arch or the side of a wall.

I always enjoyed the flight from Rome to Naples, and this occasion was no exception. The beauty of each successive scene, framed by the silver wings of my Moth as I looked from the cockpit, suggested a great painting, for the colours seemed too vivid and the range too great to be real. Flying along the coast I would cross occasional headlands and come suddenly upon a silvery strand of beach on which small fishing-boats would be drawn up and groups of fishermen busily engaged in spreading their nets. Little villages dotted the coast, and the cluster of white houses formed a striking contrast to the sapphire-blue of the Mediterranean, and the great purple, snow-capped Apennines towered away into the distance. Soon I saw the grey pennant of smoke from Vesuvius, and, arriving over Naples, altered course to cross the Apennines. I had been to Naples before too, but I never appreciated its beauty from the ground as I did from above. Seen from the air at sunset just as the tiny white lights outline the bay and the last rays of the sun tint the snowy mountain peaks, Naples beggars description. Low cloud shrouded the highest peaks, and the early morning mist had not yet cleared from the valleys. I flew high above the clouds where only an occasional peak was to be seen piercing the white carpet beneath me. Once across the mountains I met good weather, and landed at the San Vito dei Normanni Aerodrome, Brindisi, to refuel.

After lunch with the charming Italian Air Force officers I took off for Athens. Leaving the Italian coast at Otranto, I set a course over the Adriatic Sea to the island of Corfu, seventy-five miles away. A strong north-easterly wind whipped up the sea into a thousand white-capped waves, and I knew there was a rough flight ahead when I neared the mountainous coast of Greece. Visibility was good, and twenty miles away I could see the island of Corfu, and very soon the great snow-covered mountains of Greece. The magnificent grandeur of Greece impressed me deeply, and the steep mountains, rising in places sheer from the intensely blue sea, and the majestic snow-covered ranges of the interior against a background of fleecy clouds formed an unforgettable sight. Giant rocky peaks towered above me as I flew along the coast, and a small series of bumps was a sample of what was ahead.

When I rounded a rocky promontory to fly over the Gulf of Patras I experienced a bump of such intensity that had I not quickly grasped a metal longeron on the floor of the cockpit I should probably have been thrown out of the machine. For the rest of the flight to Athens I clung to the metal longeron with one hand and the lower part of the control column with the other, as the Moth was buffeted about like a feather in the boisterous wind.

Passing along the Gulf of Corinth, I felt that every mile over which I flew had played some important part in ancient history. There was rain ahead, and I flew through a severe squall when nearing the end of the Gulf.

At this stage, having passed through the squall, which was only of short duration, I had the remarkable experience of flying through a rainbow, and could see the lovely colours quite distinctly on the silver wings of the Moth. As I left the Gulf I flew over the Corinth Canal, which, although not very long, is cut from solid rock and was actually commenced by Nero, and over the little town of Corinth, to the inhabitants of which St Paul wrote his epistles.

The wind strengthened as I flew northward and approached Athens, surely one of the most beautiful cities on the face of the earth. I had been flying into the teeth of the gale and averaging only about 40 m.p.h. ground speed, and at times the aeroplane seemed almost to stand still. The aerodrome of Tatoi is in a valley fourteen kilometres north-west of Athens, and after circling a few times I was relieved to see two Greek mechanics running towards the centre of the landing area, where they stood waiting to catch the wing-tips of the Moth when I landed. As I closed the throttle to glide down to a landing the machine made scarcely any progress, and finally I was obliged to fly on to the ground. Strong arms caught the wing-tips, and the two mechanics ran alongside the Moth as I taxied into the large hangar. The wind was so strong that later when I walked along the tarmac to the customs office I was nearly blown off my feet.

My friend Mr Hill was waiting to meet me, and after all customs formalities had been completed and the engine schedule carried out we drove into Athens. On a previous visit to Athens I had stayed with Mr and Mrs Hill, and once again I enjoyed their hospitality.

At dawn the following morning I left Athens and flew over the Ægean Sea to the island of Rhodes, where I altered course for Cyprus. Athens had looked very lovely in the pale light of dawn, which softened the brilliant whiteness of the city and threw into relief the sombre green of the many cypress-trees and deepened the purple shadows of the surrounding mountains. Looking back at the sleeping city I remembered a previous visit when I had driven round Athens at night and seen the ancient and beautiful city at its best, when the great colonnades and majestic architecture had been bathed in the magic light of the full moon.

The sun rose in a blaze of gold as I flew over the many little islands of the Ægean Sea. My thoughts of ancient Greece and the mighty Colossus of Rhodes, wonder of the Old World, were dispelled as I flew over Rhodes itself and looked down on the very modern seaplane base. There was a large French flying-boat moored on the sheltered waters. A little later I passed over the island of Castelorizo, just off the Turkish coast and another possession of Italy with an equally good seaplane base. To the north the great snow-covered mountains of the Anatolian coast of Turkey towered into the sky. Seven hours out from Athens a faint smudge on the horizon resolved itself into the island of Cyprus, and as I drew nearer I experienced that sense of elation that I always feel when flying to a place new to me. The island of Cyprus is about 140 miles from east to west, and the greatest breadth from north to south is only sixty miles. Because of its geographical position Cyprus is undoubtedly destined to become an air base of strategic importance to Britain.

Crossing the limestone hills of Kyrenia I flew inland over the large plain of Mesaoria, which looked dry and parched for want of rain. It was extremely hot, and strong upward currents made the flight to Nicosia unpleasantly bumpy. On one occasion the Moth gained over a thousand feet in less than a minute, only to bump down hundreds of feet the next.

The aerodrome at Nicosia is really a natural landing-ground, and the red earth surface, blending with that of the surrounding country, would make it very difficult to distinguish were it not for the white corner markings and circle. The surface was sparsely covered with scrub, but there were no trees or buildings to hamper the approach; therefore it seemed much larger than 600 square yards, which were the dimensions given on my diagram. As I circled to land I noticed that a wind-indicator had been erected, and there was a little crowd awaiting my arrival. On taxying over the ground I noticed large flat rocks here and there, but fortunately protruding only an inch or two above the surface.

Every one was most helpful, and soon refuelling was being carried out, while I busied myself with the engine work, although I felt very hot and dusty and tempted to retire to some cool, shady spot with an iced drink. Eventually all work was completed and the Moth securely picketed for the night. When I had notified the Cypriote authorities of my intended flight to

Nicosia, in addition to arranging for the wind-indicator, for which I had incidentally to pay an extra ten shillings, I stipulated for a police guard over the aeroplane at night, as there was no hangar.

While we had been working on the engine a number of soldiers arrived, and they were soon busily engaged pegging down tents, while another group arrived with chairs, tables, cases of food, and general camping equipment. " They must think I intend staying for a month or so," I had remarked laughingly to the petrol agent. It had not been possible to drive the screw pickets into the hard ground, so we had tied the ropes to petrol-cans filled with rocks, and thus secured the Moth for the night. Every one was very pleased when the work was finished, especially Mr Ridgeway, the fuel agent, who had completed the back-breaking task of refuelling the machine with sixty gallons of fuel from four-gallon tins, which were handed up to him as he perched precariously on the wing.

As night fell I drove into Nicosia with Mr and Mrs Ridgeway, who proved good friends on this and subsequent flights to Cyprus, and at whose charming home I stayed the night.

Cyprus, I learned, numbers among its 350,000 inhabitants many Mohammedans, Armenians, and Orthodox Greek Christians, and the languages spoken include English, Turkish, French, Arabic, Italian, and modern Greek. Tobacco, cigarettes, wines, cottons, silk, oranges, raisins, flax, and cereals are the main products of this rich island, and the fact that Cyprus has changed hands so often probably accounts for the many and varied peoples living there. Richard Cœur de Lion, the Crusader, first took possession of Cyprus for England in 1191, and it was here that he married Berengaria, Princess of Navarre, thus making her Queen of England. Within a year Richard had sold the island, and it was not until seven hundred years later that Cyprus was occupied by British forces. Even then, although a British High Commissioner took over government by a convention between Britain and Turkey, the island was still really a Turkish possession. Only after the entry of Turkey into the Great War in 1914 was Cyprus annexed to the British Crown. In 1925 the island was formally recognized as a British colony.

All too soon I left Cyprus. Dawn next morning found me bidding farewell to Nicosia and setting off for Damascus. Passing over the port of Famagusta, with its palms and Byzantine churches, I saw the ancient citadel known as Othello's Tower, for it was there that the Moor was supposed to have murdered his Desdemona.

Although Cyprus is only approximately sixty miles from the Syrian coast, the direct route to Beirut took me over a hundred miles of the blue Levant. Away on the distant horizon I could see what looked like a great bank of cumulus cloud, but as I flew on I realized it was the great snow-covered range of the Lebanon Mountains. My altitude was 2000 feet, and approaching Beirut I tried to gain more height. The downdraughts from the mountains were so violent, however, that any height that the Moth gained was lost in the succession of terrific bumps which shook the machine.

Circling around Beirut for some time, I tried to gain sufficient height to cross the mountains, but it was not possible, so I flew along the coast, passing over ancient Sidon and Tyre where the great range gradually slopes away towards Nazareth. Eventually I came to a valley between hills festooned with terraces which looked so ancient that they might have been there even before Solomon took the cedars for his temple from the forests of Lebanon. On the hundreds of terraces I could see the most beautiful gardens and orderly-looking fruit-trees and vineyards. Following the valley, I came to the Sea of Galilee. To the south I could see the river Jordan, and soon approached the edge of the Syrian Desert, which stretched before me like an endless sea of sand. In the distance Damascus, on the fringe of the desert, looked like a lovely city in the centre of a vast lake. Such was the illusion created by the river Barada, on the banks of which Damascus stands, and its many tributaries and irrigation canals, which reflect the intense blue of the sky.

The French Air Force officers at Mezze Aerodrome, where I landed, were very helpful, and I lunched with the commander of the base while my aeroplane was refuelled. We discussed the next part of my flight across the Syrian Desert from Damascus to Baghdad. "Suivez la piste," advised the commandant as he spoke of the dangers of this lonely 530-mile desert stretch where sudden dust-storms and wandering Arab tribes add to the hazards of a lone flight. The track, however, was not marked on my map, nor was Fort Rutbah : in fact, nothing relieved the smooth, even yellow of several sections of the map save a few Arabic names and *wadis*, or dried-up watercourses. "You can use my map," he said, "and post it back to me from Baghdad." It was with gratitude that I took the map, for it was already past midday, and by the time I was once again in the air there might not be sufficient daylight left to make Baghdad before dark, in which case I could stop at Rutbah.

It was very hot, and my heavily laden aeroplane after covering a considerable part of the sandy surface of the aerodrome rose reluctantly above the date-palms at the far end. Skimming the tops of the palms, I flew for miles trying to coax the aeroplane to a reasonable height. The machine had risen very well considering the weight of sixty-one gallons of petrol and all the equipment aboard and the rarefied atmosphere of the aerodrome, situated as it is at 2000 feet above sea-level.

Amid the profusion of date-palms surrounding Damascus, which is reputed to be the oldest city in the world still occupied, I glimpsed white domes and turrets, and here and there a lovely garden half hidden by the leafy shade of the trees. There was a dust-haze over the desert, and it grew increasingly difficult to follow the track after I had located it at Adhra. The glare from the desert was very strong, and my throat became parched with the heat and dust. There was nothing to relieve the barrenness of the wilderness over which I was flying save an occasional clump of thorn-bushes or a stray herd of camels.

A little over three hours out from Damascus Fort Rutbah appeared through the haze. A solitary white building and a compound, a wireless mast, and rows of black Arab tents comprised this tiny French outpost. It did not look very inviting, so I continued on towards Baghdad. Flying lower and lower as the sun became merely a black disc through the sand-haze, I tried to keep sight of the track. A great yellow cloud swept across my path, and the air was filled with stinging particles of sand, completely blotting out everything, so that I was unable to see even the wing-tips of the Moth. Turning back I flew on a reciprocal course, and was overjoyed when at last I once again picked up the white tower of Fort Rutbah.

Just ten minutes before the sand-storm swept over Rutbah I landed on the barbed-wire-enclosed square of the desert that was the aerodrome. The aeroplane was quickly wheeled up to the shelter of the compound, and there was only time to peg it down and tie the canvas covers on the engine and cockpit before the storm whirled like a great wave of sand over the outpost.

On learning that petrol was six shillings per gallon at Rutbah I felt very pleased that the Moth had sufficient fuel to fly through to Baghdad.

The rest-house was quite comfortable, and when I sat down to dinner it was difficult to believe that I was in the middle of the Syrian Desert, for the *cuisine* would not have disgraced any London West End hotel. My companions at the meal were the pilots and passengers of a Dutch air liner which had also been forced back to Rutbah by the sand-storm. None of my fellow-guests appeared to speak English, and I felt too tired to attempt a conversation in French, so we just exchanged friendly nods and smiles at intervals during the meal. It was with great relief, however, that I took off into the fresh, clear air next morning, for I found the close proximity of the camels and the Arab encampment distinctly unpleasant despite their picturesque appearance.

Good weather favoured me on the flight to Baghdad. The line of demarcation between the arid and the cultivated land was very distinct as I approached the river Euphrates and flew on towards Baghdad, on the palm-fringed Tigris. Baghdad, city of the Caliphs, is a very different place now from when Haroun al Raschid ruled there, but from the air it still seems to retain a certain magic of its own. When I first sighted it in the distance I thought I had seen a mirage. From the air it appears a city of white with minarets of blue and alabaster, mosques and temples of exquisite architecture, the gleaming whiteness relieved only by the intense green of thousands of date-palms clustered thickly along the banks of the swift river Tigris, which, seemingly indifferent to the beauty of its surroundings, flows swiftly on its way to the Persian Gulf.

On approaching the city I could see many camel caravans wending their way across the desert, and wondered where they were bound for and how long they would take to reach their destination. Months probably. Some were going in the direction of Aleppo, and I thought of the time when Aleppo was the principal trading town in Syria. Hundreds of years ago camel caravans used to journey from Baghdad to Aleppo and Damascus along the same tracks that are used to-day. Their cargoes were rich, for Baghdad was once the capital of Babylonia and the principal seat of learning in the East. Long lines of camels with trappings of red and purple edged with tinkling bells and laden with fabulous wealth would arrive at Baghdad, where gold, frankincense, myrrh, ivory, and jewels used to be bartered in the market-place for exquisite fabrics from Kashmir and diaphanous silks from China, tea from Ceylon and opium from Turkey. Baghdad at the height of its glory must have been even more wonderful than the descriptions we read of it. To the north of the city I could see the great golden-domed mosque of Khadimain glittering in the sunlight. I stayed only long enough to refuel at the large aerodrome, with its modern spacious control building and hotel. Within an hour of landing I was winging my way over Iraq towards Basra.

CHAPTER IV: OVER ASIA

ABOUT SIXTY MILES SOUTH-WEST OF Baghdad I flew over the ancient city of Babylon. As one looks down on the rather pathetic ruins, none of them more than thirty feet in height, it is still possible to visualize from the foundations the immense scale on which the city must have been built. Being interested in archæology and having read a great deal about these excavations, I longed to land and investigate at close quarters the gates with their beautiful ceramic work and the foundations of the Tower of Babel of Nebuchadnezzar's city. The winds of the desert lay wreaths on the ruins of dead Babylon, and the saying that " there is no dust-cloud in all Iraq but has in it substances that were once combined in the living person of some man or woman " must be true, for this part of the world is supposed to have been the cradle of the human race.

After a hot, dusty flight with more sand-storms I arrived at Basra, and landed at the Royal Air Force aerodrome at Shaibah. Gliding down from the comparatively cool atmosphere to land on the sandy aerodrome was like entering a furnace, the heat was so intense. Both the *personnel* of the Royal Air Force and the staff of Imperial Airways were most helpful. I felt content to leave the refuelling and engine schedule to the mechanics, confident that all my directions would be carried out satisfactorily.

Flying on towards Bushire, on the Persian Gulf, next morning, I passed just south of the city of Basra. Before leaving the wide Shatt al Arab river I flew over the huge oil-tanks on Abbadan island. I had read that these great tanks have a cubic capacity of two and a half million gallons, and that the diameter of each is 116 feet. The story of Abbadan is an interesting one. Every day approximately half a million gallons of crude oil are pumped along the pipe-line from Fields, a town about 150 miles away in the Khuzistan hills, where the oil-wells are situated. There is always great activity at the big oil refineries on Abbadan, for they never close, and shifts work day and night.

Landing on the aerodrome at Bushire I had a sample of Persian officialdom. As I wished to arrive at Jask before sunset it was necessary to refuel and fly on again without any undue delay. However, after I had paid the Persian aerodrome officer the ten rials (equivalent to twenty-five shillings) landing fee, produced my bill of health from Basra, my passport and permit to fly over Persia, he declared that I could not leave before the customs officer arrived to stamp my log-book. "Where is the customs officer?" I asked after the aeroplane had been refuelled. "He is in Bushire," the official replied. Taking the thermos flask and a packet of sandwiches from the cockpit I sat down under the shade of the wing and had my lunch, while waiting patiently as the precious time slipped by. After a rather heated conversation the official, who wore a red fez and a long striped tunic, departed, eventually returning with his friend. The customs officer made no excuse for his late arrival, but stamped my journey log-book, and we all parted good friends.

To regain the time I had lost at Bushire I decided to fly a direct course from Lingeh to Jask, which would take me across the Gulf of Oman and over the northern tip of Oman. The sun beat down relentlessly, and I was glad that I had discarded my heavy flying-suit at Damascus for my white tropical suit. A little shelter was afforded by the cork helmet which had been specially made for me in London so that I could wear it in the open cockpit without fear of its blowing off.

Hours slipped by as I continued my flight along the barren coast of Persia with its peculiar rock formations, and far inland rocky mountains rose to great heights. There was scarcely any vegetation to be seen except for a few date-palms and shrubs at an occasional tiny village tucked away in a valley. Just as the sun set in a red glow Jask came into view, and I landed on the long, narrow promontory where the aerodrome is located. There was a big Fokker aeroplane on the ground, and I learned from the picturesquely clad fuel agent, whose name was Mohammed Ali, that it belonged to the K.L.M. Royal Dutch Air Lines. Years ago the Imperial Airways liners used to call at Jask, and there were then proper facilities, but nowadays they fly along the southern part of the Persian Gulf, and although K.L.M.

and Air France still use this route, they no longer stop overnight at Jask.

Mohammed Ali helped me to refuel and to picket the aeroplane down for the night; then we drove in his ancient car to the rest-house kept by a Dutchman and his wife. All accommodation in the tiny rest-house was taken, but the wife of the proprietor arranged for me to share her room. The Dutch lady was, I thought, very plucky to live in such a hot, lonely place as Jask. She spoke a little English, and I learned that every one in Jask including her husband had been ill with malaria, and that she was the only one who had fortunately escaped.

That evening at dinner I met the two pilots and the passengers of the air liner, who told me that they had heard my aeroplane and wondered who could be arriving at Jask.

I slept so deeply that night that I failed to hear the roar of the Fokker as it took off before dawn bound for Amsterdam. Continuing my flight to Karachi I was again filled with wonder at the amazing rock formations along the coast. Near Gwadar there is a great mass of rock which because of its resemblance to a cathedral is called the Cathedral Rock. Towering up to an immense height, the huge rock stands like a sentinel. I flew inland a short distance, and on looking down into the centre of a group which formed a circle I saw the most delicately shaped white rocks decorating the inner walls and appearing like exquisite lace in contrast with the sombre grey of the outer walls.

The ordinary fuel system of my Gipsy I engine was

by gravity feed from the main centre-section petrol-tank above my head. As the level in this tank became lower more petrol had to be pumped up from the auxiliary tanks situated in the front cockpit and the rear luggage locker. All the pumping had to be done by means of a lever-type hand-pump on the right side of my cockpit. The engine used five gallons of petrol per hour, so I had to work very hard pumping the petrol through at intervals. My time was fully occupied steering a compass course, checking my position on the map, making up the log, pumping the petrol, and endeavouring to have an occasional sandwich or cup of coffee.

Karachi was a welcome sight after the monotony of flying hour after hour along the barren Persian coast, and I landed there to stay the night.

At sunrise next morning I was on my way again, crossing the Sind Desert to Jodhpur. It was beautifully cool flying in the early morning, but as the sun rose higher and shone down with increasing fierceness the heat became almost unbearable. I crossed the big river Indus shortly after leaving Karachi, and until I neared Jodhpur there was nothing to relieve the parched and barren-looking Sind Desert except an occasional Indian village.

Flying over Jodhpur, reputed to be the home of polo, I soon located the large aerodrome near the beautiful palace of the Maharaja, who is a keen airman. The aerodrome, circular in shape, had a good surface and a runway of approximately a thousand yards. The instructor of the local flying club met me when I taxied up to the tarmac, and after a refreshing iced drink in the cool club-house I felt inclined to stay awhile in this interesting town instead of flying on to Allahabad in the midday heat. I was scheduled to arrive at Allahabad, 932 miles from Karachi, that evening, however, so I did not delay.

The sun burned fiercely from a cloudless sky as I flew on across Rajputana that afternoon. Altering course at Jhansi, with its British fort standing high up on the isolated rocky crag, I flew on over India. The country took on a greener look as I neared Allahabad, where the river Jumna joins the mighty Ganges. There was a thick dust-haze in the air, and the banks of the Ganges were only just visible when I flew low towards the aerodrome of Bamraoli at Allahabad.

There was the usual procedure after landing, and once again the Moth was pegged down in the open, for at that time the aerodrome boasted no hangar. I drove into Allahabad with the fuel agent, who told me that the country was badly in need of rain and every one would be thankful when the monsoon broke. " I only hope it doesn't commence before I cross India," I replied, blissfully unaware of the terrible weather I was later to encounter along the lonely Burmese coast.

On our drive to the aerodrome at dawn next morning I saw many natives padding along the road to the market. Some carried unbelievably heavy loads on their backs, and others were driving small carts filled with produce. We passed a cart heavily laden with bricks which a wretched water-bullock was striving to pull, and farther on a few blind and maimed mendicants crying for alms. I saw a sacred cow wandering unmolested along the roadway by itself. It was very hot and dusty even at such an early hour, and I was glad when I took off to feel the crisp fresh air from the slipstream against my face.

Passing over the sacred city of Benares with its burning ghats I could see hundreds of pilgrims bathing in the holy water of the Ganges. Altering course at Buddh Gaya with its beautiful Indian temples I flew on towards Calcutta. The country became noticeably greener and more densely covered with vegetation the farther I flew eastward. It was when passing over hilly country thickly covered with timber, where a forced landing would have been almost impossible, that I discovered an oil leak. Watching the gauge for the inevitable drop in pressure, for I had no idea how much oil had leaked away, I flew on, hoping that the engine would not fail me before I reached the aerodrome. At last I sighted the wide Hooghly river, and six hours out from Allahabad landed at Calcutta. On climbing from the cockpit I discovered the side of the Moth covered with oil and less than two pints left in the engine sump.

The people at Calcutta were most hospitable, and I stayed overnight at the beautiful home of Mr Matthew, superintendent of the munitions factory and an enthusiastic member of the Bengal Flying Club.

By the time the oil leak had been rectified and the engine schedule and refuelling completed and arrangements made for a dawn take-off there was no time left for sightseeing. It was most refreshing, however, after a shower to change my flying-suit for a white silk frock. Tea was served by a silent-footed Indian servant on the cool veranda of my host's home overlooking the busy Hooghly. Although I enjoyed a long sleep, that night seemed to pass in a flash. It seemed only a few minutes after I had retired that the be-turbaned Indian servant brought my breakfast, murmuring that it was time for Mem-sahib to get up. I groped through the mosquito netting for my faithful alarum-clock and reluctantly donned my flying-suit.

My host was a private owner, and he flew his own machine, accompanied by two Moths flown by other members of the Bengal Flying Club, to escort me for a few miles on my way to Akyab. I felt decidedly lonely when the pilots waved good-bye and the three machines flashed back to Calcutta. My route lay over the Sundarbans, a great stretch of innumerable islands formed by the Ganges and the Brahmaputra as they break up and flow in hundreds of tributaries into the Bay of Bengal. Crossing the Bay I altered course at Chittagong, and flew along the Burmese coastline to Akyab, where I landed for petrol. I was obliged to land cross-wind on the L-shaped aerodrome.

While I was directing refuelling operations some white residents drove up and greeted me. Among them were Mr Price and his daughter, who told me they were from my country, and laughed at my surprise, for I had not expected to meet New Zealanders in such an isolated place. They had brought some lunch for me, and as there were no buildings on the aerodrome at that time I sat under the shade of the trees with my newfound friends and enjoyed a hasty lunch.

SUPERVISING THE ENGINE WORK AT CALCUTTA

Photo Keystone

ACKNOWLEDGING THE WELCOME ON ARRIVAL AT SYDNEY

Photo "The Sun," Sydney

Continuing my flight southward that afternoon, I noticed high cumulus clouds banking up inland, although out to sea the sky was fairly clear. When I arrived at the point where I had planned to cross the lofty Arakan Yoma Mountains for Rangoon it was to find them completely obscured by great banks of cloud. I climbed up to 8000 feet before attempting to cross the range, and at that height I flew high above the clouds. When I had allowed sufficient time for the Moth to cross I experienced the awful sensation of gliding down through the cloud layers to 500 feet. At this low altitude I suddenly emerged from the hot, damp cloud to see the blurred outline of the town of Bassein.

The country over which I was flying was broken by the hundreds of tributaries which form the mouths of the Irrawaddy river. In the distance I could see the golden Shwe Dagon Pagoda, and arriving over Rangoon was able to appreciate the rare beauty of the lovely temple, which, standing on a prominence, is completely covered with gold-leaf and crowned with precious jewels.

On landing I heard the disconcerting news that the monsoon was expected to break sooner than usual. That evening I spent a delightful hour at the British Club sitting on the cool terrace sipping an iced drink and listening to the military orchestra playing on the wide lawn. Later I drove round Rangoon to see the magic beauty of the golden Shwe Dagon Pagoda floodlit, and looking at the clear, starlit sky it was difficult to believe there was bad weather ahead.

The sky was overcast when I took off from Rangoon,

and crossing the Gulf of Martaban to Moulmein flew very low to avoid the dull, leaden-looking nimbus clouds which gave the sky an ominous appearance. Instead of crossing the mountains to Bangkok I intended to fly down the western side of the peninsula and refuel at Victoria Point, a British outpost and the most southerly point of Burma. Rain commenced to fall steadily as I flew over the township of Ye, the terminus of the light railway from Moulmein. Flying through several severe squalls I continued southward over the thousands of tiny islands of the Mergui Archipelago. This line extends for hundreds of miles down the coast of Burma and Lower Siam. The islands are mostly sugar-loaf in shape and covered with dark green jungle which grows right down to the water's edge. The effect is amazing, and quite unlike anything I had previously seen. It was not until I flew back from Australia to England and had reasonably good weather on this section that I appreciated the full beauty and glorious colour of this panorama. The peaks of most of the large islands were shrouded in wispy nimbus cloud, and the high mountain ranges inland were completely covered.

Hoping that the weather conditions might improve I flew on, but the weather became steadily worse. Ahead of me, and completely blotting out the horizon, was a great bank of dark cloud, stretching like a wall far out to sea and blending with the big banks of treacherous-looking cloud covering the mountains inland. The air became rough and turbulent. I knew I was entering an intensely bad storm area. "Should I go back to Rangoon?" I thought, quickly checking up on the remaining petrol. I was five hours out from Rangoon, and there was not sufficient petrol left to return even to Moulmein. Vainly I flew on, searching for a break inland or out to sea so that I might fly round the storm, but the rain-clouds ahead were like great dark curtains screening all from view. Victoria Point was another two hundred miles farther on, and there was no alternative but to fly through the storm, hoping that it would not extend over a very wide area.

The rain thundered down on to the wings of my aeroplane like millions of tiny pellets, and visibility was so bad that the wing-tips were not visible and the coast-line was completely blotted out. It was like flying from day into night, and in the semi-darkness the luminous instruments glowed an eerie green from the dashboard. Very soon the open cockpit was almost flooded, and my tropical flying-suit wet through. The rain was blinding, and it was distinctly unpleasant flying blind at such a low altitude. The engine gave an occasional splutter, then regained its steady roar, and I marvelled how it kept going in the deluge. Through a break I suddenly saw the dark blur of the jungle beneath me, and flying lower picked up the coastline.

It was good to see something after the strain of blind flying, but I wondered if I had overshot Victoria Point in the rain. According to my watch I should be over Victoria Point in five minutes if the wind had not altered since I had last checked my position. Only the dark, blurred line of the jungle and the giant white rollers breaking on the shore were visible immediately beneath the aeroplane, and it was impossible to fly inland. Nine hours had passed since I had left Rangoon, so I decided to fly up and down that section of the coast in the hope that the rain would clear sufficiently for me to see inland. Five minutes up and five back: there was sufficient petrol left for one and a half hours' flying.

After thirty-five minutes of anxious cruising the curtain of rain lifted temporarily, disclosing the bases of the mountains. I located a clearing in the jungle which was the aerodrome, although it resembled a lake, and landed just as the rain closed in again. Great sprays of water rose on each side of the machine as it taxied to where a group of natives were sheltering under umbrellas and grass mats. A white-clad figure waded out to meet me, and I stopped the 'plane as he neared the cockpit. A big smile and two honest blue eyes looked out at me from beneath a white topee, and a big hand grasped mine in a welcome handshake. " Better take the machine over to the dry patch," he said, pointing to where the natives were huddled together. " The dry patch " was only a mere few inches deep, and I stepped out of the cockpit up to my ankles in water. Although the rain continued to teem down, we managed to picket the aeroplane and tie the canvas cover over engine and cockpit.

I learned that my new-found friend's name was Russell, and that he was in charge of a rubber plantation and was the only white man in Victoria Point. Although it was still raining it was extremely hot, and my friend removed his topee, down the brim of which the rain streamed like a veil, and mopped his brow every few minutes. I donned my raincoat, although it was not of much use, as I had been wet through for hours. Refuelling was not possible, so we drove to Mr Russell's home near the aerodrome. It seemed to be the only house there, and was built high up off the ground on supports, as is the custom in the East. After changing into dry clothes I felt decidedly happier, and gave my wet flying-suit to the native servant to dry, as anything damp becomes covered with mildew in a short time in that climate. The big living-room was most comfortable, and I enjoyed a welcome cup of tea and the most delicious egg sandwiches I had ever tasted. There was a wireless station some miles away, and I learned that Mr Russell had gone to fetch the wife of the wireless operator to keep me company.

While waiting for my host to return I looked over the great pile of English magazines that I concluded he had reserved to pass away the time during the incessant rains of the monsoon season. I walked out on to the veranda and surveyed the scene. The rain had lifted, to reveal the panorama of the thick tropical foliage. Near the house great drops of water slid down from the glistening leaves of the tall palm-trees and flopped to the wet earth beneath with thudding precision. Wispy grey cloud still hid the tops of the mountains from view, and thin columns of steam rose here and there from the thick jungle.

Mr Russell returned with the shy little dark-eyed wife of the wireless operator, and as the rain had stopped we went on to the aerodrome. Refuelling was a lengthy procedure from two-gallon tins of petrol, and owing to the state of the ground I decided to take a very light load—just sufficient with a slight margin to enable me to fly to Alor Star, where I could refuel and proceed to Singapore.

During the night I awoke to hear the rain thundering down on to the roof, and despaired of ever being able to take off from Victoria Point. Next morning, however, the rain stopped, and although the aeroplane had been out in the open and exposed to the full force of the deluge, we were able to coax the engine to life. The cockpit was flooded, but at least the upholstery was dry, as I had taken the cushions to Mr Russell's house the previous evening.

The take-off was a most anxious one for me: the small aerodrome was fringed with trees, and a mountain overhung one end. The ground was very wet, and I was extremely doubtful if the aeroplane would lift in time to clear the high palm-trees. Two sprays of water rose on each side of the machine as I gave the engine full throttle, and the aeroplane lifted just in time to clear the trees. Circling the aerodrome to gain height I saw the white-clad figure of Mr Russell waving, and felt a tremendous admiration for him. I felt the same about all the white people I met at these outposts—shut off from the world yet going on with their jobs, and incidentally keeping the flag flying. Mr Russell would probably be cut off from the rest of the world until the rains ceased several months later. With the exception of the wireless operator and his wife and an occasional visitor to Victoria Point from the tin-mines on the islands farther up the coast, he would have no company save the natives. In addition to supervising the rubber plantation he was in charge of the aerodrome in a purely honorary capacity, and took it upon his good-natured self to attend to the needs of any aviators who landed there.

Hundreds of miles of jungle stretched ahead, and there was no sign of civilization to be seen except a stray native village. Over Lower Siam I met several severe squalls, but as I neared Malaya the weather improved. At Alor Star I refuelled, and when taxying out to take off the aeroplane became bogged in the wet ground. Stepping out of the cockpit I waded round to the front of the machine, and saw that only the tops of the wheels were visible above the mud. Every one was most helpful, and the superintendent requisitioned a number of natives to pull the aeroplane out of the mud. The machine was eventually lifted on to a dry patch, and I took off for Singapore. Isolated storms loomed ahead, looking like giant mushrooms, but I was able to fly round them. Despite the fact that my shoes were covered with mud and my feet wet through, I felt very happy as I speeded towards Singapore. On this section I passed over great rubber plantations and saw many homesteads and small towns. Roads were a welcome sight too, and Malaya seemed to have many good highways. Just as I crossed the railway bridge which connects Singapore island with the mainland the sun sank in a golden glow, and a few minutes later I landed on the beautiful R.A.F. aerodrome at Seletar.

There were a large number of R.A.F. men in spotless white tropical suits waiting on the tarmac with cameras as I taxied up to the hangars. I sat smiling from the cockpit until I hoped they had exhausted all their films, then climbed out to display my once white suit and shoes caked with Alor Star mud. Group Captain Sidney Smith, whom I had met in England, was in charge of the base, and I received a cordial invitation from him and Mrs Smith to stay at their bungalow. Very soon I was enjoying the luxury of a bath. I greatly appreciated the hospitality of my charming hosts, and felt thoroughly rested and refreshed next morning. The Air Force mechanics had carried out the engine schedule, and I felt grateful when I climbed into the cockpit and tested the engine, which also seemed to have gained vigour during our short stay. The aerodrome was circular in shape with a diameter of a thousand yards, so it was a pleasure to take off from its smooth surface.

Leaving the island of Singapore I flew over myriads of little islands forming the Rhio Archipelago on a course for Batavia. About sixty miles south-west of Singapore I crossed the equator and flew along the coast of Sumatra. The jungle looked particularly thick, and the trees so close together that I doubt if sunlight ever penetrated to the earth beneath. As I flew low over the jungle, occasionally great flocks of brightly coloured parakeets would rise up from the trees, evidently startled by the roar of my engine. On the muddy banks of the great rivers I saw many crocodiles sunning themselves. Upon the aeroplane's approach they would invariably slither off the bank into the river, down which floated *débris* of every description. The high mountains of Java were visible some distance away, and as I crossed the strait from Sumatra to Java I thought how strange it was that of these two islands, so close together and both belonging to Holland, one should be almost completely claimed by the jungle and the other so intensely cultivated. Java has a population of 40,000,000 people, hundreds of miles of beautiful roads, large cities, and a general air of prosperity. Approaching Batavia I flew over miles of cultivated fields with elaborate irrigation canals, and when the capital itself came into view was surprised at its size. The aerodrome was very large, with modern-looking administrative buildings, and I found Mr Smet, the fuel agent, there to welcome me.

I stayed for the night at the home of Mr and Mrs Smet. These most hospitable Dutch people soon made me feel at home. The flight from Singapore had been very hot, and I welcomed the thought of a refreshing bath. Mrs Smet laughed at my surprise on seeing the bathroom, which I found later was typical of the Dutch East Indies. The floor was tiled, and along one side of the wall extended a deep stone container, filled with cold water. Alongside were two pitchers. The procedure was to stand beside the stone container and tip water on oneself with the pitchers. Although this required a certain amount of dexterity, nevertheless it was the next best thing to a shower and most refreshing.

Mr Smet proved himself a good friend by returning to the aerodrome that night to repair the cracked air-intake pipe on my engine.

CHAPTER V: ARRIVAL IN
SYDNEY

WHEN WE ARRIVED AT THE AERO-drome next morning it was to find a thick layer of fog covering the ground. I despaired of being able to take off until the sun had dispersed the fog later in the morning. Mr Smet, however, declared that although it was so dense the fog was not very thick through. "I shall drive my car at full speed up and down a section several times and clear a pathway through the fog," he said. "Then if you are quick you can take off down the path before the sides close together."

The scene assumed an air of unreality. There we were standing beside the aeroplane, which looked ghostly in the poor light, and hardly able to see each other when wisps of fog drifted across the vision like smoke—there we were, talking about clearing a pathway through the fog. Alice in Wonderland would not have been more surprised at the idea than I. Mr Smet, who was most enthusiastic, however, and eager to try his scheme, drove the car alongside my aeroplane. I shook hands with him, and climbing into the cockpit ran the engine up.

Arranging everything for the take-off and strapping myself in securely I called to him that all was ready. The fog was so thick that I could only just distinguish the dark blur of Mr Smet's car as it raced forward and disappeared into the fog. I had visions of Mr Smet driving blindly along at full speed, becoming lost somewhere in the middle of the aerodrome, but suddenly the car reappeared, turned, and raced back again. It seemed hopeless, and yet after many similar dashes the fog thinned out in the path of the car, and gradually began to look as if some one had sliced it with a knife. The effect was really extraordinary, with the high walls of fog on each side, and reminded me of a Biblical picture I had seen as a child depicting the crossing of the Red Sea. Mr Smet shouted to me to get ready as he made a final dash down the rift he had cleared. Although he had insisted that the fog did not extend up to any appreciable height, it was with a certain amount of misgiving that I pushed the throttle lever forward and guided the aeroplane through the rift. Just as I neared the end of the pathway the machine left the ground and the walls closed together. The fog enveloped everything in a dense whiteness.

Climbing the machine gently, for there was a heavy load of petrol aboard, I wished desperately that I had not attempted to take off. Suddenly I was almost blinded by a strong glare as the machine penetrated the fog layers and emerged into the brilliant sunlight and a blue sky. Beneath me stretched the white carpet of fog, completely covering the ground, and, knowing that Mr Smet would hear the roar of my engine and realize all was well, I set a course for Soerabaya. Inland great volcanic peaks towered to unbelievable heights, and the mist cleared to reveal miles of green fields intensely cultivated. Aerodromes were numerous, and every town of any size seemed to possess one. All the landing-grounds were marked with a white cross, and the majority were the shape of a Maltese cross with wide runways. I frequently flew over emergency landing-grounds, consisting of two-way strips marked with the inevitable white cross. Quaint Javanese villages and prosperous towns passed beneath my wings, until, eight hours out from Batavia, I landed at Soerabaya.

While we were refuelling the aeroplane two English-men arrived. One of them explained to me that they were playing golf and had seen my aeroplane land. Leaving their game unfinished they had driven over to ask if I needed any help. They were both very hospit-able, and insisted on taking me to Soerabaya to lunch at their very beautiful home. Much as I should have liked to stay in Soerabaya I decided to keep to my sche-dule, and an hour later took off for Rambang. Flying on towards the eastern end of Java I passed Mount Merapi, over 8000 feet high and the most easterly of the great chain of volcanic mountains which extends from one end of the island to the other. A strong south-easterly wind was blowing, and as I left Java and crossed the open sea to the island of Bali I experienced some terrific bumps. In a down-draught from a mountain towering over 9000 feet high on that island the aeroplane dropped 1000 feet within a few seconds.

A chain of smaller islands extends from Java to

Timor, and on some of them volcanic peaks rise to a height of over 9000 feet. Flying from one to the other I was exposed to the full force of the boisterous wind, which tossed the aeroplane about as if it were a cork in a rough sea. Three hours after leaving Soerabaya I flew over the island of Lombok. On the north-east side of the island a great mountain reared itself to a height of nearly 10,000 feet and hid its peak in the clouds. The southern part of the island, however, was flat and intensively cultivated. I flew over miles of neat little rice-fields and quaint native villages.

The wind was blowing fairly strongly when I arrived at Rambang, and I felt hot and tired after the rough trip from Soerabaya and in no mood for a cross-wind landing on a strange aerodrome. There was no alternative, however, and after circling a few times I gently slipped the machine over the palm-trees and landed.

There was a small grass hut in the corner of the aerodrome, and a native surrounded by a number of small children stood in the doorway. Taxying the aeroplane over, I turned it into the wind and switched off the engine. The native regarded me with faint surprise, but could not speak English, so all my questions fell on deaf ears. I felt like a person from another world; in fact, I might have landed from Mars, for none of the small crowds of natives who were gathering understood a word I spoke. The only thing to do was to sit down and wait for some one to arrive, for I had flown over the village, and the fuel agent must have heard the aeroplane. Eventually a truck loaded with four-gallon drums of petrol and crowded with natives drove up. One of the natives greeted me and proudly pointed to a red gilt badge on his breast and bearing the name of the Shell company, which he represented. The language problem seemed an insurmountable obstacle until the agent produced an effective solution. He walked over to the truck, and returned with a notebook in which a number of questions and answers were written in Javanese with English translations. Very soon we were carrying on a silent conversation. I would point to a question written in English and the agent would read the Javanese translation, then delightedly point to the answer. Unfortunately, however, the list was all too short and soon exhausted.

Refuelling was soon being carried out by the natives, while I perched on top of the engine adjusting the tappets, magneto points, and attending to the numerous other items of the schedule. The sun slipped down, leaving us to complete the task of pegging the machine down in the darkness. As the only means of communication seemed to be the list of questions and answers I took charge of the precious book. Scanning the list by torchlight I pointed to a line reading, " I want a watchman to guard my aeroplane for the night." The agent read the question and entered the grass hut in the corner of the aerodrome, emerging almost immediately accompanied by a native, whom he sat down beside the aeroplane. I explained to the watchman by sign language what would happen if he whiled away the hours by smoking, and stressed the importance of my instructions by using phrases which were not in the agent's book, but which nevertheless seemed to be perfectly understood by all present. Taking my bag from the aeroplane, and also the upholstery and movable equipment from the cockpit, I boarded the truck, and we set off for the village of Selong, seven miles distant.

There was a pasangrahan, or rest-house, in the village, and I was impressed by the cleanliness of the room to which I was shown. The floor was bare, and there was little furniture. An oil-lamp on the wall provided the only light. In the centre of the room stood a large bed draped with a mosquito net. The bathroom was similar to the one in Mr Smet's house, and after I had bathed and changed into my white silk frock I felt decidedly refreshed. The faithful agent was waiting on the veranda to receive final instructions for the morning. He seemed mildly surprised when I managed to make him understand that I was hungry and wanted my dinner. Calling the natives in charge, he was soon in deep conversation with them. It was quickly apparent, and the proprietor made it quite clear, that there was no food to be had in the pasangrahan. My spirits sank as I thought of the few dried-up sandwiches I had brought with me from Batavia, and the thermos flask, half full of cold black coffee. The milk tablets, raisins, barley sugar, concentrated meat tablets, and the rest of my rations had been left in the aeroplane. Not that I regretted the fact particularly. During the flight when breakfast or lunch-time came round I would place a meat tablet in my mouth and try hard not to think of roast chicken or a porterhouse steak, and attempt to console myself with the thought that each tablet contained the equivalent nourishment.

I was never quite able to convince myself that the milk tablets with which I rounded off the meal were really the equivalent of the large glass of iced milk I visioned as I sucked the tablets. That was all very well in the air, but I had no intention of dining off tablets when on the ground.

"Are you sure there isn't any food at all?" I asked the dusky Mother Hubbard. Before he had time to reply we heard steps on the path and voices. Two white-clad figures approached, and as they stepped on to the veranda the lamplight caught the gold buttons and epaulettes on their uniforms. "I am so sorry that we were not at the aerodrome to meet you, but we did not know you had arrived," said one of the visitors, who proved to be the Dutch Superintendent of the island, as he shook my hand and introduced his companion. Their blue eyes twinkled as I told my woeful tale of the total lack of food in the pasangrahan. The Superintendent was not at all surprised, and explained that it was the custom for travellers to bring provisions with them or send the proprietor of the pasangrahan to the market to purchase food. "We have brought some 'flesh and fowel' for you," he said.

In answer to a command from my Dutch friend, and almost as if by magic, a native servant appeared with a hamper, which when opened disclosed all manner of good things. The table was set, and I was soon enjoying what the Superintendent had called "flesh and fowel" and the delicious fruits which, I learned, grew in abundance on the island. After giving the proprietor orders for my breakfast and arranging to drive me to the aerodrome the tall, fair Superintendent and his friend departed.

My Dutch friends arrived punctually next morning, and we drove to the aerodrome, to find that the fuel agent had already removed the screw pickets. A little crowd of admiring natives watched me turn the propeller over, and fortunately the engine fired the first time I swung it on contact. While the engine was warming up I bade farewell to the faithful fuel agent, paid the native watchman, and thanked my Dutch friend for his hospitality. The two beautiful little coloured native baskets containing sandwiches and some mandarins which the Superintendent had given me were packed in the cockpit, together with the flask of coffee and maps for the day's flight. Climbing into the machine, I tested the engine, and waving a farewell to the little group took off for Timor island.

Crossing the Alas Strait I flew along the southern coast of Soembawa island, meeting occasional rain-squalls of varying intensity. The weather cleared as I passed over the little island of Komodo, where huge lizards resembling dragons are reputed to live. Mr Smet had told me of one captured for the Batavia Zoo, and a photo of it showed its remarkable resemblance to a prehistoric animal. A low flight over the island, however, failed to reveal any trace of the Komodo dragons, so I continued my flight over Flores island.

At Ende the magnificent spectacle of a volcano in eruption met my eyes. The sea reflected the crimson glow which tinted the sky, and great clouds of smoke rose from the crater. I flew near the mountain to get

75

a better view of this awe-inspiring sight, but when a cloud of smoke and fine ash temporarily obscured my view I decided I had seen enough and headed out to sea on a direct course for Kupang. There was a fresh south-east wind blowing, and the sea crossing from Flores to Kupang took a little over two hours. Visibility was good, and some distance away I sighted the mountainous island of Timor. As I drew near I saw an occasional native fishing-boat. I was soon flying over tiny Semaoe island, just off Kupang. The smooth water of Kupang Harbour was an indescribable shade of green and wonderfully transparent. As I looked down, admiring the beauty of the scene, I saw a black dorsal fin cleave the water, and near the shore shadowy forms of several sharks moving slowly beneath the surface. The charming Dutchman who met me at the aerodrome when I landed seemed mildly surprised that I should mention the sharks in Kupang Harbour. This surprise was not to be wondered at really, for there was nothing particularly remarkable about sharks in tropical waters. Moreover, some of the largest sharks ever captured, and weighing over 800 lbs., have been caught off the coast of my own country, New Zealand. The coast of Australia, as I later saw for myself, is infested with these loathsome monsters, and in Sydney an efficient aerial shark patrol of the beaches is maintained every week-end during the summer.

We refuelled the aeroplane, and I worked until sundown carrying out the engine schedule and a detailed inspection. When the aeroplane was securely picketed down and a native appointed to guard it I drove to the rest-house at Kupang. The pasangrahan was most comfortable, and every one very hospitable. When I entered up my log-book that night I found it difficult to contain my joy at the knowledge that Australia was now only 530 miles away and a record almost achieved.

Dawn next morning found me at the aerodrome making final preparations for the flight to Darwin. The weather report was handed to me, and I saw that apart from head winds the weather would be mainly fair, with dust-haze near the coast of Australia. Drafting out a telegram stating my estimated time of arrival and the course I intended steering, I handed it to the agent to send to the authorities at Darwin. The aerodrome was L-shaped, and the rough surface covered with fairly high grass. Nevertheless the aeroplane rose easily despite the heavy load of petrol. Circling to gain height before crossing the mountains, I looked down and saw the little group of people waving farewell. I did not know then the utter loneliness I was to endure for almost eight hours steering my frail low-powered aircraft into the teeth of a strong south-easterly wind over the Timor Sea.

As I left the coast and headed out over the open sea I looked back and tried to check the drift of the fast-receding land. The magnetic course was 104°, and I flew very low so that I could gauge the direction and strength of the surface wind, and make adjustments to the compass course to compensate for drift. Hour after hour slipped by, and I began to long for the sight of land. I seemed to be in a world of my own. As far as my eye could see there stretched the blue expanse of the Timor Sea, and overhead the sun burned fiercely down from a clear sky. Six hours passed, and I broke the monotony by having lunch. I took as long as possible over the meal, and finished with a cup of coffee and an orange. I had been so occupied trying to peel the orange that I had not noticed the sky become overcast and a dust-haze gradually obscure the horizon. Seven hours out from Kupang I pumped the remaining petrol into the main tank and strained my eyes ahead for some sight of land. Time dragged on, and every minute now seemed more like an hour. The haze lifted slightly, and a dark smudge on the horizon seemed to become more definite as I flew on. Land! It was really land ahead this time, I assured myself, not just another misleading cloud-bank.

Some seconds elapsed before I grasped the fact that my eyes were not deceiving me. My feelings were indescribable as I sat watching the Australian coastline become more definite, until I could discern the actual contours and then the dark green of the bush. Very soon I was looking down on Darwin Harbour, and the little pearling luggers looked like toys on the calm, azure waters fringed with thick green tropical foliage that spread over the country like a great carpet and seemed to stretch into infinity. Circling the township I located the aerodrome, and when I shut off the engine to glide down to a landing I could still hear its full-throated roar, so accustomed had my ears become to its steady note.

I received a warm welcome from the Darwin residents who had assembled at the 'drome to see me land on that memorable day of May 23, 1934. I was deeply conscious of the joy of achievement when I realized that my time of 14 days 22 hours 30 minutes lowered by over four days the time established by Miss Amy Johnson. Although I always thought of Darwin as my goal, nevertheless it was by no means the end of my flight. The long journey of 2200 miles across the continent of Australia to Sydney lay ahead. Before leaving England I had realized that the final stage would be one of the most difficult, owing to the almost complete absence of landmarks. Great was my joy when I learned that Lord Wakefield had arranged for an escorting aeroplane to accompany me on the flight to Sydney. My machine was refuelled and pegged down, for at that time Darwin Aerodrome did not boast a hangar.

I sank into the comfortable seat of the car on the drive into Darwin, and experienced a feeling of deep contentment as I closed my tired eyes and felt the cool breeze against my face. On arrival at the hotel I was delighted to find a great sheaf of telegrams and cables of congratulation awaiting me.

At sunrise next morning I took off from Darwin followed by the escort machine. After the ten thousand lonely miles of my flight from England I greatly appreciated the company of the other aeroplane. Leaving Darwin we flew southward over thickly timbered country, keeping within sight of the ribbon-like clearing where the single-track railway line wound like a serpent through the bush. Gleaming white among the dark green of the tropical foliage, dozens of gigantic anthills stood out like great cones. As we neared the township of Katherine the escort 'plane flew alongside mine, and the pilot signalled that he was going to land for petrol. We had been flying into a strong south-easterly wind since leaving Darwin, and this reduced ground speed considerably. My aeroplane, with its auxiliary petrol-tanks, did not require more fuel, but the escort 'plane, with its higher-powered engine and consequent greater fuel-consumption, had to land frequently for petrol.

The landing-ground at Katherine was very rough, and I had to watch carefully for anthills and guide the machine over a number of gum suckers before touching down on the rough surface. My annoyance at the unscheduled stop and subsequent delay gave way to pleasure at the cheery welcome I received from the willing helpers who carried the heavy tins of petrol to refuel the escort machine.

I met Dr Fenton, " the Flying Doctor," about whom I had heard so much. No distance, it seemed, was too great for "the Flying Doctor," who, piloting his own Moth, visited isolated stations in the Northern Territory to render aid. These people in the " Never Never " regard the aeroplane as a necessity, and it certainly is, for in the rainy season some of the stations are inaccessible by any other means. I found later that some children on the stations of Central Queensland, who were quite used to the arrival of the mail 'plane, had never seen a train or a boat.

As we flew southward I began to wonder how people ever managed to exist on the isolated ranches of

Northern and Central Queensland before the advent of the aeroplane. After another stop for petrol at Daly Waters, where we found a good aerodrome, we located the track, and followed it as it wound through the bush towards Newcastle Waters. The railway we had left at Birdum, where it terminated, 275 miles south of Darwin, and until we reached Cloncurry, 700 miles farther on, the only means of finding our way was by stock routes and water-bores. It is extremely unwise to steer by compass when flying across the featureless country comprising the greater part of the Central and Northern Territory of Australia if the aeroplane is not fitted with radio.

The arrival in Sydney was a triumph. I found several thousands of the warm-hearted Australian people waiting to greet me at the Mascot Aerodrome, and I shall always remember that particular reception, for it was a big milestone in my career: not only for the fact that I had made my first big solo flight, but I had gained valuable experience. On my arrival I had no idea that I should be asked to make a speech, having never before even attempted to speak in public. I listened with growing uneasiness to the various speakers, until at last a great roar went up from the crowd, and I found myself standing alone in front of the microphone being filmed making my maiden speech. That marked the beginning of a great series of receptions given in my honour at which I was to receive the warm hospitality of the Australian people.

CHAPTER VI: INTERLUDE

AFTER A WONDERFUL TIME IN SYDNEY, during which I was entertained by the leading clubs and societies and a reception held for me at Parliament House by the Premier of New South Wales and members of the Cabinet, I visited Brisbane and Melbourne, where the enthusiasm and hospitality equalled that of Sydney. A luncheon was given in my honour at Canberra by Mr Lyons, Premier of the Commonwealth, and his Ministers, and I returned to Sydney to take the ship to my home in New Zealand. Much as I should like to have flown on to my homeland, it was quite impossible in the tiny, low-powered Moth, with its range of only 800 miles. The Australian flyer Flight-Lieutenant Charles Ulm was a fellow-passenger on the ship, and we used to have long talks about the great part aviation would play in linking up our respective countries with England and America. Little did I realize that within six months gallant Charles Ulm was to perish in the Pacific wastes while on an attempt to span the Pacific from America to Australia.

A great welcome awaited me on our arrival in New Zealand, and I was glad to be home again. All the boats in the Auckland harbour were decked with streamers and bunting, bands played, and the streets were packed with cheering crowds. I was made a guest of the New Zealand Government, and amid scenes of tremendous enthusiasm at the civic reception in Wellington the Prime Minister, Mr Forbes, announced that the Government wished to show its appreciation in a practical manner, and that I was to receive a grant of £500. My aeroplane was taken off the ship, where it had perched with wings folded on a hatch of the U.S.S. *Aorangi* during our voyage from Sydney. In the company of a New Zealand Air Force aeroplane which the Government had sent to escort my own I commenced a six weeks' tour of my homeland. During my stay in Wellington I had been a guest of the Governor-General and Lady Bledisloe, who were wonderfully hospitable. They were both present at the aerodrome to see me take off for the South Island. The flight round New Zealand gave me a wonderful opportunity of studying flying conditions and the progress of aviation in the Dominion, and I landed at over twenty towns during the course of the tour. At most places I found an aero club and many enthusiastic pilots, both men and women.

New Zealand is a most fascinating country to fly over, but I had never before realized what a very mountainous country my homeland is. The scenery of the North Island differs greatly from that of the long South Island, and beyond the rich pasture-land stretch great mountain ranges heavily timbered and covered with the dark green sub-tropical foliage of the native bush. The

island is of volcanic origin, and Rotorua, my birthplace, is situated, as I have mentioned, in the centre of
the thermal region, where there are many mineral
springs, pools of boiling mud, and geysers. This region
extends over an area about a hundred miles long by
twenty wide. Some one once aptly remarked at a dinner
given in my honour that it was most appropriate that I
should be born in this thermal district, as everything
there was sure to go up into the air at some time or
another. The view of this region from the air is most
majestic, and not far away the snow-covered mountains of Ruapehu, Tongariro, and Ngarahoe thrust their
great peaks into the sky, towering above the surrounding country. Although all three are snow-covered,
Tongariro and Ruapehu, which towers to 9000 feet,
are now quiet, but Ngarahoe still smoulders in sup-
pressed anger and emits a pennant of smoke from his
crater.

The big South Island is different again, although
Nature was just as lavish with her gifts, and the magnificent splendour of the scenery in both islands is beyond
description. The mighty Southern Alps form the back-
bone of the South Island, rearing their majestic snow-
covered peaks to the clouds. On the western side of the
island several giant glaciers press towards the sea, and
at the base of the Alps Nature has thrown a luxuriant
mantle of dark green forest. Here tall trees rise above
the dense undergrowth, and fairy-like ferns and starry
white clematis grow in profusion, and the tui, bell-bird,
and the rest of the shy bird family compose symphonies
in the solitude. The vast Canterbury Plains form a

striking contrast on the eastern side of the Alps, and the rich pasture-land, reminiscent of England, extends from the mountains to the sea. In the centre of the southernmost part of this island are a cluster of lakes that vie with each other for sheer beauty. From a height of 10,000 feet in winter they resembled a number of uncut sapphires thrown at random on the carpet of snow that lay right down to the water's edge. They all bear Maori names. Manapouri, Te Anau, Wakatipu, Wanaka, and Hawea are the largest, and some of them are more than 1500 feet deep.

Crossing Cook Strait on the first day of the flight I saw that all the great ranges were mantled in white. It was terribly cold flying in an open aeroplane during July, which is mid-winter in the Southern Hemisphere. Even the foothills were carpeted with snow, and as far as my eye could see there stretched snow-covered ranges which in the interior rose to such heights that their summits were lost in the clouds. When I landed at Christchurch I found the sheltered plains were clear of snow, but farther south the whole country was mantled in white.

During the tour I had the interesting experience of taking an old lady aged 101 years for a flight. She was one of the earliest pioneers, and clearly remembered the arrival of the first Governor of New Zealand, Governor Hobson, in 1840. The old lady had a great sense of humour, and remarked to me that she had flown when much younger. On being asked at what age she had first flown she laughingly remarked, "Oh, only ninety-nine."

In such a mountainous country it is not to be wondered at that some of the roads and the railways which spiral up mountains, go through unbelievably long tunnels, and bridge giant chasms and gorges are great feats of engineering. All the main towns are linked by rail, although, for the size of the country, comparatively speaking there are not a great number of railways. With the exception of the excellent thoroughfares in the cities and on the plains, the majority of the roads, owing to the nature of the country, are tortuous and winding and sometimes very steep. Because of these facts and the time taken to traverse difficult country there is a very big future for aviation in New Zealand. Apart from its importance from a defence point of view, aviation has tremendous commercial possibilities. The main cities are widely separated, and the fact that the country is divided by Cook Strait enhances the value of aviation as a means of transport, not only of mails and passengers, but also of freight. Using surface transport a person wishing to travel from Auckland to Dunedin, a distance of approximately 800 miles, is obliged to make a long and tedious journey. First there is a long journey by train to Wellington, then a trip by steamer across Cook Strait to Lyttelton, near Christchurch, then another long train journey for the rest of the way to Dunedin. By air line it is now possible to combine speed with comfort and make this journey in a few hours. The fleet of modern air liners which operates between the main towns not only enhances the prestige of the Dominion in the aviation world, but also fills a long-felt want for speedy transport. The operating companies more than deserve a handsome Government subsidy, without which at present they gallantly operate at a considerable loss.

The tour proved to be as enjoyable as it was strenuous, and during the six weeks I made approximately a hundred and fifty speeches. In addition to flying to the various places I attended many banquets held in my honour. I was entertained by civic authorities, aero clubs, rotary clubs, and various women's clubs and sports associations and societies, visited schools to address the scholars, and also found time to visit many hospitals. At the conclusion of the tour I decided to revisit Rotorua, my birthplace, and take a much-needed holiday. During my stay a *hangi* or native feast was held in my honour by the Maoris at the village of Whakarewarewa. On my arrival I was met by the famous guide Bella Papakura, and entered the village through the great carved gateway, on which was the word *Haremai* (" Welcome "). Before the reception I was taken to see the preparations for the feast. In the centre of a clearing Maoris were busily engaged placing wood on a fire which burned fiercely beneath a large heap of stones. When they were red-hot the wood was removed and water dashed on the stones to clean them. Taking the meat which was to be cooked they laid it on wirenetting over the stones, then threw a large cloth over all. Quickly the stones were covered with earth, until all that was to be seen was a large mound. The kumeras, a variety of sweet potato, were prepared in similar fashion, and it was not until some hours later that the earth was removed. In the beautifully carved native meeting-house the chief of the Arawa tribe, Mita Tau-popaki, greeted me in true Maori fashion and in the poetic language of his race. Placing a rare greenstone Tiki (Maori god) round my neck he said that the Maori people would always think of me as the shining gem of New Zealand. After the native songs and dances of welcome the feast was held. The meat and kumeras were served in little plaited flaxen baskets, and every one thoroughly enjoyed themselves.

About this time an air race from England to Australia was being organized in connexion with the Melbourne centenary celebrations. There was a tremendous amount of interest in the race, and aeroplanes from many different countries were entered. The race was scheduled to start on October 20, 1934, from Mildenhall Aerodrome, Suffolk. I planned to be in Melbourne to see the finish of the race, which promised to be a very thrilling one, as there was just that spice of international rivalry so necessary to the success of such an event. On my arrival in Sydney I received an offer to visit Melbourne and broadcast a commentary on the race for a network of radio stations. This proved to be not only interesting, but very hard work. My first broadcast was from the Melbourne Town Hall just after the competing aeroplanes had left England, and for the next ten days I gave several broadcasts each day on the progress of the various competitors.

Unfortunately a number of entrants withdrew, and Australians were disappointed that Sir Charles Kingsford Smith was not able to compete. However, twenty entrants started from England. On the first day there

A MAORI GREETING

Photo C. Troughton Clark , Rotorua, N.Z.

TAKING OFF FOR ENGLAND

Photo Topical Press

[*See p.* 95]

were many surprises and thrills : several machines were forced down in France with bad weather, and the American entrant, Miss Jacqueline Cochran, and her co-pilot gave up at Budapest. Others retired for various reasons, Mr and Mrs Mollison with a Comet abandoning the race in India. After the first day it became increasingly apparent that the race was between Charles Scott and Campbell Black, flying a De Havilland Comet, and the Dutch competitors Parmentier and Moll, in a Douglas, closely followed by Roscoe Turner and Clyde Pangbourne, in a Boeing.

As the 'planes neared Australia the interest became greater and the excitement intense, and as I sat at the microphone broadcasting, telegrams and cables would be handed to me stating the positions of the various competitors. Two airmen crashed in Italy and were killed, and a machine flown by the Dutch pilot Geysendorfer caught fire at Allahabad, fortunately without loss of life.

In the amazing time of a few minutes under three days Charles Scott and Campbell Black, flying the Comet, were first to flash past the winning line at Melbourne, and an immense crowd of people assembled to see them land. I clung gallantly to my microphone, and tried to continue the broadcast as calmly as possible as the great crowd, pushing and jostling, surged forward towards the Comet. I was one of the first to greet the winning airmen, and at a special broadcast had the pleasure of introducing them to Australian listeners on our network of radio stations.

Crowds waited all night for the arrival of the Dutch pilots, and I remember sitting on the wheel of a Moth machine in a hangar waiting patiently to broadcast the landing. Shortly after midnight the news came through that the Douglas had landed on a racecourse in frightful weather and would fly on the following day. It was not expected, however, that they would be able to start so early, and when I received a telephone message to go to the aerodrome and broadcast the landing they were already nearing Melbourne. I had overslept considerably that morning, so, hastily dressing and forgoing breakfast, I drove as quickly as possible to the aerodrome. As I sped along at over seventy my spirits sank, for in the distance I saw the giant silver machine circling the aerodrome to land. Dashing through the gates, scattering the surprised sentries, I left the car and quickly ran to the tarmac. Arriving breathlessly just as the hangar doors closed behind the Douglas I was just in time to hear the announcer, who had been frantically trying to fill in time until my arrival, say, " And now, ladies and gentlemen, here is Miss Jean Batten, who will give you a graphic description of the landing." As I tried to regain my breath and give a vivid account my rivals, shaking with amusement, nearly split their sides laughing.

Later, however, I made what we considered a big *coup*. Immediately each competing aeroplane landed it was wheeled into the hangar, where the handicap times were checked. All doors were guarded, and no Press representatives or radio announcers admitted. Receiving an invitation to meet the Dutch pilots, I arranged for the electricians to run the leads up to a small window. Once inside the sanctity of the hangar I climbed on to a work-bench, and the precious microphone was handed to me through the window. Imagine the thrill all my listeners received when I announced that Messrs Parmentier and Moll would speak over our stations. These two pilots were great sports, and I asked Parmentier to speak in Dutch and Moll to translate what he said into English. The big Boeing machine was given third place. The chief pilot, Roscoe Turner, reputed to be a lion-tamer, was a veritable hero with the children, who liked his colourful uniform. He used to carry a walking-stick made of a complete lion's tail everywhere he went.

The only person flying solo in the race was Jimmy Melrose, the young Australian pilot, who flew out in eight days to win the handicap prize.

I continued my broadcasts for some days after the arrival of the winning Comet, then had the pleasure of flying to Sydney in the Douglas, piloted by Parmentier and Moll, with Roscoe Turner, Clyde Pangbourne, and a few other people as passengers.

An air-mail service was to be commenced between Australia and England, and I flew my Moth to Brisbane to be present at the inaugural ceremony, which was performed by the Duke of Gloucester.

The Jubilee of King George V was to take place in May 1935, and I decided to fly to London to witness the wonderful pageant. I thought very deeply about buying a new machine for the flight, or at least a new engine, but decided instead to have a complete overhaul carried out and to conserve the engine as much as possible during the flight. It was quite capable, I thought, of taking me safely back to England in reasonable time. Once there I would be in a better position to purchase a new machine for the flight I was even then planning to South America.

Before leaving Australia for England I returned to New Zealand to say good-bye to my people. Imagine my surprise when on driving to the boat I saw contents bills flaming the words "Will Jean Batten marry?" Quite dazed, I stopped the car and purchased a paper. There were all the details of my recent engagement laid bare in black and white. It appeared that a rumour had been circulated that I was flying back to England to be married. Before leaving England I had become engaged, but on arrival in Australia realized that I should have to choose between matrimony and my career. What made the situation rather difficult on this occasion was that my *fiancé* had been interviewed in London about the reason for my forthcoming flight a few days before receiving my letter suggesting that we should break off our engagement. I really felt that if I married at this stage I could not devote myself so wholeheartedly to the programme I had planned for the next few years. Not that my *fiancé* actually objected to any further flights. Quite the contrary was the case, for he had given me vital help after the forced landing in Rome. I was able to repay him a few days after my arrival in Sydney when I cabled the amount I had borrowed. Now that I had tasted the fruits of success and felt the urge to rise to even greater heights, any responsibility, however light, that would in any way hinder or deter my progress was not to be considered. In short, I suppose ambition claimed me, and I considered no sacrifice too great to achieve the task I had set myself.

From the day when I had my first flight I had been fired with the idea of making the first direct flight from England, the heart of the Empire, to New Zealand, my own country, and the farthest-flung Dominion. My flight to Australia made me realize that I would not be satisfied merely to fly out, taking a long time over the flight. If I were able to accomplish that flight I wanted to demonstrate the practical value of aerial travel between the two countries so widely separated. This could only be achieved by a rapid flight reducing the four to five weeks taken by ship by a handsome margin. To attain this I would need not only a great deal more long-distance flying experience, but also a fast modern aeroplane capable of nearly double the speed of my trusty Moth, which was then nearly six years old.

The flight to Australia had not been a great financial success, but I had managed to clear expenses, and by doing a lecture tour of New Zealand was able to pay off most of my debts. The New Zealand Government had given me, as previously stated, a grant of £500, and I decided to put this towards the purchase of a new machine, although it would be whittled to a forlorn £375 by the exchange when turned into sterling. By lecturing, broadcasting, writing, giving passenger flights, and advertising various products I managed to put some money aside for my dream aeroplane. If I were able to fly successfully back to England I thought it might be possible to sell the Moth; then I should just about have enough sterling to buy a new machine.

CHAPTER VII: RETURN FLIGHT

I N SYDNEY I MADE MANY FRIENDS, AND THE few weeks before my return flight were among the happiest of my life. The Moth had been overhauled, and I organized the flight down to the smallest detail, and felt that everything humanly possible had been done to make it a success. I was very reluctant to leave Sydney, however, and right up to the moment when I climbed into the cockpit to take off for England I thought seriously of cancelling the flight and remaining in Australia. Fate evidently ordained otherwise, however, and one lovely morning in April 1935 I set off for England. Good weather favoured me on the 2200-mile section across Australia to Darwin, and after the first day out I began to enjoy the flight. There had been a drought in Central Queensland, and I would pass over lonely drovers with great herds of cattle trekking southward to the greener country. It was a terrible sight to fly over dried-up water-holes and see scores of dead cattle lying around them.

The flight was an eventful one, and on April 12 I took off from Darwin and met with a terrible experience. The wind was south-easterly, and blowing great clouds of fine red dust from the Australian continent reduced visibility to a minimum. So that I might fly in clearer atmosphere and also take full advantage of the following wind I climbed up to 6000 feet and set off across the Timor Sea for the island of Timor. Below me floated a cloud carpet tinted orange by the dust, and occasionally through a gap I would glimpse the sea. About 250 miles from land the engine suddenly gave a cough. Were my ears deceiving me? I listened intently. There it was again—a sudden falter which seemed to shake the entire structure of the machine. The engine gave a final cough, then there was dead silence. A terrible feeling of helplessness swept over me as the machine commenced a slow, silent glide towards the cloud carpet. "Perhaps it is only a temporary petrol blockage," I thought, as my brain worked like lightning trying to find a way out of the predicament. I gave the engine full throttle, but there was no response. There was no sound to relieve the terrible silence except the whirring noise like a sigh as the lifeless 'plane glided down. "Surely this can't be the end!" I thought. "No, it's impossible; there must be some way out."

Almost fascinated, I watched the altimeter—5000, 4500, 4000 feet. I was in the cloud layer now—it was not very thick though, and at 3000 feet I emerged to see the blue expanse of sea stretching into infinity. This was agonizing—I must try to land the machine on the water as best I could. Undoing my shoes and flying-suit I reached for the small hatchet which I carried in case of emergency and placed it in the leather pocket at my side. There seemed a desperate chance that if I were able to land the machine on an even keel I might be able to cut one wing away and float on it.

The last few minutes were torture as I neared the water. The propeller was still just ticking over, and in a last desperate effort before attempting to land I opened and closed the throttle lever—without success. Suddenly, with a noise that was nearly deafening in the stillness and like a great sob, the engine burst into life again. I sank back greatly relieved, scarcely daring to breathe lest I should break the spell. As the engine regained its steady note I gradually coaxed the aeroplane up to 6000 feet again. For the next three hours, however, until I was flying once more over land, my mind was tortured with doubt.

On landing at Kupang I offered up a prayer for my deliverance, and the kind Dutch people listened with ashen faces as I told of my experience. We agreed, as was probably the case, that some foreign matter, possibly dust, had caused a temporary blockage in the petrol system. I cleaned the filter and jets while a weather report was obtained for the next section of 550 miles to Rambang, on Lombok island. My experience had shaken me more than I cared to admit or fully realized, and I did not feel my usual confidence return until I neared England towards the end of the flight.

From the time I crossed the equator until the end of the flight I had to battle with head winds which at times reduced the speed of my machine until it seemed to be making no headway at all. Seventeen days and fifteen hours after leaving Australia I landed my veteran Moth at Croydon on April 29, having completed the first journey to Australia and back by a woman pilot.

London was seething with excitement, and thousands of visitors were arriving daily from all parts of the world for the Jubilee of King George V and Queen Mary.

My flight had been a test of endurance, and crossing France I had been delayed some days by fog. On the last section I had felt so bitterly cold that I made an unscheduled landing at Abbeville to spend my last two francs on a cup of coffee.

The morning after my arrival I rose at 6.30 A.M. to give an Empire broadcast from the B.B.C. This was the first time I had broadcast from London, and the experience was an interesting one. A few nights later I spoke again on the "In Town To-night" programme.

The Jubilee celebrations exceeded my greatest expectations, and at the invitation of the Countess of Drogheda I watched the brilliant procession from the balcony of a lovely house in the Mall. Shortly afterwards I visited Scotland as guest of Viscount and Viscountess Elibank, and spent several happy days at their lovely home in Peebles.

Not very long after my arrival in London I signed a contract with Gaumont-British to give talks with a new film which had just been completed. The film was called *R.A.F.*, and, as the title suggests, gave a portrayal, and very vividly, of life in the Royal Air Force. The cream of British aviation was present at the *première*, and the newly appointed Air Minister, Sir Philip Cunliffe-Lister (later created Viscount Swinton), introduced the film. I felt very proud to be associated with it. At this time the great Air Force expansion scheme was just about to be launched, and I used to preface my talks with a few words stressing the vital importance of the R.A.F. and the necessity for expansion. Each day for two weeks I gave three talks, which evidently bore fruit, for, to the disgust of the theatre manager, but to my undisguised joy, the operator left to join the R.A.F.

After a considerable amount of thought and studying of the various types of light aircraft on the market I decided to sell my Moth and buy a new Percival Gull aeroplane. This proved to be easier said than done, however, and I ordered the new machine before I had managed to sell the old one, and consequently spent many weeks wondering how I could make ends meet. Eventually I sold the trusty Moth to a pilot in whose ownership I could rest assured it would spend its remaining days being treated with the respect and dignity that its great career merited. I took delivery of the new machine on my birthday, and the sleek silver monoplane fulfilled all my expectations when I took it for a trial flight.

Nearly all my time was occupied in organizing a flight to South America, studying maps and charts of the route, and collecting all available meteorological data for the South Atlantic Ocean. On this flight of nearly 8000 miles from London to Brazil and Buenos Aires I would have to fly over eight different countries, and the regulations to be complied with were legion. The French Government wisely insisted that I should

carry a revolver in case I was forced down in the in-
hospitable Riff territory in West Africa. On the other
hand, I learned that the importation of firearms into
South American countries was forbidden, and was notified that in no circumstances should I be in possession
of a revolver on arrival in South America. I spent
months unwinding red tape, interviewing consuls and
Air Ministry officials, who were most helpful, and
waiting for various permits. At last, however, all
preparations were completed, and it only remained for
me to fly my Gull to Lympne Aerodrome and clear
customs for South America. It was a wrench saying
good-bye to my mother, however. I felt that everything
possible had been done to make the flight a success, and
all depended now on a steady hand, a clear head, and a
modicum of luck to win through.

I flew the Gull to Lympne and made final preparations for the flight, arranging for a special weather
forecast to be sent to me from the Air Ministry at 3.30
on the morning of my proposed departure. At that
very early hour on the appointed day my alarum-clock
awakened me with a start, and hurriedly throwing a
coat over my nightclothes I crept downstairs in the
darkness to listen with bated breath to the forecast for
the England–Morocco section of my flight to South
America. Picking up the receiver I wrote down the
report as it came through: "Patches of fog over the
Channel; clouds 10/10ths at 1000 feet; early morning
mist in Northern France; wind at 1000–1500 feet, S.W.,
at 15–20 m.p.h., changing to westerly over Spain and
increasing in velocity; isolated storms on the Spanish

border and possibility of hail." The voice at the other
end of the line rapped out each word with military-like
precision. "And Morocco?" I asked hopefully, the
very name conjuring up visions of warm southern sunshine, palms, and strangely garbed people. The visions
quickly disappeared as the voice continued, "Conditions over Southern Spain, Strait of Gibraltar, and
Morocco more favourable, but wind S. to S.W. at 10–15
m.p.h." "Do you think——" I began, but the receiver
had already banged down, and I was left to make my
own decisions.

Should I go? Back in my room I perused the report.
Throwing open the window wide, I looked out, and was
met with an icy blast, which quickly dispelled any
further desire for sleep.

Anyway, what was the use of wasting time looking at
sleeping Hythe when I had to cross four countries to
reach my first stopping-place, Casablanca, 1400 miles
away. After all it was November, and the weather as
good as could be expected for that time of the year.
November . . . With a start I realized it was Armistice
Day. That anniversary, synonymous with courage and
quick decisions, decided me. Yes, I would go. . . . No
use hoping for better weather to-morrow. Who was it
said, "To-morrow never comes"?

Hastily donning my flying-suit and coat I collected
my few belongings, charts, and maps and hurried downstairs. As I sipped a cup of tea my gaze wandered
round the hotel dining-room to the opposite wall, where
hung a large coloured print of the dawn breaking over
the gigantic waves of an ocean. So big and powerful

were the waves that they seemed to threaten at any moment to flow from the frame and engulf the room. The picture had fascinated me the previous evening. It seemed to lend itself for contemplation, and was the sort of painting about which one could weave all sorts of stories—especially when about to attempt a solo flight across the Atlantic. What was the inscription beneath the 'picture, I wondered. Kind friends were waiting to drive me to the aerodrome, the car was ready, time was flying with incredible rapidity, but I must see what that inscription was before I left. Hurrying across the room as a voice from outside inquired for a third time if I were ready, I peered in the semi-darkness at the inscription, which read, "The Ocean, lonely, wild, unconquerable." Well, we would see about that, I thought.

As we drove towards the aerodrome we could see the tiny red lights like a ruby necklace round the boundary of the aerodrome, and from the Duty Officers' room a single light reassured me that everything was in readiness for my early start. There were no customs formalities to be gone through, for in my blue journey log-book the previous night the customs officer had placed the Government stamp beside the entry Lympne–Casablanca, and G-ADPR had been cleared by his Majesty's Customs—outward bound for South America on November 11, 1935.

The big hangar doors swung back, revealing a low-wing monoplane. Its silver surface, glistening and gleaming under the powerful electric lights, made it look like some lovely thoroughbred groomed and polished in readiness for some great race and straining to be away. 'In readiness,' yes, for had I not for six long months been organizing this flight? More than once I had sat up studying charts, maps, aerodrome and meteorological data till long after midnight, determined to plan every tiny detail so that when the time came to take off I should go knowing that I had done everything possible to make this flight a success.

While the engine was warming up I glanced anxiously at the wind-indicator, and found that I should have to take off towards a long row of ominous-looking pine-trees on a property bordering the aerodrome. How I hated those trees! They brought back vivid memories of my take-off for Australia the previous year when the little low-powered, five-year-old aeroplane heavily laden with petrol had climbed so gallantly over them, but laboriously enough to make the watchers below hold their breaths. My fears were groundless, however, for even while I taxied across the aerodrome the wind changed slightly, so that when the aeroplane had taken off straight and swift as a silver arrow the trees were soon far below.

CHAPTER VIII: SOUTH
AMERICAN FLIGHT

Iset my stop-watch and air-log as I left
Lympne Aerodrome. The time was exactly 6.30 A.M.,
G.M.T. I did not follow my usual practice of circling
the aerodrome to gain height, but set straight off across
the English Channel, as I had no time to waste if I were
to make Casablanca before dark with this head wind.
Climbing gradually to gain altitude, I was soon high up
above the mist and cloud in a world of my own. I had
set a compass course for Biarritz, and could only navi-
gate by dead-reckoning as seconds resolved into minutes
and minutes into hours, until now I was more than two
hours out and still above the clouds.

Blue sky and sunshine above, and below as far as I
could see stretched a white carpet. Sometimes it was
smooth as ice, and at other times ruffled like swans-
down. For company I watched the shadow of my aeroplane on the clouds beneath. Often on my flights
I had watched that shadow speeding along, sometimes
silhouetted against the sands of the Syrian Desert,
sometimes on white clouds such as these high above
some lonely part of the world. Something dark caught

my eye—a gap in the clouds. Very soon more gaps
appeared, and here and there I caught glimpses of the
pasture-lands of France as hour after hour slipped by.

When nearing the Spanish border I expected to see
the great snowy peaks of the Pyrenees silhouetted
against the skyline. To my consternation there was not
a mountain to be seen—only dark, treacherous rain-
clouds which I knew were concealing the peaks. Heavy
raindrops splashed on to the windscreen, to be whipped
into tiny rivulets by the slipstream of the propeller as
the aeroplane plunged into the storm. Visibility became steadily worse as I flew south, and the raindrops
formed a prelude to thousands of tiny silver arrows
which beat against the cabin windows as if vainly seeking admission. Hail . . . I thought of that voice rapping
out the weather report . . . "possibility of hail."

Flying lower and lower that I might see the coast, I
suddenly lost it completely as the machine nosed into
the rain-clouds. This would never do. I was flying into
a trap. Only a few hundred feet up and heading at
150 m.p.h. straight for the mountains. Wheeling the
machine about I turned back. Should I return to
Biarritz and wait for the storms to clear? Over the Bay
of Biscay the low rain-clouds foretold more storms to
come, and if this flight was to be a record every minute
was precious. I decided to keep to my schedule. There
was only one alternative, and that was to climb up
above the clouds before attempting to cross the mountains. I wondered to what height the clouds extended.
Giving the engine full throttle, I turned the machine
back on to its course and put it into a climb. Up and

up I climbed . . . 5000 feet . . . 6000 feet . . . 7000 feet.
As soon as I would rise above one layer of cloud it was
only to find another above. I watched the needle of
the altimeter creeping steadily higher as my trusty
aeroplane roared upward through the great cloud-
banks. Twelve thousand feet—surely the clouds could
not be much higher. Outside the cabin the grey and
white mass seemed to press against the cabin windows
of the machine and threaten to engulf it completely.
I began to despair of ever penetrating the sea of cloud.
Suddenly at 14,000 feet I emerged in brilliant sunshine.
How wonderful to see the light again after that dark,
choking mass which made me shudder at the thought
of it! Able to relax now after the long climb, I
realized how cold I was. My fingers gripping the control column were numb, and I welcomed a drink of hot
black coffee from my thermos. I seemed to be in a
world of my own, for as far as my eye could see there
stretched a vast, billowy carpet of cloud. It was bitterly
cold, and at such a great height I wondered if conditions were favourable for ice-formation. I anxiously
glanced out at the wings of the aeroplane, but was reassured by the answering gleam which flashed back at
me from the smooth silver surfaces of the wings. I became overwhelmed by an intense feeling of loneliness
which only the long-distance flyer knows, and found
myself listening intently to the rhythmic beat of the
engine and trying not to think what the consequences
of an engine-failure now would mean . . . the thought
of gliding down through that white carpet beneath me
that hid the mountains, where it would be almost im-

possible to make a forced landing. It seemed strange that I should be crossing a great mountain range like the Pyrenees without glimpsing even one mountain peak.

Away to the east of my course the clouds seemed to assume fantastic shapes, rising and falling like waves. I wondered what strange currents caused such peculiar formations. Suddenly I realized that these irregularities in the billowy cloud carpet were in reality snow-capped mountain peaks. They looked cold and unfriendly, these great snowy peaks rearing themselves majestically above the sea of cloud like giant sentinels.

My spirits rose as I flew southward, and the clouds were lower, enabling me to descend to 10,000 feet, where it was not quite so cold. Gradually the billowy carpet beneath me began to break up, and here and there I caught glimpses of the earth and was able to check up my position. Through one break in the clouds I looked down into the yawning gap of a deep, grey, rocky crevice. So deep it seemed that I thought it must surely descend hundreds of feet into the very bowels of the earth. Another time I caught sight of a precipitous mountain with a narrow road winding up to a castle and looking just like a strand of white cotton thrown haphazard on to the mountain-side. Very soon the clouds disappeared, giving way to a vast panorama of purple-grey mountains and green valleys. Occasionally I would fly over villages with their tiny houses clustered together. What was that open space in the shape of a circle that seemed a feature of every village? Of course . . . the bull-ring.

Sunny Spain ... Half-forgotten tales of my childhood came back to me—tales of adventure, hidden treasure, and Spanish galleons; of flashing swords and chivalrous *conquistadores* who fought to defend some lovely princess in a lonely castle. There were the castles all right. Even now I was passing over one high up on a mountain. It might have been an abandoned medieval fortress long since forgotten, but it was evidently inhabited, for a tiny flag fluttered from the turret. "I should see Madrid soon now," I thought, scanning the rugged mountainous country ahead. My eyes swept across the instrument-board. All was well: oil-pressure, 42 lbs.; engine revs., 2000; altitude, 9000 ft.; air speed, 150 m.p.h. Leaning down to reach a petrol-cock on the floor of the machine I switched over to the port wing-tank. Number 2 tank I called it, for there were five tanks in all to watch and switch from one to another as the indicators of the little gauges on the wing-tanks neared the red zero mark as the petrol was consumed by the engine, which purred faithfully on hour after hour. I had to be quick, though, to switch over, then turn off the cock of the empty tank so that the two automatic pumps on the engine should not draw air and, forming an air-lock, cause an engine-failure. On the right side of the cabin was an auxiliary oil-tank, and every hour I would pump air into the tank from where the oil flowed out under pressure to the main oil-tank in the starboard wing, where there was yet another gauge to be watched. I checked up my position and jotted it down in the log-book strapped to my knee.

I was soon approaching the lovely, undulating purple

line of the snow-capped Sierra de Guadarrama. Above the highest peak a solitary fluffy white cloud floated like a pennant. Villages and roads became more numerous, and now I was beginning to enjoy the flight. In the distance to the westward of my course I saw the great white city of Madrid, and felt tempted to alter course and explore the beauties of the Spanish capital. I made a resolve to return one day and learn more of this fascinating country. How strange it seemed that on my first visit to Spain I should fly the full length of the country with no intention of landing. Why, even Don Quixote would have raised his eyebrows at the very thought of such a journey. The vast plateau over which I had been flying was 2000 feet above sea-level, and although I was nearing the edge of it there were still more mountain ranges ahead. The country beneath reminded me somewhat of my own homeland, New Zealand, with its majestic mountains and fertile valleys. Frequently I would fly over the acres of orderly dark green trees of orange groves.

Crossing the broad, sweeping curves of the Guadal-quivir river to the east of Seville I continued on, until at last I sighted the blue waters of the Strait of Gibraltar. The mountains here were lower, and the country became much greener as I neared the southern coast of Spain. A strong westerly wind and myriads of white-crested waves were my impressions of the Strait as I left the coast of Spain east of Cape Trafalgar and crossed to Northern Africa. I had my first glimpse of Morocco nearing Tangier, for although the wind was strong there was a slight dust-haze which limited visibility. Tangier . . . The graceful curve of a sapphire-blue harbour backed by green hills. What an exquisite setting for such a gem! White, flat-roofed houses, with here and there a Moorish tower or dome; wide, cool terraces sloping down to the sea, and palms and flowers in profusion.

The sun beat fiercely down as mile after mile of the sandy coastline slipped beneath the silver wings, which reflected the glare and shone like burnished steel. England seemed a long way off . . . 1200 miles away, for I was now eight and a half hours out. Only another 190 miles or so to Casablanca, I thought, pulling on my cork sun-helmet and wondering how I should stand the sun on the next day's flight to West Africa.

The country was flatter now and much greener than I had expected. I was passing over a fairly large town. Picking up my map I read " Rabat." A sleepy-looking place with square white, flat-roofed houses and narrow streets. It seemed to be completely deserted, but then I was too high up to distinguish any figures, and the only sign of life seemed to be a herd of animals wending their way along a street leaving the city. Glancing back I decided Rabat looked interesting and rather pretty, probably worth a visit some day. I flew much lower, and was able to distinguish the figures of some Arabs, their draperies flying in the wind as they galloped their horses along the beach. Approaching a lighthouse I saw three tiny native fishing-smacks, and far ahead the white buildings of Casablanca gleaming in the strong sunlight. Well named . . . Casablanca, for almost without exception it seemed that every flat-roofed house was white. So strong was the light that I could easily distinguish people walking about the streets, and as I flew low over the aerodrome could see the little crowd that had gathered to welcome me and speed me on my way.

Shutting off the engine, I glided down to land; then as the wheels touched down started to taxi across to the hangars. I paused for a moment and made a hurried entry in the log-book: "Landed Casablanca 04.15 P.M., G.M.T. Day's run, 1350 miles." Arriving in front of the hangar I switched off the engine exactly nine hours and three-quarters after leaving England, and opening the door of the cabin stepped out. I felt a little stiff as I climbed down off the wing, to be immediately surrounded by a group of friendly French people. Handshakes and congratulations, murmurs of " Bon voyage ! " and " Bonne chance ! " " Why, I've only just started the flight," I began. " This is the first stage." " *Ah, oui*, but what a record to start out with ! Non-stop from England to Casablanca in nine hours and three-quarters ! " Yes, of course, I had not thought of that, for there were the preparations for the next stage to think about. Phew ! It was hot. Discarding the heavy woollen coat in which I had set out I felt the sun burning my shoulders through my white flying-suit. Accompanied by the president of the Aéro-Club de Maroc, I walked across to the customs office, where once again G-ADPR was cleared outward bound, but this time for Rio de Oro, where I had arranged for a supply of petrol to be ready for me at the tiny Spanish outpost of Villa Cisneros. Willing hands pushed the machine into the shade of the hangar. A French mechanic was waiting to give any help I should require with the engine, for I was not going on again without first servicing the machine and having some food and sleep. There was another flight of some 1600 miles ahead before I reached the taking-off point for the final stage of the flight across the South Atlantic Ocean nearly 2000 miles to Brazil. I must conserve my energy, for the successful navigation of that ocean depended on a clear brain and a steady hand. A cup of tea and some ham and salad in the club-house was a welcome interlude. There was a considerable amount of talking going on in the adjoining room, and it did not occur to me that I was the subject of the discussion. The President left me to finish my belated lunch, and joining the group was himself soon engrossed in the deep discussion. As I was finishing the meal he returned and said that the health officer wanted to know if I had been vaccinated. Giving myself a mental pat on the back for my careful organization I searched through my papers until I came to a medical certificate attesting that I had been vaccinated for smallpox. No, that would not do, it appeared. I must produce a certificate stating that I had been inoculated against 'pest.' What was 'pest,' I wanted to know. It was not mentioned in the long list of " conditions to be complied with in flights to French West Africa " that had been sent to me from the Air Ministry before my departure. Had I not complied with all these regulations, and already shown the customs officer the mooring equipment, signal pistol complete with red and green rocket cartridges, the insurance policy for 100,000 francs to assist in paying for a search in the event of a forced landing on the lonely stretches over which I must fly to reach Thies? There were also the big two-gallon water-containers, the packets of emergency rations sufficient to last for fourteen days, the 20 per cent. petrol margin, the glass tubes containing chemicals to indicate wind-direction on impact with the ground, and, of course, the heavy Service revolver with twenty cartridges. I thought with a twinge of regret how these new regulations had already delayed the start of my flight for one month. Surely there could not be anything I had overlooked. No, no, I must not misunderstand them, the President assured me with a smile. I had certainly complied with all the regulations. The health officer had received notification that plague had broken out in Senegal, and no one who was not inoculated against 'pest' could enter Moroccan territory from there.

"I don't want to," I began. "You see, I am flying on from Senegal to South America, and will only land at the military aerodrome of Thies."

"Yes, but you run a terrible risk, and once having entered Senegal it would not be possible for you to return to Morocco should any contingency arise and you wish to do so. It is wiser that you wait in Casablanca for a few days and be inoculated before proceeding."

I closed my eyes for a second: the bottom seemed to be dropping out of my world, so disappointed did I feel. "There must be a way out," I thought, determined not to give up.

" Can I go to Villa Cisneros? " I asked. " That's Spanish territory, and the authorities there might let me proceed to Senegal." If not I had decided to return to England on the following day and make the flight in another month or two. To my mind that seemed the only solution, for apart from the record the thought of being inoculated in the unaccustomed heat of Morocco for such a horrible plague as ' pest' seemed to be, and immediately afterwards attempting an Atlantic flight, was not to be entertained.

The President promised to see if there was any alternative, and departed to the adjoining room, to return almost immediately with a man whom I took to be the health officer. They were not at all happy as they told me that if I liked to sign a document to the effect that having been warned about the plague I proceeded entirely at my own risk I should be allowed to fly on to Senegal. Ah, fate was kind. Yes, I would sign the paper, I declared happily. They all looked at me in astonishment. I had no first-hand knowledge of plague, and did not realize the terrible scourge that it was, so the thought that I might encounter the deadly ' pest' did not enter my head.

Once the document was signed we returned to the machine. Refuelling operations were soon in full swing; the mechanic, eager to carry out any work I could give him, busied himself draining the oil, cleaning filters, and refuelling the petrol-tanks.

At last everything was in readiness for an early start, for I proposed leaving about an hour before dawn in order to arrive at Thies before sundown. Taking the thermos and the small leather bag containing my few belongings from the cockpit, I smiled at the crowd, who seemed so genuinely pleased that everything was going to schedule. Several people had already offered to drive me into the town, and after arranging for a guard to watch the machine I departed, leaving the aeroplane still surrounded by an admiring group.

Leaning back in the deep seat of the sports car I breathed a sigh of contentment. The flight so far had kept to schedule, and now I was able to relax for a few hours. We were approaching the outskirts of the city, and the sun, setting in a blaze of gold, tinted the low white houses shades of pearly iridescence. The car flashed past a herd of native cattle jolting along the road, and farther on passed two Arabs riding on donkeys and picturesquely clad in hooded garments of orange and black striped cloth. As we drove through the deep shadows of the narrow streets at times we would have to stop as crowds of natives made way for the car. In some of the doorways Arabs were squatting cross-legged smoking pipes, and here and there the rays of an odd lamp would catch the handsome features of some Arab youth padding noiselessly along the street or jogging homeward on a mule.

With a jolt we pulled up outside a large white building, which was appropriately enough called the Hotel Atlantic. A native wearing a long striped garment and a red fez dashed forward to carry the luggage, and I laughed at the look of amazement and incredulity on his face as I emerged carrying the thermos and tiny leather bag. My kind friends agreed to call for me at

3.30 A.M., and after ordering some dinner to be sent to my room I retired.

The furnishings of the room to which I was shown were typically Moroccan. The floor was tiled and partially covered with several beautifully coloured native rugs. The main feature of the bed was a large mosquito net, which completely enveloped it, and the orange and black striped coverlet was of woven cloth.

By the time I had dined, checked over the maps for the next section of the flight, arranged to be called at 3.30 A.M., and instructed the native attendant in the art of filling a thermos it was nearly midnight. As soon as my head touched the pillow I fell into a deep sleep, only to be awakened three and a half hours later by the shrill note of my alarum-clock. Sitting up reluctantly, I groped about for the clock that I might silence its impatient ringing. Where had I put the wretched thing? Before I had disentangled myself from the folds of the mosquito net and discovered the clock on the floor the impatient screaming had terminated abruptly. "Every one in the hotel is probably awake by now," I reproachfully told myself. I listened for the angry muttering and smothered oaths that these early notes of my alarum-clock usually brought forth from disgruntled guests in adjoining rooms, but there was not a sound to be heard. It did not take me long to struggle into my flying-suit, and after a hasty cup of tea and some biscuits I joined my friends, who had arrived punctually and were awaiting me in the dimly lit hall. The native attendant had faithfully carried out my instructions, and had the thermos, filled with coffee, and some sandwiches ready for me.

We were soon on our way to the aerodrome. The white houses looked quite ghostly in the moonlight as we drove through the sleeping city, and the deep silence was only broken by the occasional distant howl of a dog. With the deserted streets to ourselves we made good progress, and soon arrived at the aerodrome. There was my passport to retrieve from the customs officer, so while the aeroplane was being wheeled out of the hangar I walked across to the control office and collected it, also obtaining a weather report for Agadir. Bidding good-bye to my French friends I climbed into the cockpit, ran the engine up, and, releasing the brakes, taxied slowly across the aerodrome and turned into wind. I carefully checked over the instruments on the dashboard once again, setting the stop-watch and air-log and adjusting the illuminated compass, which shone up at me like a circlet of diamonds from the floor of the cockpit. Switching on the navigation lights I took off.

As I gave the engine full throttle and gently pushed the control column forward the aeroplane roared across the aerodrome. The tail lifted, and as I eased the stick back the Gull rose, climbing high above the red boundary lights. Rapidly gaining height I throttled the engine down to cruising revolutions and turned to fly back across the aerodrome. Even in the darkness Casablanca looked white—almost like a fairy city with its myriads of tiny sparkling lights. Unless the light southerly wind increased in strength I should pass over Mogador at about 6.45 A.M., G.M.T.

The time factor is a great problem on such long flights, for each place has its own local time, and as I was flying gradually westward—that is, travelling with the sun—I was actually gaining daylight. On the Australia flight exactly the opposite had been the case, for with every thousand miles I had flown eastward approximately an hour's daylight had been lost. To prevent confusion I made all my calculations in Greenwich Mean Time, and this also enabled me to know to the minute the number of hours of daylight there would be for each day of the flight. There were two clocks on the instrument-board, one which was set to Greenwich Mean Time, and the other I altered at each stopping-place to the local time, for naturally the authorities at each aerodrome had to know my estimated time of departure in their own local time.

CHAPTER IX: SAND AND SUN

I LOOKED BACK AT CASABLANCA, WHICH IN the distance, with all the lights blurred together, looked exactly like a great, sparkling diamond. The brightness of the city was accentuated by the fact that apart from the aerodrome there was not another light outside the boundary of the town, and the surrounding country was in pitch darkness, for by this time the moon had set. Leaning forward I turned off the navigation lights to conserve the battery, and switched on to the rear petrol-tank. The aeroplane roared along like a steady ship cutting through a calm sea.

It was impossible to distinguish anything in the blackness which enveloped the earth beneath. The sky, clear and exquisitely lovely, was encrusted with stars, like myriads of diamonds scattered at random across the vault of heaven. One by one I watched the stars fade before the oncoming dawn, and gradually the darkness gave way to a cold grey light, through which I began to distinguish the country over which I was flying. Miles and miles of sandy ridges met my eye, with here and there a rocky patch sparsely covered with vegetation. To the east the dark outline of the Atlas

Mountains towered high in the sky. It was growing rapidly lighter, and from behind the purple shadows of the Atlas a single ray of gold pierced the sky. The effect was unbelievable; the sky was tinted with the most gorgeous colours—layer upon layer, from deep crimson to exquisite shades of rose, all wonderfully blended. A solitary little cloud high up in the greeny blue above the strata of colour became a pale gold as one by one the rays pierced the sky and the sun rose from behind the mountains. Paling the rich colouring to pastel tints it shone down, completely dominating the clear blue sky.

I was passing over Mogador, and ahead were the rocky peaks of the Atlas Mountains as the range terminated abruptly at the coast. The towering peaks looked like great giants whose progress farther westward had been checked by the mighty Atlantic. What a huge range it was, too, for even here by the coast where the mountains were lower they rose to a height of over 2000 feet, while about a hundred miles inland some of them reached a height of over 12,000 feet. The mountains rose in some places almost sheer from the sea, and I decided to fly some little distance from the coast so that I should be sheltered for the next sixty miles or so from the piercing heat of the sun, which was now burning down with fierce intensity.

It was time for breakfast: so absorbed had I been in watching the sunrise and sighting Mogador that hunger had been forgotten. I now thought longingly of bacon and eggs, crisp toast, and a cup of hot tea. This being out of the question, I surveyed the contents of the larder. On the floor of the cockpit was a box I named the tucker-box. It was well within my reach, but unfortunately near enough to the auxiliary tanks to allow all the food to be permeated by the unappetizing odour of petrol and oil. The contents of the box formed the daily rations, which consisted of ham sandwiches, ordered overnight, chocolate, which was now in a state of liquid, milk tablets, apples, dates, barleysugar, raisins, cereals, cheese, one thermos flask of black coffee and one of water. Not a very long list for breakfast, lunch, and tea in the air. The other things would keep, I decided, selecting a ham sandwich. Holding the control column in my left hand I managed to sip some coffee from the flask without spilling a drop on my white suit. Fortunately the air was calm here in the shelter of the mountains, for this was an extremely difficult feat to perform. To hold the control column in the left hand, keep one eye on the instrument-board and the other on the compass, and while keeping the aeroplane flying straight and level attempt to pour out a cup of coffee from the thermos flask is no easy task. More than once in the past when trying to perform this feat in bumpy weather a shower of hot coffee had been precipitated over me, so nowadays I usually drank out of the thermos itself after leaving the cap off for some time previously to cool the liquid.

After finishing my breakfast with an apple I felt decidedly refreshed. I was then flying over a rocky promontory and rounding the curve of the mountains to Agadir. Should I land at Agadir and obtain a weather report for Villa Cisneros, for the report given to me at Casablanca only covered the route as far as this French military outpost? It was already 7.30, G.M.T., and if I was to make Thies before sundown, allowing for one hour on the ground at Villa Cisneros, there was no time to be wasted. In any case, I thought, if the sand were blowing there would be a sufficient margin of petrol left for me to turn back to Cape Juby, which would be the next landing-ground I should pass over about three hundred miles farther on.

The farther southward I flew the more wild and barren became the country, until it was so featureless that there was nothing to look at but mile after mile of sandy coastline. It was easy to realize now why I had been ordered to carry all the additional equipment. There was no sign of civilization to be seen: no living thing apparently existed on this forsaken-looking country. Even a stray herd of camels would at least have relieved the monotony of the yellow sandy expanse. Opening both windows that I might gain some respite from the close, suffocating heat inside the cabin, I struggled to remove my heavy coat. The monotony was not to last long, however, for soon a series of bumps which seemed to shake the whole structure of the aircraft roused me from my lethargy. The sky was partially covered with fluffy cumulus clouds, above which I climbed in an endeavour to reach calmer atmosphere.

Almost two hours out from Agadir I caught sight of a small encampment through a gap in the clouds, and shutting off the engine glided down so as to make sure I had not passed over Cape Juby without checking it. There it was, a group of square white houses and a landing-ground marked with a circle—a welcome sight to a lonely pilot. Setting a direct course for Villa Cisneros I climbed once more above the clouds, which were assuming a yellowish tinge with the dust which a fresh wind was whirling up from the desert. It looked rather like a storm blowing up, and I hoped the weather would hold at least long enough for me to fly through to Villa Cisneros, another 350 miles farther on.

An hour later I decided it was a case of jumping from the frying-pan into the fire. Above the cloud layer I avoided the bumps and bad visibility, but the sun was scorching, and looking down on to clouds was even more monotonous than the barren desert. Gliding down through a gap I found the clouds offered a certain amount of shelter from the sun, and although it was bumpy visibility had improved considerably. I strained my eyes for some sign of an Arab encampment, remembering all the tales I had heard about the Riffs, who apparently lived in this part of the world. Years ago when the French were surveying a route over the Sahara Desert, and across which they now operate two motor-car services and a regular air service, they experienced a great deal of trouble with the natives. On this west coast route, however, the natives had been the most troublesome, for they seemed particularly cruel and warlike. During those pioneering days aeroplanes had frequently been forced down on this territory, and some of the men captured by the Riffs had been cruelly tortured. Eventually the French Government had made the Riffs understand that an aviator was worth money to them if delivered safe and sound. Nowadays the worst that could happen to any aviator who made a forced landing on this desolate stretch would be that if captured by the Riffs he would be held to ransom. That may have had something to do with that 100,000-franc guarantee that I had to arrange, I thought, wishing the time would pass more quickly, so that I could once more reach civilization. All the same, my curiosity prompted me to wish for one peep at a Riff. Not a horde of them such as I had seen in Foreign Legion pictures, where thousands dashed across the screen, but just one or two viewed from 1000 feet couldn't be very dangerous. However, they were either very elusive or encamped in the sandhills farther inland, for I failed to see any sign of life whatever, although I knew from past experience how natives could apparently spring from nowhere when a stranger landed on their territory.

To the west stretched the mighty Atlantic, with its blue expanse seeming to stretch into infinity. Although it provided a certain relief from the intense glare of the desert, I viewed it with some uneasiness. It was a constant reminder of the 100 per cent. efficiency that would be demanded of the trusty engine which purred so happily hour after hour. I wished that the taking-off point for the South Atlantic crossing were not so far from England. The three thousand miles to West Africa seemed a long, gruelling flight in itself rather than a prelude to an Atlantic flight. Neither the engine nor myself could be expected to be quite as fresh as when we left at the commencement of the flight. A severe test was in store for the aircraft too, and for the big auxiliary eighty-gallon petrol-tank, which almost completely filled the cabin, leaving me only just sufficient room to climb in front of it to take my place at the controls. For the flight across the Atlantic Ocean it would be necessary to fill all five petrol-tanks to capacity, so that the aircraft would be very heavily laden for the take-off. For the flight to the military aerodrome of Thies, from where I proposed crossing to Brazil, it was not necessary to fill all the tanks, for there were aerodromes at reasonable intervals where it was possible to refuel. For the 1907-mile flight from Thies to Natal it would be of the utmost importance to have a safety margin of petrol.

The horizon was blurred by a yellow dust-haze, and visibility became steadily worse, until at last I was forced to fly very low over the coastline so that I might not lose sight of it altogether and perhaps miss Villa Cisneros. After flying so low that at times I was obliged to hurdle the machine over rocky boulders on the shore at last the air became clearer, and running parallel with the coastline I noticed a line of fairly high sandhills. These hills were of peculiar undulating formation, and were marked on my map as "Las Almenas," terminating about twenty-five miles north-east of Villa Cisneros.

Very soon I was passing over a long, tapering sandy stretch, its golden yellow accentuated by the deep blue water of an inlet which almost severed it from the mainland. Picking up the map I read, "Ed Dajla Sahria Peninsula," and looked ahead for a glimpse of Villa Cisneros, which should be at the southern end of the peninsula. Early adventurers in these parts had evidently mistaken the large inlet for the mouth of some great river, and not bothering to explore the blue strip had given it the name of Rio de Oro ("River of Gold") and sailed away. I wondered whether there was really gold there, or whether the name referred to the golden sands on each side of the inlet.

To the south of the sandy strip I could see the radio masts of Villa Cisneros, and was soon flying over the rows of tiny black tents of an Arab encampment. After circling the square white tower of the fort I flew across the aerodrome. There were wheel and tail-skid marks on the ground, so evidently the surface, if hard, was crusty or covered with a soft layer of sand, I thought, shutting off the engine. The aerodrome was really a large part of the desert fenced off with barbed wire, and as I glided down to land it was as if I were entering a furnace, so intense was the heat.

It is extremely difficult after being hours in the air to judge accurately one's height above the ground when landing on sand. Especially is this so at midday, when the sun has reached its meridian and there are practically no shadows. The heat rising from the sand made little waves in the atmosphere just like the ripples above a fire. As I rubbed my eyes and stared down at the golden surface the heat-waves gave the illusion of sand-hills, and for one frightful second I imagined that they were real hillocks which would overturn the machine. Touching down near the hangar I switched off the engine, for there was a regulation forbidding taxying on this aerodrome owing to the miniature dust-storm created by doing so. Mechanics wheeled the machine

into the shade of the hangar, and at once commenced
refuelling.

I did not intend staying long on the ground, for there
was another 680-mile flight to Thies, where it was imperative that I should land before sunset, as no night
landing facilities were available there. I watched the
native boys busily straining the petrol through the
chamois-leather filter, and wondered idly why it was
necessary for twelve of them to cluster round each tank
as it was filled, whereas the refuelling could have been
finished in ten minutes had they distributed themselves
and filled all tanks simultaneously. As each was filled
there was a loud shout from all twelve as the petrol
overflowed and poured down the wing. A lot of talking
ensued as the cap was replaced, and exactly the same
process repeated at the next tank. I had salvaged the
packet of sandwiches before the petrol-tin being hoisted
on to the side of the machine overbalanced and distributed part of its contents into the tucker-box. Opening the packet I found that the bread had dried up, and
just as I had finished the ham and thrown the bread
to some persistent native dogs a motor-car pulled up
outside the hangar. From it stepped a Spanish officer,
who saluted and explained in French that the hospitable Governor sent his compliments, and would be
very pleased if I would join him at lunch. I looked at
my watch and wondered if I could really afford the
time for lunch. Where was the house? Was it far away,
I inquired of the officer. He pointed to the square
white house just outside the boundary of the aerodrome, and I decided to accept the invitation.

As soon as the refuelling was finished I accompanied the officer to the house, where the Governor and his wife were waiting to receive me. The large white house was typically Spanish with its arched doorways and cool blue-and-white-tiled floors. How restful, I felt, sinking into a deep chair and sipping a cool drink and conversing with the Governor and his wife in my best Spanish. Each of the children was presented to me, and looking at the four bright little faces I wondered how it was they were so healthy in this great heat. "I flew right over your country yesterday," I told the charming little wife of the Governor as the silent-footed servant served the lunch. She was surprised and rather sorry that I had not landed in Spain. Would I not care to stay and rest for the night, she inquired. I had a vivid mental vision of the cool room where I had bathed my sunburned hands and face on my arrival as I reluctantly declined her invitation. The time was passing all too quickly, so, thanking the Governor's wife for her hospitality, I bade good-bye to my new-found friends.

Although it was so hot in the open the Governor kindly offered to accompany me to the aerodrome, where the machine was quickly wheeled out of the hangar and the engine started up. The slipstream from the propeller was whirling up the sand, which looked like a smoke-screen behind the machine, and the fine, choking dust was blowing into my eyes and mouth, so that I could even taste the grit between my teeth. Quickly bidding good-bye to the Governor, I climbed into the cockpit and took straight off. As I turned to fly back across the aerodrome the cloud of sand defined my line of take-off, and through the yellow haze I could see the white-clad figures on the ground waving good-bye. Not River of Gold, but Hearts of Gold they should have called this place, I thought, remembering the kindness of my new-found friends, living so far away from their own country in this lonely outpost.

For the next three hundred miles the route lay inland, but as visibility became steadily worse and the yellow dust blotted out the horizon I decided to alter course and steer for Port Étienne, where I could land if the sand-storms were blowing farther south. Mile after mile of barren sandy desert slipped past, with never a tree or bush or even a blade of grass to relieve the monotonous yellow. I felt very lonely flying over this vast stretch, for utter desolation reigned supreme, and not a sign of civilization was to be seen anywhere. The wind was northerly, about 40 m.p.h. I estimated, as the machine sped southward, covering the next two hundred miles in just over an hour. I did not fly over Port Étienne, but cut across the top of the peninsula and continued on down the coast, leaving Spanish territory and crossing the border to French Mauritania.

A name on the map caught my eye, "Île des Pélicans," and gliding down I flew low over the island, in the hope of seeing some sign of life, but it seemed just as desolate as the rest of the coast. A hundred miles farther south I could hardly believe my eyes when a flock of about a thousand flamingos rose like a lovely veil of pink tulle from the islands over which I was flying. Shortly afterwards I saw a small fishing-smack, and when a little native village with three men on camels riding towards it came into view I considered this must be quite a thickly populated district.

The heat was terrific, and it was almost with feelings of relief that I hailed the sight of an approaching rain-storm. "It would at least cool the atmosphere," I thought, flying low along the coast as the heavy tropical rain pelted down so fiercely that I could only just see the white line of rollers breaking on the beach beneath. When the rain had almost ceased I removed my topee, and putting my head out the window let the rain drench my hair and cool my burning face. The rain was refreshing, and my weariness left me as I once more donned my sun-helmet and estimated the time when I should pass over the town of St Louis, at the mouth of the Senegal river.

The country was becoming greener, for the sandhills were sparsely covered with vegetation, and occasional clumps of trees dotted the landscape. As I flew over a vast swamp in the centre of which was a lake hundreds of wild birds, evidently disturbed by the noise of the engine, rose like a cloud from the green reeds.

Quite suddenly I came upon the river Senegal wending its way southward through the thick dark green vegetation. My course lay parallel to the river, and it was not until nearing St Louis that I actually crossed it and was able to see the many palm-trees and the jungle *débris* floating down the muddy waters to the sea.

St Louis, with its shady trees and white houses, looked

a prosperous and busy town. In the centre was a railway station, for a line connected Thies and Dakar with St Louis, and I guessed that the arrival of a train was quite an event. The sea for some considerable distance from the shore was discoloured by the muddy waters of the great river as it flowed into the blue Atlantic. The sun was low on the horizon, and I expected to arrive at Thies just before sundown, for I knew from experience how little twilight there is in the tropics. The wind had dropped completely, and the tree-tops of the dark green jungle which covered the flat country were thrown into relief by the golden rays of the setting sun.

In the fast-fading light I saw the railway fork at Thies, and immediately sighted a large clearing in the jungle, which was the aerodrome. Circling the hangar I pulled back the throttle and glided down to land. As I crossed the boundary it seemed impossible to lose speed, and the aeroplane, flying just above the ground, was rapidly approaching the high trees at the end of the aerodrome. Quickly I opened up the throttle: the machine roared over the trees. Whatever had happened, I wondered, circling to attempt another landing. Exactly the same thing occurred again, and I found that the throttle lever had jammed, and it was quite impossible to pull it right back.

The light was fading fast; I must get down somehow. There was only one thing to do, and that was to switch off completely. Leaning forward I knocked the two little switches on the dashboard down, and as the roar of the engine ceased glided silently towards the aerodrome. The aeroplane seemed to sink heavily through the still air, and the now lifeless metal propeller caught the last rays of light. It was imperative that I make no error now, for there was no engine to help me if I undershot the aerodrome. Manœuvring the machine so that I should land well inside the boundary I glided silently over the trees and landed near the hangar. A group of mechanics who had gathered outside the hangar while I had been circling were now running across to the machine. Opening the door, I climbed out, feeling decidedly stiff after the 1600-mile flight from Casablanca. The aeroplane was pushed into the hangar and soon surrounded by an admiring group of mechanics. Several French officers congratulated me on my fast flight from England, and I now realized for the first time that it was only thirty-six hours since I had left England, three thousand miles away.

CHAPTER X: SHOCKS AT THIES

My original plan before leaving Lympne had been to fly to West Africa, rest for a day or two and await favourable weather, then attempt to lower all records for the fastest flight across the South Atlantic Ocean. If I were to fly straight on across the Atlantic to Brazil there was every possibility of my lowering by almost a day the record for the only other solo flight from England to South America.

"You will rest in Thies for a few days before continuing your flight?" asked one of the officers.

"No, I have decided to fly straight on, and if the weather is not too bad will take off before dawn tomorrow morning," I told the astonished officer.

"We have no night-flying equipment here," they told me, in answer to my request for a flare path. "You should have gone to Dakar: they have all facilities there, and good all-weather runways."

Before leaving England I had made exhaustive inquiries as to the best aerodromes along the route, and had been told that the runways at Dakar were not yet completed, and it seemed that the military aerodrome of Thies, forty-five miles inland, was the most suitable.

On good authority I had been told that Thies was exceptionally large, and as the aeroplane would be heavily laden with petrol for the Atlantic flight of almost two thousand miles it had seemed the better of the two for my purpose.

I looked across the aerodrome, which was sparsely covered with long grass. It had been large at one time, but it appeared that since the Air France company had moved their headquarters to Dakar only a square in the centre of the big aerodrome had been kept cleared, and the rest was now overgrown and covered with scrub and hillocks. Yes, it was only too plain now that I should have gone to Dakar, for it was also on the coast, and would have shortened the flight to Brazil by forty-five miles. The fact that Thies was so much farther inland meant that by leaving from there I was really handicapped by approximately fifteen minutes for the record which I hoped to establish for the Atlantic crossing. It was too late now to fly on to Dakar, for the sun had long since set, and if I were to lower the England–Brazil record I should have to take off in the dark hours before dawn to arrive at my destination before nightfall. Special permits had been granted for me to land at Thies, and I had arranged for fuel supplies to be sent there for me. Great was my surprise and disappointment on being told that no supplies had arrived.

"They must have thought you would go to Dakar," said one of the officers.

"No, all arrangements for me to land here were made months ago," I protested. "Would you please telephone Dakar for me?" I asked the officer, giving him the telephone number and name of the agent, which I had fortunately obtained before leaving England.

Just then a motor-car drove up, and out stepped the Commandant of the base, who proved to be as kind as he was efficient. As soon as I had explained the situation to him he ordered the officer to telephone immediately. It was imperative that the fuel should arrive that night if I were to lower the record, and this delay only made me more determined than I might otherwise have been.

"Would you care to have something to eat, and are you not in need of rest?" inquired the Commandant.

"Yes, I would like some sandwiches," I replied, but rest was out of the question, for there was the engine schedule to be done and the throttle lever to be adjusted, I explained.

"The military mechanics will help you," said the Commandant, calling up three smart-looking men.

I was determined to arrange everything in readiness for the early take-off before leaving the aerodrome.

The officer arrived back to say that the agent had not expected me so soon, and that the supplies would arrive in the morning.

"That's no good!" I cried. "They must start immediately. It is imperative that the supplies arrive to-night. I don't care if they do have to drive sixty-five kilometres from Dakar in the darkness," I said, as the thought occurred to me that there were probably wild animals lurking in the dark green jungle I had seen from the air. "I haven't flown three thousand miles to be held up by a wretched agent," I continued. "Anyway, this will teach them a lesson."

It was difficult to control my anger, for I was tired and hungry, and this hold-up was quite unexpected.

"I will speak to the agent myself," promised the Commandant, "and we will have the supplies here for you to-night somehow or other."

As soon as he had left I walked over to the aeroplane, where the mechanics were waiting for me, and removed all the cowling from the engine, which was still warm. "I think we will start with the filters," I said, taking the tool-kit from the locker and handing a pair of pliers to one of the mechanics. "You fetch an oil-tray and drain the main tank," I told the second man, "and you can help me remove the oil-cups from the cylinder heads," I said to the third. We were soon hard at work cleaning jets, petrol-filters, oil-filters, and removing plugs, adjusting magneto points. Progress was a little slow, for no one spoke English, and although I managed to make myself understood quite well in ordinary conversation it was difficult to explain the technical terms in French to the mechanics. However, we managed quite well, and when the Commandant returned he found us all busily working. "They are starting immediately with the supplies of fuel," he said, "and expect to arrive in about four hours, so *tout est bien qui finit bien*," he added with a smile.

I put down the set of clearance gauges and got up from my position under the engine, wiping the oil from my hands with a piece of waste cloth. "It was very kind of you to speak to the agent for me," I told the Commandant. "I do indeed feel grateful to you."

"There is no need for you to do the work on the engine yourself; you must be tired," he said, calling up two more men. "We have many mechanics, and you can sit down by the engine and supervise the work."

A box was brought, and I was thankful to sit down and eat the sandwiches which had arrived from the Commandant's bungalow.

At about 10.30 P.M., when the engine schedule was almost completed and one of the mechanics was in the cockpit adjusting the throttle, we heard the throb of an engine, and a vehicle pulled up outside the hangar. The big doors had been shut to keep out the night insects, and when they were now pushed back they revealed a lorry, from which stepped the agent and a number of native boys, who commenced lifting down the big petrol-tins which contained the precious fuel supply.

Overjoyed at their arrival I unfastened the caps on all five tanks, and refuelling operations were soon in full swing. It was a slow business though, and took quite an hour, for the tanks had to be filled by means of a hand-pump, which the native boys took turns at working.

At last the work was completed, and all the native boys crowded into the lorry, where it was decided they should sleep for the night, as it was too late for them to go to the village. The headlights of the lorry could be requisitioned too, and with those of the Commandant's car would help to light a path for the take-off. The tanks were filled to their capacity of 140 gallons of petrol, and I felt anxious about taking such a heavy load off the aerodrome, which was barely big enough to allow as long a run as I should have liked.

The night was very calm, and the wind-sock on the hangar hung limp and motionless. "If only a wind would spring up it would help the take-off tremendously," I said, looking up at the sky. The moon had risen, and was shining down through a gap in the clouds, which pressed in unending procession across the sky. The air seemed very still and almost foreboding.

"Do you think there will be a storm?" I asked the Commandant.

He looked up. "I think it will rain," he answered; then, as if to reassure me, added, "but it will probably pass over before you are ready to start. Anyway, if there is no wind you can take off from corner to corner, and that will give you a much longer run."

I was not at all happy about the take-off. We must lighten the machine somehow. Climbing into the cockpit I removed the heavy signal pistol, my revolver and the rockets and cartridges, and the torch. Putting the things on the floor of the hangar, I opened the locker, and very soon all the movable equipment was in a heap on the ground. I had decided to leave everything except absolute necessities at Thies. The two firearms, cartridges, tool-kit, and spare engine parts alone weighed many pounds. The big water-drums I presented to the

Commandant. Smiling at my own optimism I surveyed the assorted collection and selected two evening dresses, which weighed practically nothing, and to the surprise of all present put them back into the locker. After all, if I crossed the Atlantic successfully they would be more useful than the tool-kit, I explained to the Commandant. If I didn't—well . . . He turned away, and I bent once more over the varied assortment. Only the log-books, the emergency rations, thermos flask, and my little bag of personal effects went back into the aeroplane. The agent, who proved a good friend, took charge of the jettisoned equipment, and promised to send everything back to England for me.

All was now in readiness for the start. It all depended now on a steady hand and accurate navigation, for I was sure that the engine on which I pinned my faith would not fail me, and every inch of the sturdy silver wings of the aeroplane looked the very essence of power itself.

Stepping into the car I drove with the Commandant to his bungalow, where it had been arranged I should stop for the night, as the village was too far away and I had not forgotten the declaration about the plague which I had so eagerly signed at Casablanca. It was only a few minutes' drive to the white bungalow, and as we stepped up on to the veranda a negro boy hurried forward to open the double wire-gauze doors, leading into a room much more comfortably furnished than I had expected. It was good to rest on the soft divan while the Commandant prepared a cool drink for me and ordered the native servant to serve dinner. I should have been quite happy to go to sleep immediately, but the Commandant wisely insisted that I should eat first. Reluctantly I rose to my feet, and taking my bag went into the tiny bathroom. A curtained-off corner of the room disclosed a tiled square on which was a large can of water with a dipper. This was something like the baths I had encountered in Java, where the water-containers had been much larger and of stone, and there had been two dippers, with which one tipped the water over oneself. Feeling decidedly refreshed after the bath I slipped into a white frock and put some sun-burn cream on my face, which was hardly recognizable in the mirror.

At dinner the Commandant told me how much he was looking forward to his leave, when he would return to France and see his wife and children. The dinner was excellent, and when we had finished the Commandant asked if I would like to see the cook. All the native boys in the kitchen had been very excited at my arrival, he explained, and it was only their good manners which prevented them from satisfying their curiosity by peeping through the grass curtain in the doorway to see the white woman who had flown all the way from England.

" Yes, I would like to see him," I said, and at a word from the Commandant the chattering in the next room ceased, and the bamboo curtain parted to reveal the tall figure of the cook. He was a negro boy pure ebony in colour and quite six feet in height, and smiled shyly, disclosing a perfect set of white teeth. Clothed in a white tunic with a red sash, he was barefooted, and I could hardly believe my eyes, for on his curly head was a pale pink turban.

The Commandant spoke to him in his own tongue. " He thinks you are very brave," said my host, who had evidently told the boy that I intended to fly on across the ocean, for the cook rolled his big, soft, expressive eyes at me with such a look of terror that the Commandant hastily changed the subject by calling for the rest of the staff. Three ebony faces came from behind the curtain. None of these boys was quite as tall as the cook, and their close-cropped curly heads were bent as they smiled shyly at me and stood nervously changing from one foot to another, until the Commandant dismissed them and they hurried back to the kitchen, where, said my host, I should be the main topic of conversation for some time to come.

It was agreed that the Commandant should have my alarum-clock, which we set at 3 A.M. so that he could rise first and receive the weather forecast which was to be sent through by Air France from Dakar, and also arrange for some sandwiches to be made up for me and the thermos filled. " That will enable you to sleep for half an hour longer. You must have all the sleep you possibly can, and I won't wake you until the last minute."

It was midnight when I turned out the lamp. Lying down on the divan I fell asleep as soon as my head touched the pillow.

The piercing note of the alarum-clock, which must have resounded throughout the wooden bungalow, failed to wake me, and it was 3.30 A.M. when I sleepily opened my eyes to see the Commandant lighting the oil-lamp, which slowly flickered to life. For a moment it was difficult for me to think where I was as I lay watching the flickering shadows on the ceiling; then, as the Commandant left the room, the full realization of the flight I was about to undertake dawned on me. "If only I could have slept for another hour or so," I thought, rising reluctantly from the divan and pulling on my flying-suit.

Going to the wire-gauze door I looked out. The night was very dark, for low clouds hid the moon from view, and by a ray of light from the oil-lamp I saw that fine, misty rain was falling. This was terribly disappointing, for had I not waited a whole month so that the flight would coincide with the full moon, which I had hoped would help light me on my way? How different this was from the night I had pictured for the take-off across the Atlantic! I had imagined a lovely tropical night with a sky like dark blue velvet, studded with millions of stars like diamonds, and a bright full moon to guide me.

"Do you think it will clear?" I asked the Commandant, joining him at the light breakfast the cook had prepared.

"The weather forecast states that this extends for several hundred miles from the African coast, where you will have dull but fair weather for a stretch until ten degrees north of the equator," he replied.

"What then?" I inquired. "May I see the report?"

He spread it on the table, and for a few minutes we both read intently. The report, which was written in

French, gave an approximate forecast and the probable velocity of wind to be encountered for every 200 kilometres across the Atlantic. The worst section appeared to be in the doldrums, or region of calms just north of the equator, where a deep depression was located.

" I had intended to fly low in any case on account of the drift," I said, pointing to the passage which read, " Dépression entre équateur et 10 degrés nord et entre 18 degrés et 32 degrés ouest. . . . Intérêt à voler bas jusqu'à 4 degrés nord." This was evidently the region which the French pilots had named the " Pot au Noir," and it seemed a vivid and unpleasant memory to any people with actual practical experience of South Atlantic flying conditions, for, as its name implied, the region was one of black storm-clouds and heavy rain. With radio it would be possible to make a *détour* round the centre of this permanent depression, which apparently moved up and down in that region, but my funds had not extended to a radio-set, and to deviate a fraction of a degree from the corrected rhumb line I intended steering might have spelled disaster. To try and fly round bad weather in mid-Atlantic, then attempt to regain the original course, was unthinkable, and would probably mean complete loss of bearings. " Anyway, the weather is much better near Brazil," I said, putting the report in my pocket and finishing a cup of tea.

The Commandant went to start the car, and hastily collecting my belongings I joined him, and we set off for the aerodrome. " The cook has prepared a nice lunch for you," he said, indicating a neat parcel, which, to my delight, proved to contain some sandwiches and a whole chicken. I smiled as I visualized the cook in his pink turban preparing the chicken at midnight.

It was still raining when we arrived at the aerodrome, and the mechanics pushed back the big hangar doors while I put my things in the aeroplane and by the light of the torch gave the engine a final check over. The machine was wheeled out on to the wet tarmac, and after flooding the carburetters I climbed into the cockpit. One of the mechanics turned the propeller over two or three times, and at the word "Contact" swung the airscrew once again; the engine started with a roar. I could not afford to waste a drop more of the precious petrol than necessary, so, leaving the engine just ticking over to warm up, I climbed out to make final arrangements about the take-off. The Commandant ordered two of the mechanics to go ahead with torches and guide me to the far corner of the aerodrome and as near the rough ground as was possible. "I will drive the car to the other end," he told me, "and turn it so that the headlights will point towards you. The lorry will do the same, and you should have a good idea of the distance you will be able to run the aeroplane before trying to lift it off the ground. We shall be right back against the boundary, so don't think you can run any farther," he added. "If the machine doesn't lift by the time you are almost level with the lights you had better switch off and try to stop it as best you can."

Rain continued to fall, and clouds still hid the moon from view, and there was not a breath of air even to stir the long grass on the aerodrome. I was feeling really anxious about the take-off, for, although I had realized before leaving England that taking off with such a big load of petrol in the rarefied air of the tropics would require all the skill I possessed, I had not counted on an overgrown aerodrome and a total lack of wind. Supposing the machine would not lift? Quickly putting the thought out of my mind I determined to give the Gull as long a run as I dared before even trying to take it off the ground. "Au revoir et bonne chance, mademoiselle!" shouted the Commandant above the roar of the engine as he grasped my hand and I climbed back into the cockpit.

The needle of the revolution-counter rose as I ran the engine up, until at full throttle it wavered at 1830 revolutions per minute. "Good, that's more than usual," I thought, glancing at the oil-gauge, which registered a steady 42 lbs. pressure. Bending down I adjusted the compass. The magnetic course was exactly 242 degrees, 15 minutes. Strange how my daily life for some time past had seemed almost to revolve round those figures, and at last I was actually setting the course for the flight to Brazil. Flashing the torch round the cockpit I placed the charts, maps, and notes well within reach. The light fell on the notebook, and I read, " ½ degree of deviation to north or south of magnetic track = error of approximately 17 miles." "There isn't going to be any error, for I shall steer the machine straight as an arrow," I decided, releasing the brakes and taxying slowly behind the two mechanics, who walked in front with torches.

Turning the machine round when they stopped I pointed the nose a little to the left of the headlights, which shone towards me from the far corner of the aerodrome. "Can't I go farther back?" I shouted to the mechanics.

"No, it's bad there—no good!" they shouted in reply, gesticulating and shaking their heads to make sure I understood.

Holding the control column fully forward I gave the engine full throttle, and the Gull roared towards the lights. Would the tail never lift, I wondered, as we plunged across the dark aerodrome. At last, as I felt it rise, I tried to lift the aeroplane off, but it sank heavily back to the ground. I had to think quickly now. . . . "Forward with the control column again, and give it the full length of the aerodrome," I decided, keeping the nose still pointing to the left of the lights, which we were rapidly nearing. The Commandant's words rang in my ears: "If the machine doesn't lift by the time you are almost level with the lights you had better switch off and try to stop it as best you can."

The aeroplane roared on through the darkness, and just as the car headlights flooded the cabin, almost dazzling me by their nearness, the wheels lifted as in a final effort I heaved the machine off the ground. I kept the nose down for a few seconds to gain flying speed, then eased the aeroplane up into a gentle climb and rose above the dark shadow of the jungle. Just skimming the tree-tops I flew for miles before gaining sufficient height to turn the aeroplane back towards the aerodrome. As I searched the darkness beneath it seemed that I had lost the aerodrome completely, until in the inky blackness I saw the lights of the Commandant's motor-car as he drove back to the hangar.

CHAPTER XI: ACROSS THE
SOUTH ATLANTIC

A DREADFUL FEELING OF LONELINESS almost overwhelmed me as I left the African coast and steered the aeroplane out into the blackness of the Atlantic on a course for Brazil, nearly two thousand miles away. To the north I could see the blurred gleam of the lighthouse at Dakar sending its friendly beam out into the night. I switched off the navigation lights, for the lighted cabin seemed to make the darkness outside more intense as I peered vainly through the windows trying to distinguish the horizon. "It must get light soon," I thought, glancing at the clock, to realize that it was only twenty minutes since I had left Thies. It was no use looking at the clock, I decided: it only seemed to make the time pass more slowly. What was that? Did I imagine it, or were there really lights in that black void below? Yes, it was a ship. "Looks like a steam-yacht," I thought, glancing down at the small lighted vessel. I flashed the navigation lights on and off a few times, hoping for an answering signal, but there was none. They seemed very close to the coast, and must have been making for Dakar, and I envied the sleeping passengers on board.

The rain continued to fall, and thick clouds at a thousand feet forced me to fly low, so that all my concentration was focused on keeping the machine level and straight on its course while I patiently waited for the dawn to break.

Gradually and almost imperceptibly a grey light stole into the cabin, and I began to distinguish the white tops of the waves beneath. The rain had ceased, and as the light became stronger the scene which unfolded itself before my eyes in that grey dawn was one of majestic beauty. The sky was completely overcast, and in every direction there stretched the vast blue expanse of the mighty Atlantic. Not a ship in sight, nor any sign of life whatever. My only company was the roar of the engine as the aeroplane winged its way low over the ocean like a solitary bird. So completely isolated did I feel that to all intents and purposes I might have been the only person in the world.

The clouds began to break up, and soon the sun shone down from a clear blue sky with such fierceness that the heat in the cabin became quite suffocating. Visibility was good, for the horizon was a deep blue against the paler blue of the sky, and by the white-capped waves I saw that a north-east wind was blowing. Not that I should benefit very much from it because of the low altitude at which I was flying, and I knew it would drop completely as I neared the doldrums region.

The engine purred faithfully on, and with everything going so smoothly I was able to relax and eat some of the sandwiches that the Commandant had given me. The weather was too good to last, however, and a hundred and fifty miles out from Africa the sky became flecked with clouds and gradually completely overcast. Great black, ominous clouds were banking up ahead, and in the distance the leaden sky seemed to merge with the grey sea. The wind had by this time dropped altogether, for the sea was calm, looking almost as if oil had been poured on the angry waves, and all was still except for a long swell which gently rose and fell.

My position was 200 miles north-east of the equator, and I was entering the doldrums, or region of calms which had always been such a nightmare to mariners in the days of sailing-ships. As a child I had listened spellbound and thrilled to the tales of how my own grandparents had set sail for New Zealand. Their ship, after being becalmed in the doldrums for weeks and encountering a fierce storm, had run aground, nearly being wrecked on a reef off the coast of Brazil. The ship had been floated off, however, and undaunted they had continued their voyage. During a terrific storm off Cape Horn, when giant seas had swept the decks of the little ship and the sails had been torn to shreds, the captain had died. After further adventures the ship had eventually arrived in New Zealand six months out from England.

The heavy rain-clouds ahead seemed to open and pour their contents down with such force that the rain resembled a great black curtain. The Pot au Noir. . . . Could I go round the storms? I wondered how far south they extended. No, that was out of the question.

Altering course without radio to check one's position would only result in being lost in mid-Atlantic. Could I fly above that dark mass directly in my path? I remembered the weather forecast: "*Intérêt à voler bas.*" Either go back now while there is time or go through it.

Before I could think any more about it I had plunged into the pouring rain. Flying so low that at times I must have been less than fifty feet above the surface I tried vainly to keep the sea directly beneath in view, but suddenly lost sight of it altogether. For one terrible moment I thought the aeroplane would plunge into the water before I gave the engine full throttle and pulled the machine up into a climb. If I had to fly completely blind I should do so at a reasonably safe height.

The Gull roared up through the dark mass, until at 1000 feet I put the machine on an even keel and flew on. With both feet braced against the rudder-bar and my hand firmly gripping the control column I concentrated all my attention on the blind-flying instruments and the compass. Relaxing my grip on the control column every now and then so that I should not in my anxiety over-correct any slight error in steering, I flew on, unable to see a yard outside the windows, against which thundered the heavy rain, almost as if bent on destruction. Every minute seemed like an hour. Would I never penetrate that dark curtain of rain which seemed drawn round the machine?

Suddenly I saw the compass needle swinging slowly round the dial. " It must be imagination," I thought.

Drawing my hand across my eyes I felt the tiny beads of perspiration on my forehead as the needle continued its ghastly movement. I was lost. . . . If I followed the compass now I should go round in a circle. "It is all up now," I thought frantically. The compass had swung round about 180 degrees. If only I could see the light instead of this terrible blackness enveloping the machine. I almost prayed to see the sky and sea again. No, I should not give in now: there were still the blind-flying instruments, and the machine was flying a straight course by the bank and turn indicator. "I must not lose faith now," I told myself. My eyes were staring at the turn indicator, but I realized that unless the compass righted itself it would not be possible to steer another thousand miles to Natal on that alone. This was torture. The strain was terrific. The perspiration was trickling down into my eyes, and every muscle and nerve in my body was alert. . . . Were my eyes again deceiving me, for slowly but surely the compass needle was swinging back to its former position? Thank God I was saved, and within a few minutes the darkness outside the cabin gave place to light, and once more I saw the calm sea beneath.

All the muscles that had been taut for so long relaxed, and I sank back in the seat breathing a prayer of thanks. Taking out my handkerchief I mopped my forehead, and throwing open the windows let some air into the stifling cabin. I saw the compass needle steady, and once more thanked God for my preservation. I realized by my clock as I entered up the log that I had crossed the equator during the storm. The sky was still overcast, and my spirits sank as I saw more storms looming ahead. Very soon I plunged once more into a succession of heavy rain-storms, and although they were not so thick through, it was a strain blind-flying for so long. As soon as I would emerge into the light again from the nerve-racking experience of one storm it was to see another ahead. They looked something like huge black mushrooms, seeming to come up from the sea to join the clouds, resembling photographs I had seen of cloudbursts.

When at last I entered a fine zone I felt thoroughly worn out, but after some lunch and a drink of black coffee felt quite refreshed again. My altitude was 600 feet, and I calculated my position as about 1100 miles out from Thies. That meant approximately another 800 miles to the coast of Brazil.

The sun had penetrated the clouds, and was burning down on to the blue sea, which had lost its calm look and was now capped by myriads of white-topped waves. The sea became more turbulent, until at last huge waves left great trails of spray, which the wind caught and carried along like thousands of streaming white pennants. The strong south-easterly wind was now increasing in strength, and by aligning the nose of the aeroplane against the waves I could see that the machine was drifting northward. Even at the low altitude at which the Gull was flying I calculated that the present rate of drift would carry me well off my course. There was not another aerodrome north of Natal for hundreds of miles, and the petrol margin was not great enough to allow for any but the smallest error in navigation.

Apart from this there was the record to consider, and any error meant loss of time, for as I was endeavouring to break the record of a multi-engined flying-boat equipped with radio and a crew of experienced men every mile I drifted northward of the course meant precious time wasted.

I spent the next few minutes trying to ascertain accurately the amount of drift, and calculated it at eight degrees to starboard. I decided to alter course eight degrees to port to compensate for the drift. This should take me to Cape San Roque, where I expected to make landfall. Leaning forward I unlocked the compass verge ring and set the machine on its new course. Vainly I searched the horizon for some sign of a ship, but there was no trace of any vessel. Time slipped by, and I felt very lonely, but comforted myself with the thought that after my terrible experience in the storms it was good to see the sun, the sky, and the sea again. "Nine hours out from Thies," I wrote in the log, and hopefully thought that if visibility were good I might see the coast of Brazil in under four hours.

Scanning the horizon for the hundredth time I caught sight of a small dark object in the distance. Were my eyes deceiving me or was it really a ship? Yes. As I drew nearer it was possible to distinguish the masts and funnel of a boat. It seemed too good to be true. For almost eleven hours I had been completely isolated from the rest of the world, with no one to talk to, no sign of life. The blue sea everywhere made me long for the sight of other human beings, a ship, or anything to relieve the monotony of the vast blue waste stretched before me. Jungle or desert stretches would be a pleasure to fly over compared with this.

The sea was becoming rough, and huge waves seemed to rise beneath the Gull, as if stretching up in an effort to grasp the machine which flew contemptuously out of reach on its lonely way. The ship was quite near now. It was a cargo vessel, evidently bound for Dakar, and my course lay right along the ship from tip to stern. I was almost breathless with joy, for the ship must have come from Natal, in which case I was absolutely on the right course. "Unless it is from Pernambuco," I thought, and a shade of doubt entered my mind, for perhaps the drift was not as strong as I had estimated and eight degrees' compensation was too much to allow. Glancing at my chart I saw that Pernambuco was 160 miles south. No, it was unthinkable that I should be that much off my course. The ship was definitely from Port Natal, I decided. As my altitude was still only 600 feet it was quite easy for me to see the name of the vessel, which I read with such joy and eagerness that it must be stamped on my heart for all time. The name painted on the bows read *Belgique*.

Figures on deck were waving wildly, so taking off my scarf I held it out the window and let it trail in the slipstream, and also dipped the aeroplane in salute over the ship. How I longed to circle, for although the crew must have been excited to see a small silver monoplane winging its way over their ship so far from land, their feelings were not to be compared with mine, so overjoyed did I feel at sighting the vessel. "Wish I had

radio and could ask them what port they are from," I
thought longingly as another doubt assailed me that
they might be from Ceará or Maranhão, both hundreds
of miles north of Natal. Thrusting the doubt from my
mind, I decided not to let anything mar my joy at
seeing the ship and at the realization that I was only
about three hundred miles from land. Several times I
looked back, until the ship was merely a speck in the
distance.

Time seemed to drag terribly now, but perhaps soon
I should sight Fernando Noronha island. This small
volcanic island was shown on my chart as being about
twelve miles long, with a cone rising to a height of over
a thousand feet. In good weather it should be visible
from a great distance, although, looking closely at the
chart, I saw that it lay almost fifty miles south of my
course and about a hundred and fifty miles from the
Brazilian coast.

The sky was growing once more overcast, and I was
not going to reach the land without another battle
with the elements. For the next two hours I flew
through one tropical deluge after another, until I felt
terribly disappointed at missing a sight of Fernando
Noronha island, and very tired at the continual blind
flying, which after twelve hours in the air seemed even
more difficult than ever.

Emerging once more into the light after a particularly heavy downpour I saw a faint yellow line on the
horizon ahead. Was it really land, I asked myself.
Glancing round the skyline I saw a similar line, and
realized that the intense glare from the silver engine

cowling coupled with the strain of staring at the blind-flying instruments was tiring my eyes.

Twelve and a half hours out from Africa. . . . Surely I would see land soon. Vainly I searched the horizon for some sign of the coast. Bending down I switched on to the last petrol-tank. Petrol for only one hour more, and still no sign of land. . . . Even though I was flying so low, surely I should be within sight of land now.

What was that faint yellow line? Surely my eyes were deceiving me again. No, this time it was real. Land . . . land . . . I shouted aloud for sheer joy. Nearer and nearer the land drew, until it was possible to distinguish the sand-dunes on the lonely coast of Brazil. Very soon I was within gliding distance of the undulating sandy coast, and at last flew over the long line of foamy white Atlantic rollers sweeping up on to the beach. About half a mile to the north I saw a slight promontory . . . a sandy stretch covered with coconut-palm trees. . . . " Cape San Roque! " I cried, hardly believing my eyes. It seemed too good to be true that after steering for thirteen hours over almost two thousand miles of ocean I had made landfall within half a mile of the point I had been aiming for. But was it Cape San Roque? My chart showed a lighthouse; there was none to be seen here. Silhouetted against the sandy background I saw the wire framework of a red-painted structure which evidently held the fixed light—a strange, lonely-looking edifice, but nevertheless a lighthouse, I decided. Yes, it was Cape San Roque—an exact likeness of the little photograph in my pocket that I had taken from a book. During the last few months I had looked many times at the lonely palm-fringed point depicted in the photograph, and at the last minute had thrust it into my pocket for a mascot. Now that my position on the Brazilian coast was quite definitely fixed I turned southward for Port Natal. "Only a few minutes now," I thought, skimming low along the line of sand-dunes as the sun sank lower in the western sky.

Crossing a hilly part of the coast I suddenly came upon an inlet and a white lighthouse, then saw the buildings of a town. "Port Natal!" It was like a dream to see real houses and civilization, and passing over the town I gave another shout for joy.

"Aerodrome, 15 kilometres S.S.W. Natal, near Lake Parnamiram," read my notes, as I steered the machine past the outskirts of the town and over the jungle, where I quickly picked up the large clearing in the dark green tropical vegetation. Having circled the aerodrome, I shut off the engine and glided down to land. Immediately the wheels touched the ground I checked the stop-watch, which registered 13 hours 15 minutes, my time for the flight from Thies Aerodrome. It was exactly 7.45 P.M., G.M.T., on November 13, so my total elapsed time from England to Brazil had been 2 days 13 hours 15 minutes. A wave of pleasure overwhelmed me as I realized I had lowered the record from England by a margin of almost a day, and had also crossed the Atlantic in the fastest time in history.

As I climbed out of the cockpit all my tiredness left me, and I was immediately surrounded by an enthusiastic crowd which had been awaiting my arrival.

There were a number of the Air France pilots and mechanics, who warmly shook my hand, and I realized they were genuinely pleased.

Their enthusiasm surprised me. It was not until later, when I had met more French people and had come to love France almost as if it were my own country, that I fully realized what wonderful sports the French are. In their earnest desire for the advancement of aviation they realize that speed means progress and competition prevents stagnation.

On hearing of my terrible experience in the doldrums when I thought my compass had failed me one of the pilots assured me that in the electrical storms peculiar to that region he had known of similar experiences.

The group of people assembled to welcome me included an Englishman and his wife, who were overjoyed at my arrival and invited me to stay with them at their home. "We had not been out here at the aerodrome very long when we heard the roar of an engine, then suddenly saw your silver aeroplane fly over Natal," said the Englishwoman. "It was a wonderful sight," she kept saying. "To think that a little over sixty-one hours ago you were in England!" and her eyes glistened at the thought of her beloved country.

"We are very proud that it's a British machine," put in the Englishman as we walked across to the hangar.

When the refuelling was completed we left the aerodrome and drove towards Natal. The car was well sprung, and sinking deep into the comfortable seat I breathed a sigh of relief. Closing my eyes, I could still hear the roar of the 200-h.p. engine, and it was difficult to realize that the flight was over and I was really in South America, and not still over the ocean. The terrible storms seemed a long way off now. I must have slept for a few minutes, for on opening my eyes I saw that we were driving along a track above which the dark green trees of the jungle towered like a great arch. The road was not good; it was fortunate that the car was so well sprung. At one stage to pass another car we had to mount the bank by the roadside and drive along at an alarming angle.

"What a terrible road! Is it the main one, and do they drive the air line passengers along this to the aerodrome?" I inquired.

"There aren't any regular passengers," said my companions. "You see, the transatlantic 'planes don't take passengers—only mail—and the Clipper ships of the Pan-American Airways are flying-boats, and they land down at the port."

As we were about to enter Natal the car was stopped by an armed guard. My friends were closely questioned. I was very glad that I had left my revolver at Thies, for in all probability it would have been confiscated. It appeared that special precautions were being taken because of recent trouble and the imminent possibility of a revolution. On being assured that the car contained no firearms the soldiers allowed us to drive on into the town. We stopped outside a large house, and traced our way through a garden the beauty of which I did not realize until next morning, when daylight revealed it in all its glory. After a refreshing bath I changed my flying-suit for a frock and joined my friends, who were genuinely surprised at the sudden transformation of the tired aviator.

"If you listen to the radio you may hear the announcement of your flight being broadcast from London," said my host, looking at his watch. "It's just about time for the news broadcast," he added.

Drawing a chair close up to the radio-set I sat down and listened intently. I could still hear the roar of my engine, which had made me practically deaf.

"There it is," said my friend, and through the roaring far, far away I heard a voice speaking. There was a pause, then quite clearly the voice came through again: "Miss Jean Batten successfully completed her flight from England to South America by landing at the aerodrome at Port Natal, Brazil, this afternoon. Her total time for the flight from England was 61 hours 15 minutes, and this lowers by almost a whole day the record previously held by Mr James Mollison." The voice paused again, then continued broadcasting the rest of the news.

I turned to my host. "It is wonderful to think that within a few hours of the landing the news is being sent out from London." Until I heard the voice broadcasting the news it had all seemed unreal and more like a dream, but now the realization that the flight was accomplished came to me, and I experienced once again the greatest and most lasting of joys: the joy of achievement.

CHAPTER XII: RIO DE JANEIRO

O N ARRIVAL AT NATAL I HAD CONSIDERED the idea of flying on to New York and seeing the United States, but owing to the further expense involved decided instead to fly southward and see Rio de Janeiro, Montevideo, and Buenos Aires before shipping the Gull back to England.

The flight southward was an interesting one: storms had been forecast, but I was not expecting the series of fierce tropical rain-storms which I encountered. More than once I nearly turned back. The storms, although of almost monsoonal intensity, did not extend over a very great area, however, and it seldom took more than ten or fifteen minutes to fly through one of them. On one occasion, flying low over the tree-tops, I opened the windows, for the heat was intense and great columns of steam arose from the hot jungle. A strong, exotic perfume was wafted into the cabin, and I realized that among the trees of the steaming jungle must be thousands of glorious orchids. Often I would look down and search the dark green, tropical vegetation for some glimpse of the lovely flowers. Although I knew that some of the rarest of orchids were to be found growing on the tree-tops there was no sign of their exquisite colouring in the jungle beneath. Here and there I would see great purple patches of bougainvillæa.

Gazing down on the tropical vegetation as mile after mile slipped by on the long flight southward, I began to realize the vastness of the great country to which I had flown. I tried to remember some of the overwhelming details I had come across while studying the flying conditions in Brazil before setting out from England. The fourth largest country in the world, with an area of 3,300,000 square miles, approximately four-fifths the size of Europe, with a seaboard of 4000 miles, there seemed very little that the great country was unable to produce. With the rarest of orchids and exquisite Morpho blue butterflies (whose wings are used for jewellery), the wonderful mineral riches and infinite variety of precious gems, the huge coffee and cotton plantations, great cattle stations, and the thousand million acres of timber-producing forest area which form only a percentage of its vast natural resources Brazil seems to the flyer almost a world in itself. I remembered how my host at Natal had smiled at my disappointment when it was found that there was no room for the huge pineapples which had been brought to the aerodrome for me. " Perhaps one will be all right there," I had said, balancing one of the large fruits on top of the auxiliary oil-tank, where it had looked so comical. Realizing that it might fall forward and interfere with the controls I reluctantly removed it from the cockpit. There were plenty of pineapples to be had in Rio, my friend assured me. A ripple of amusement ran round the crowd at my astonishment on learning that nearly ninety million pineapples were exported each year from Brazil.

Innumerable little islands dotted some of the great rivers as they curved towards the Atlantic. Flying low over them, I searched vainly for a glimpse of any crocodiles such as I had seen on my flights over Sumatra, in the Dutch East Indies. There was no sign of life, however, but swimming in the deep waters were probably shoals of the deadly little native fish which live in many of the Brazilian rivers. These fish, although so tiny, swim in vast shoals and are particularly vicious. They will set upon any living thing entering the water, and within a few minutes will have nibbled every ounce of flesh off its bones. One story I heard was of a man who, when trying to cross a river, was attacked by a shoal of these fish and dragged under the water. Only a few hours later his skeleton was found without a single piece of flesh left on the bones.

One of the most interesting-looking cities over which I flew was San Salvador, or Bahia as it was marked on my map. There were innumerable churches to be seen, and it is said that at one time there was a church for every day of the year. I believe the full name of this city, the third largest in Brazil, is Bahia de São Salvador de todos os Santos, meaning " Bay of the Holy Saviour of all Saints." At one time Bahia was the capital of Brazil, long before Rio de Janeiro was discovered by the Portuguese sailors, who thought that the harbour was the mouth of a great river and named it Rio de Janeiro—" River of January."

Flying over Bahia I saw that it was built partly on the side of the bay and partly on a plateau about two hundred feet high. Connecting the lower part of the town to the upper I could see a high white lift. It appeared to be a very prosperous town, and I learned later that it is the centre of the cacao and tobacco trades, also that it was from Bahia that the navel orange was transplanted to California.

Only fifty miles north of Rio a bad petrol leak exhausted my fuel supply; fortunately I was able to land safely on a beach. I telegraphed to Rio, and kind military pilots from the Campo dos Affonsos air base brought succour on this occasion. When the thirsty Gull was replenished I flew on to the Brazilian capital.

Never shall I forget the magnificent scene which met my eyes when I arrived over Rio de Janeiro. The sun was setting, and the last rays picked out the red wings of the escorting military aeroplanes, which followed the Gull in perfect formation. As we crossed a promontory where the green-clad mountains rose sheer from the sea I suddenly beheld a sight which made me hold my breath. Rio de Janeiro . . . lovely, colourful, unbelievably beautiful Rio . . . well worth flying nearly seven thousand miles from London to see. The great blue harbour was shown on my map as being about fifteen miles long by seven wide. Rising sheer to a height of 1000 feet at the entrance of the harbour was a great granite rock, which I immediately recognized as the famous Sugar Loaf. Many green-clad islands dotted the harbour, looking almost like peaks of some subterranean mountain range. On a strip of land about six miles long between the great jungle-covered mountains and the sea lay the city of Rio de Janeiro. It looked almost as if the towering mountains had drawn back to allow this exquisite gem of a city to be displayed in this superb setting. Accentuated by the last rays of the sun, the Organ Mountains, thirty miles away, looked close enough for me to lean out of the cabin window and touch one of the fantastic peaks, soaring over 7000 feet into the sky, to earn the apt description of " the fingers of God." Towering above the palatial villas, gardens, and plazas in the centre of the city was a jagged rocky peak—the Corcovado (Hunchback) Mountain, well over 2000 feet in height. As I gazed in wonderment at the great mountain I was fascinated and could scarcely believe my eyes, for on the summit stood a gigantic white figure of Christ, seeming to dominate completely the surrounding country.

The city was suddenly transformed into a fairy city, for almost as if by magic myriads of tiny white lights flashed on. Rio . . . exquisitely beautiful by day, wondrously so by night. The thousands of lights outlined the city, and hung like festoons round all the silvery beaches and coves. In the fast-fading light I could just distinguish the long promenades, and the wide, straight line of the most beautiful of all avenues, the Avenida Rio Branco, over a mile in length, with its three rows of tall, stately palm-trees.

There was a large crowd at the military aerodrome of Campo dos Affonsos. As I landed and taxied up to the tarmac the aeroplane was quickly surrounded by enthusiastic people, while dozens of cameras clicked a welcome. From that moment until I left Rio and flew on to Buenos Aires some days later I received the most wonderful hospitality from the people in Rio, including a large number of British residents. A big reception was given at the British Embassy. The scene was one of great brilliance, for there were many lovely women present, and their beautiful gowns and exquisite jewellery were admirably set off by the smart uniforms of the men. I learned that the British Ambassador, Sir Hugh Gurney, was to present me to the President of the Republic of Brazil, Dr Vargas, who had taken a great interest in my flight from England to his country.

High up in the mountains, at a restaurant set amid the most glorious scenery, with a superb view of the vast Atlantic, a luncheon was given in my honour by Colonel Ivor Borges and the officers of the military air force and their wives. As I turned my gaze from the magnificent scenery and walked on to the wide, cool veranda I was deeply moved by the genuine enthusiasm and the smiling faces around me. The scene was again a brilliant one, the women in their bright colours looking like so many orchids amid the smart gold-trimmed white uniforms of the officers. It was announced that I was to be made an honorary officer of the military air force, and I felt very proud of the lovely gold badge which was presented to me.

That night a dinner was given by the Royal Empire Society at which several hundred people were present, including the British Ambassador and Lady Gurney. Speeches were made by the President and the Ambassador, and I felt deeply moved by the poetic text of a speech delivered by the head of the Brazilian Press, who spoke in fluent English. During the evening I was presented with an exquisite Brazilian diamond set in a platinum brooch by the British community as a token of admiration for my flight, which, it was said, not only demonstrated the capability of the modern aeroplane and engine, but did a great deal for British prestige in South America.

The following day I visited the Director of Civil Aviation and heard all about the wonderful new aerodrome being made in Rio. The site for this aerodrome, which was already in course of construction, was on a promontory near the wide Avenida Rio Branco, and almost in the heart of the city. Part of the harbour was being reclaimed, and the aerodrome when finished promised to be one of the largest and most modern in the world. "You must fly back to Brazil when it is ready," the smiling Director of Aviation said, as he gave me a design of the projected airport.

Just before leaving I learned that the *fonctionnaires*— the girls working in the Department of Aviation— wished to meet me. I was delighted by the warmth of their welcome as they crowded round and congratulated me. Suddenly there was a hush, and the group of pretty Brazilian girls parted to allow their spokeswoman to come forward. Although she spoke in Portuguese it was not difficult for me to interpret the words, for her lovely dark eyes alone were eloquent enough. She handed me a small case, and on opening it I saw a most exquisite aquamarine. The girls were pleased at my appreciation of their gift as I gazed entranced at the gem. Resting on the pale satin lining of the case it resembled the translucent blue of the water lapping up on to the creamy beaches of Rio, where its shallowness and transparency toned the sapphire shade of the deeper waters almost to pastel tints.

A visit to the headquarters of the naval air force followed, and to my joy I learned that it was the intention of the Aviação Naval to make me an honorary officer in the force. The naval air base was on the large island of Gobernador, and I learned that British aeroplanes were used for training purposes.

The following morning a flight of aeroplanes from the naval base flew over to the military aerodrome of Campo dos Affonsos, and officially I was presented with the gold wings and diploma making me an honorary officer of the force. The Colonel and officers were very charming, and I accompanied them back to their base in my own aeroplane. It was a glorious afternoon, and the city was bathed in strong sunlight, so before returning to the military aerodrome I decided to fly once more over Rio and explore the numerous little beaches, coves, and islands with which the great harbour abounds. Leaving the island of Gobernador and the naval base I flew first round the Sugar Loaf rock, guarding the entrance to the harbour, then low along the silver strand of the Copacabana beach. Speeding back, I passed once again over Rio and along the palm-lined *avenidas,* and circled the site for the new airport.

I put the machine into a climb and soon gained height, then at an altitude of well over two thousand feet flew round the shoulders of the giant Christ on top of the Corcovado Mountain. At close quarters it appeared to dwarf everything in the city so far below. I felt almost awed by the immensity of the majestic figure, standing as it does two hundred feet high on the peak of the mighty Corcovado. Gliding down again, I flew for miles up the harbour, passing over unbelievably beautiful little palm-fringed islands encircled by silvery beaches. On some of the islands were coconut plantations, and I could see the tall, graceful palms clustered closely together as if afraid of slipping into the limpid sapphire water surrounding them.

Turning back at length to the military aerodrome I landed, and then drove into Rio.

An English lady had kindly offered to lend me several light frocks, for the costume I had brought with me was too warm for Rio. The heat seemed very sudden, for only a few days previously I had left the chilly autumn of the Northern Hemisphere. It was with a very critical eye that I surveyed the gowns, for that day was to be a momentous one in my life. I was to be presented to the President of Brazil that afternoon, so the selection of a suitable frock had assumed a position of great importance.

With a spray of orchids adorning my dress, I went to join the Ambassador at the appointed hour. We drove along the wide, palm-lined *avenidas* to the President's house. On entering we were shown into a large cool room with a highly polished parquet floor. The

THE PRESIDENT OF BRAZIL, DR VARGAS, CONFERS UPON ME THE ORDER OF
THE SOUTHERN CROSS

MY ARRIVAL AT BUENOS AIRES

Associated Press Photo

furniture was upholstered in brocade, and between the large gilt-framed mirrors on the walls were several portraits in oils. An attaché in a dazzling white uniform embroidered with gold cord escorted us into another room, where we awaited an audience with the President. It was only a matter of a few minutes before the door opened and a man wearing a tropical suit advanced and warmly greeted the Ambassador. It was the President. On being presented I found him charmingly natural and unaffected as he spoke to me of my flight and congratulated me on the record I had established. He said that the Brazilian nation wished officially to show its appreciation of my achievement. It had been decided to confer on me the decoration of Officer of the Order of the Southern Cross in recognition of my flight, which had linked England with Brazil in the fastest time in history. Taking a green and gold leather case from the desk by his side the President opened the box and produced the insignia of the Order of the Cruzeiro do Sul. It was an exquisitely designed gold cross with a centre medallion of blue enamel, on which were embossed in gold the stars of the Southern Cross constellation. The cross was joined to a pale blue ribbon by a green enamel link representing a laurel wreath. Pinning the decoration to the bodice of my dress the President shook my hand warmly. The first British person other than royalty to receive this decoration—no wonder I felt pleased. Although the President was such a busy man he courteously agreed to pose for a photograph, which was taken on the terrace of his beautiful house.

The following day I drove to the aerodrome and made preparations for refuelling the aeroplane, as I had received cordial invitations to visit both Uruguay and Argentina before leaving South America.

I felt very reluctant to leave Rio de Janeiro, for apart from the fascination I felt for the beautiful city I had made many friends and enjoyed wonderful hospitality during my stay. Although it was very early when I arrived at the aerodrome a large crowd had assembled to see me take off on my flight to Buenos Aires, 1350 miles farther south. As strong head winds were predicted I wished to take off at dawn in order to arrive at Buenos Aires in daylight.

The aeroplane looked like burnished steel when it was wheeled out on to the tarmac, for it had been carefully washed and polished, and the windows and metal fittings were gleaming. The blue-and-green star symbol of the Brazilian Air Force had been painted on the rudder, and I had never seen the Gull look so smart. A squadron of aeroplanes was to escort me for a few miles, and the Colonel had detailed a fast fighting machine to accompany my aeroplane as far as Santos, 200 miles south-west of Rio. After shaking hands with all my friends and bidding them good-bye I was just about to step into my aeroplane when an officer hurried forward and asked me to wait for a few minutes, as the Colonel wished to make a presentation. Almost before the officer had finished speaking the Colonel appeared and walked across the tarmac towards us. He was carrying something in his arms, and as he drew near I saw that it was a beautiful bronze statue. " On behalf of the officers of the Aviação Militar I wish to present you with this trophy as a token of our great admiration of your magnificent flight from England," said the Colonel.

I looked at the statue which he presented to me. It was an exquisitely wrought bronze female figure. She was poised on a globe representing the world and on which were embossed the stars of the Southern Cross. In one hand was an olive branch of peace, and in the other a scroll on which the words " Conquête de l'Air " were written. The statue was mounted on Brazilian marble, and a gold plate bore a suitable inscription.

I was quite sure that all the British people present felt as proud as myself at this signal honour. " I wish it was possible to take the statue with me," I said.

" Yes, do," said some one in the crowd, who added, " then your aeroplane won't take off and you will have to stay in Rio."

" That's a very good idea," I replied laughingly, and handed back the lovely trophy, which was so heavy that I could scarcely lift it.

It was arranged that the statue would be safely packed and sent to England for me. Thanking the Colonel for the beautiful present, and once again for the kindness I had received from the Aviação Militar, I bade farewell to my friends and climbed into the cockpit. Waving a final farewell I taxied to the end of the aerodrome, and took off to join the squadron of military aeroplanes circling overhead. Rounding the high mountain almost overhanging the aerodrome I drew level with the other machines and recognized the pilots, whom I now knew quite well. We flew in formation for some distance, then one by one the escorting machines flew close to my aeroplane, while the pilots waved a last good-bye and flashed back to the aerodrome.

CHAPTER XIII: BUENOS AIRES
AND MONTEVIDEO

WHEN THE LAST MACHINE HAD GONE I felt again an overwhelming sense of loneliness. How bitter-sweet it all was, I reflected—flying about the world, visiting these great cities, meeting many people, making many friends, then having to fly off again. I consoled myself with the thought that I always saw the very best side of everything, and seldom stayed long enough in one place to have any illusions or ideals shattered. Therefore when I do fly away I take with me an exquisite cameo of impressions and recollections which will remain with me for ever.

Deep in reflection I suddenly saw something flash past my aeroplane. It was the fast fighting machine which the Colonel had sent to accompany me as far as Santos. My spirits rose and the loneliness left me as I waved to the smiling pilot in the other machine. It was great fun flying along together and holding conversation from time to time by gesticulations.

There were many islands dotted about, and we soon neared a large one, the Ilha Grande, which towered thousands of feet up from the blue sea. The country near Rio had been mountainous, but this was even more so, and for the next two hundred miles there was scarcely a level stretch. The mountains on the coast rose sheer from the sea, and range upon range stretched inland, the jungle-covered peaks seeming to vie with each other for supremacy. The coastline was very broken, and I experienced many terrific bumps when crossing some of the rocky promontories jutting out from the land. The very strong south-westerly wind which was blowing greatly impeded progress, and I calculated my ground speed at approximately 120 miles per hour. "If this head wind persists I shall have to land for petrol before reaching Buenos Aires," I thought.

The wind increased as we flew on, and over San Sebastian, an island just off the mainland and towering to an immense height, the ground speed dropped to a hundred miles an hour. I could see the other machine rising and falling in the vertical currents and battling against the head wind, which was over fifty miles per hour. There was no aerodrome or landing-ground between Rio and Santos, and we had not expected to meet quite such a strong head wind. With all my auxiliary tanks I had a good margin of petrol, and it would not delay me very much to land at one of the aerodromes farther along the route and refuel before flying on to Buenos Aires. The escort machine was not, to my knowledge, equipped with extra tanks, and I wondered if it could reach Santos on the petrol in its main tank. The military machine was a single-seater fighting aeroplane with a powerful engine, which would consume much more petrol than my own. Flying along-

side, I asked the pilot in sign language if he had plenty
of petrol. Yes, he reassured me with a wave, he could
make Santos all right.

So strong was the wind that at times the machine
seemed to stand still, and it was with a sigh of relief
that almost two hours after leaving Rio de Janeiro I
sighted Santos. Having been delayed nearly an hour
by the strong head wind I could not spare the time to
circle Santos. The leading coffee port of the world,
it is built on a flat island, and is about three and a half
miles from the sea. I wondered how the large ships
managed to negotiate the winding channel leading
from the open sea to the port. "Perhaps the current
is not very strong," I thought, looking down on the
muddy channel and the occasional stretches of palm-
dotted sandy beach.

We had passed the town and were approaching the
aerodrome when the escort machine flew up close to
my wing. "Good-bye!" waved the pilot. "Good luck!
Hasta la vista!" he seemed to say. I waved an answering farewell, and he flashed back to land.

It had been good company having another machine
flying alongside, and I felt very grateful to the Colonel
for sending the escort so far. There was still nearly
another 1200 miles to fly to Buenos Aires, and as I flew
on alone I missed the company of the other machine.

The wind dropped a little fifty miles to the south of
Santos, and I climbed above the heavy mist hanging
low over a huge swamp area. The mist gave way to
low clouds, and for the next hundred miles I flew above
a billowy white carpet punctured here and there by

a green-clad peak rising above the cloud layers. My position at this stage was 350 miles south-west of Rio, and as I had to change course for Florianopolis at the 400-mile mark it was most important to descend below the clouds before doing so. Not knowing the exact height of the cloud layer above the ground, and considering the mountainous country beneath, I decided to fly out to sea for a few miles before gliding down. Altering course due east I flew for five minutes, until I caught a glimpse of the sea through a hole in the clouds, and gliding down through the gap flew back to the land.

Before me there stretched a great blue lagoon-like bay, which I recognized on the map, and turning the machine I continued southward towards the island of San Francisco. The country near the coast became flatter and the head wind dropped a little, and I was now averaging about 120 miles per hour. As I was crossing a promontory something prompted me to look back, and to my surprise I saw a large seaplane skimming low over the water. The machine, which I recognized as being of German design, was evidently bound for Florianopolis. It was good to see another aeroplane, and I glided down to allow the big seaplane to draw level. "No, you can't pass me," I smiled, waving to the pilot as I shot ahead. Passing over Florianopolis I looked back again, and saw the seaplane alighting on the harbour.

Situated on the western side of Santa Catharina island, Florianopolis looked a prosperous town. Linking the port with the mainland was a big steel bridge.

The island was large and fairly narrow with a blue lagoon, sheltered on one side by a range of irregular hills, the highest of which was almost a thousand feet. On the eastern side, about thirteen kilometres from the city, was the sandy aerodrome. I felt tempted to land and explore this lovely island, and see for myself if the city lived up to its name—"City of Flowers."

The wind increased in strength, and when flying across to the mainland I could see myriads of waves being whipped into a white, foamy mass by the wind, which swept up the narrow channel between Santa Catharina and the mainland.

The country over which my course now lay was comparatively flat and intersected by innumerable streams and rivers. Inland the mountains rose to great heights, and 120 miles beyond Florianopolis I left the state of Santa Catharina and crossed into the rich Rio Grande do Sul state. Although the head wind had dropped a little, its velocity was still about thirty miles per hour. As my progress had been considerably impeded by the wind I decided to gain time by taking a direct course to the deep-sea port of Rio Grande instead of flying over the big modern city of Porto Alegre, as had been my original intention.

Lakes of various sizes studded the land I looked down upon, and very soon I approached the swampy area adjoining Lagoa dos Patos. This large freshwater lake, although less than forty miles across at its widest point, was very long, and I skirted its shores for well over a hundred miles. It was pleasant flying along the strip of land separating the huge lake from the sea, and

I counted many lighthouses, dotted at intervals. The presence of these lighthouses was explained by the channel at the southern end of the lake enabling ships of limited draught to sail up to the wide Rio Guahyba, which flows into the lake, and thence to Porto Alegre, a journey of 190 miles or so.

Flying on, I soon approached another lake, shown on my map as Lago Mirim, and as the time was nearly 2 P.M. decided to have lunch.

I was now crossing into Uruguay, one of the smallest but most modern and progressive republics of South America. The country had gradually become less mountainous, until at this stage, with the exception of an occasional line of hills, it was comparatively flat. The wind was still south-west, and I wondered if the dreaded pampero, a dust-laden wind from the plains, was blowing in Argentina. The constant head wind had seriously impeded my progress, although I had travelled nearly a thousand miles since leaving Rio, and had been ten hours in the air. Taking stock of the petrol in each tank I decided to land and refuel at Pando, an aerodrome nearly a hundred miles farther on, and used by the Air France company. Innumerable little lakes showed along the route as I skirted the hills of Minas and steered for Pando. Ten hours twenty minutes after leaving Rio I arrived over the aerodrome. As I glided in to land a swarm of insects like a great dark veil rose from the long grass and enveloped the aeroplane. The machine touched down, and, applying the brakes, I brought it to a standstill. The dark insects outside were beating against the windscreen, and some of the heavy, cumbersome objects flopped into the cockpit through the open window. Locusts . . . ugh! I shuddered, hoping that they would not fly into the air-intake. The propeller was cutting through the swarm as I taxied up to the hangar, and the locusts were whirled back and fell heavily against the windscreen and on to the wings.

The kind Air France mechanics soon refuelled my aeroplane and helped clean the locusts off the silver wings. "I do hope the swarm has gone now," I thought, taxying out to take off for Buenos Aires. The air was quite clear, and I flew on towards Montevideo without encountering any more locusts. As I particularly wished to make the flight from Rio de Janeiro to Buenos Aires in one day, it had been arranged that I should visit Uruguay after staying a few days in Argentina.

The solitary mountain to which Montevideo owes its name seemed to dominate the surrounding flat country as I approached the city. In the strong afternoon sunlight Montevideo looked like a fairy city with its flat-roofed white houses and lovely gardens. I was enchanted, and circled the town several times. From among the houses rose the dome of a large cathedral, and near by a particularly high building, towering up like a skyscraper. Turning towards the outskirts of the town I flew low over the military aerodrome in salute and on towards the civil aerodrome. To my surprise there were hundreds of people assembled on the ground to see me pass over on my way to Buenos Aires; so I glided down, and flew low across the aerodrome to enable the people, who were all waving enthusiastically, to see the aeroplane at close quarters. I felt terribly sorry to fly on without landing, but the reception committee was waiting at Buenos Aires, and had I landed at Montevideo there would not have been time to fly on that night.

Setting a direct course for Buenos Aires I flew across the River Plate. The air was heavy with dust-haze, and flying into the strong rays of the sinking sun I had great difficulty in distinguishing the sky from the shallow, muddy water of the river. My intention had been to land at the military aerodrome in Buenos Aires, but just before leaving Rio de Janeiro I had received a telegram from the Aero Club of Argentina asking me to arrive at the civil aerodrome of Moron, as a big reception had been arranged in my honour. My map of Uruguay and Argentina was of a very small scale, eighty-three miles to the inch, which contrasted strangely with the large-scale four-mile-to-the-inch maps used for flying in England. When there were so many other aerodromes on the outskirts of the big city trying to find the specified one with this tiny map was going to be like finding a needle in a haystack. The instructions vaguely stated that the Moron Aerodrome was fourteen kilometres south-west of the centre of Buenos Aires.

The wind had now dropped completely, and as visibility was so poor I began to wonder when I should reach the other side of the great river, which measures over fifty miles across, and is more like an inlet. The distance to Buenos Aires on the direct course I was flying was a little over a hundred miles. There were many ships sailing up the River Plate to Buenos Aires, and I was overjoyed when I sighted the big capital of Argentina. Visibility had improved a little, and as I flew over the large docks I was astonished at the size of the city, the biggest of the Southern Hemisphere and the sixth largest in the world. It was totally different from any other capital I had seen.

High white skyscrapers reared their sleek lines above the delightful parks and plazas and the wide *avenidas*, along which the lovely blossom of the jacaranda-trees showed vivid purple.

Leaving the city, I flew in a south-westerly direction, keeping a sharp look out for the aerodrome. As far as my eye could see there stretched the vast, rolling, grassy plains of Argentina. The country was perfectly flat, and I decided that here indeed was an aviators' paradise. A forced landing could be made safely in almost any of the large fields, which seemed to gain in size as I flew inland. There was an aerodrome ahead, but was it the right one, I wondered. Yes, it coincided exactly with the description, and looking down I saw a vast crowd thronging the field, and hundreds of motor-cars lined all the streets approaching the ground.

Having landed I started to taxi the Gull slowly towards the enclosure. As I neared the tarmac the crowd broke through the barriers and, accompanied by a number of mounted police, who were unable to check its progress, surged towards the aeroplane. Quickly I switched off the engine, and only just in time, for within a few seconds the Gull was surrounded by the cheering throng. Hats were thrown into the air and

arms raised in salute as I looked out of the window.
For a moment I felt helpless, for it seemed that if I left
the cockpit I would surely be crushed, and if I remained where I was my beautiful aeroplane would be
unintentionally damaged by the enthusiastic crowd,
which evidently meant to give me a welcome I should
never forget.

The mounted police were powerless to clear a passage
through the cheering people, who, apparently oblivious
of the rearing horses, were pressing forward. The police
were using their whips now. Hoping that if I left the
machine the crowd would follow I opened the door and
stepped out on the wing. Great bouquets were thrust
into my arms, and I was literally pulled off the wing
on to the shoulders of the crowd and carried in
triumph to the reception in the club-house. "My aeroplane!" I gasped to the smiling people around me.
"*Mi aeroplano!*" But the words were drowned by
thousands of lusty voices expressing their joy at my
arrival. Looking back, I saw the machine, safe and
sound, being wheeled across the aerodrome towards the
hangars. "What a welcome!" I thought, waving to
the happy people.

As we neared the enclosure the crowd assumed even
greater proportions. The girl who had thrust the
bouquets into my arms was one of Argentina's own airwomen, and near the club-house she helped me to the
ground. I was greeted by the reception committee, including a number of British residents. The President
of the Aero Club of Argentina gave me the medal of
the Gran Premio de Honor on behalf of the club to

commemorate my flight, the first by a woman from England to Argentina. It was engraved with the date of my landing at Buenos Aires: November 24, 1935. I was also made a life member of the Aero Club and received the gold badge.

In a short speech of thanks I said a few words in Spanish. The crowd was delighted. Camera men had wrenched one door from its hinges and broken several windows in their enthusiasm to take photographs, and every few seconds the click of their cameras punctuated the speeches of welcome. Once again I was lifted shoulder-high and carried to a motor-car, for which mounted police endeavoured to clear a path.

"I want to get my luggage from the aeroplane," I said to the British Air Attaché, who was near me at the reception. He kindly offered to bring my kit to the hotel for me.

The car proceeded at a slow pace through the unending line of smiling, waving people, and it was almost dark when we finally arrived in Buenos Aires. I heard later that it took several hours for the crowd to disperse, and until late that night the cars were streaming back to the city.

"What a magnificent welcome!" I said to members of the British community who accompanied me in the car.

I had accepted a very cordial invitation from the Commander of the military air base of El Palomar, Colonel Zuloaga, to fly my aeroplane over to that aerodrome, so the following morning I drove out to the civil aerodrome. The military aerodrome was only a few miles distant, and it was arranged that the British Air Attaché, Wing-Commander Park, who spoke Spanish fluently and proved a very good friend, should drive over and meet me with the car.

Climbing into the cockpit I waved good-bye, and taxying to the end of the aerodrome turned into wind and took off. It was a lovely sunny morning, and within a few minutes I arrived over the military aerodrome of El Palomar. Landing I taxied up to the big tarmac, on which were assembled a large number of officers in smart khaki uniforms. As I switched off the engine and stepped out of the cockpit one of the officers stepped forward and addressed me in Spanish. It was the Commander of the base, and after congratulating me on my flight and welcoming me to El Palomar he called forward some of his officers and introduced them. Would I care to accompany him to the mess and take some refreshment, asked the Commander. It was very hot in the sun, and I was delighted to accept his invitation.

As we neared the officers' mess we walked through a most beautiful garden. Roses grew in profusion, and there were cool palm-trees at intervals.

" What a beautiful aerodrome ! " I cried, stopping to admire the abundance of flowers.

" There is also a swimming-pool," one of the officers told me, as I remarked on the modern aerodrome and we entered the cool lounge of the low, flat-roofed white building.

It was not long before Wing-Commander Park arrived, and to my delight the Commander announced that a luncheon was to be given in my honour at El Palomar one day during my stay.

That night a reception was held by members of the large British community resident in Buenos Aires, and I met the British Ambassador, Sir Nevile Henderson, who had taken a great interest in my flight.

The next few days were crowded ones. Many other receptions were given in my honour, and at one of them I met several of my own countrymen and women, and was surprised to find that so many New Zealanders lived in Argentina.

One evening I dined at the British Embassy, and was very pleased to hear that the Ambassador intended to present me to the President of Argentina, Señor Justo.

Wonderful hospitality was shown to me by the British and Argentine people, and those happy days will live long in my memory. One firm presented me with a complete wardrobe, and managed as if by magic to make a tailored linen suit for me almost overnight.

Buenos Aires has been called "the Paris of the Southern Hemisphere," and although I do not like comparisons I saw that a large number of the beautifully dressed Argentine women wore Paris gowns. The shop-windows looked very inviting, and I noticed that several English firms had large branches in Buenos Aires. I was very sorry that time did not afford me the opportunity of exploring the interiors of some of the big shops.

One day, in company with Wing-Commander Park and his wife, I drove to El Palomar for the luncheon which the Commander, Colonel Zuloaga, and officers had arranged in my honour. We were met on arrival by the Commander himself and introduced to some of the officers' wives. The Commander's wife, who was particularly charming and spoke a little English, told me that although her husband had been Commander of the military base during the whole of their married life she had never before been inside the officers' mess.

The lunch was a very enjoyable one. After the many toasts I was surprised to see about three-quarters of the men present stand on their chairs, and with one foot on the table drink my health. My Spanish vocabulary was not large enough for me to understand what the smiling Commander was trying to explain to me, so I appealed to the Air Attaché. " All the bachelors here are toasting your health," he said, as the men, amid much laughter, sat down again.

After lunch we walked through the lovely rose-gardens and inspected the aeroplanes. Just before leaving the base the Commander told me that he and the officers wished to make me an honorary officer in the Argentine Air Force, and would like me to accept a souvenir of their admiration of my flight from England, and which should be also a memento of my visit to El Palomar. One of the officers then brought forward a large box, which the Commander opened, to disclose an exquisitely designed large silver plaque with the emblem of the Argentine Air Force embossed in gold in the centre and the engraved signatures of the heads of the Air Force and Air Ministry. It was indeed a beautiful present, and a wonderful memento of my visit, I told Colonel Zuloaga and his officers as I thanked them.

The day on which I was to be presented to the President I drove with the British Ambassador, Sir Nevile Henderson, to the Government House, called La Casa Rosada because of its rose colour. As we walked through the hall I noticed several very beautiful pieces of statuary, and the room in which we awaited the audience was exquisitely decorated, and the Louis XIV furniture upholstered with blue brocade.

The President was most charming, and congratulated me on my flight, talking about aviation at great length. As we were about to take our leave he walked across the cool room to a stand on which was a large vase of magnificent carnations. With a spontaneous gesture he took the flowers from their vase and, bowing, presented me with the lovely bouquet. He was most courteous, and I received quite a shock on learning that an attempt had been made on his life that very afternoon as he left the Casa Rosada.

Shortly afterwards an alfresco luncheon was arranged by the Rotary Club of Argentina. The meat for the luncheon was cooked in the open. Great fires had been lit, and on a frame half-carcasses of beef were roasted whole. This was certainly a novel way of cooking meat, and it was just as well that the luncheon was held in the open, otherwise in the intense heat all present would probably have evaporated. I was the only lady present, and the luncheon was attended by hundreds of Rotary members. It was at this luncheon that I first heard " For she's a jolly good fellow " sung in Spanish. The occasion was a most memorable one. The President, at the conclusion of his speech of welcome, announced that the club had decided to give me the name of Clavel del Aire ("Flower of the Sky"), by which name the people in Argentina would always remember me.

When I rose to reply I was given an ovation, and before taking my leave was presented with a silver plaque for my aeroplane and a small Argentine flag, with the request that I should take it and a message of goodwill to the Rotary Club of New Zealand when I returned home.

There were, as I have said, many receptions given during my stay, and I thoroughly enjoyed every one of them.

It was a lovely morning when I drove out to El Palomar to fly to Montevideo, and the sun shone brightly as I stepped into my aeroplane, on the rudder of which had been painted the emblem of the Air Force of Argentina. All my friends were there to bid me good-bye, although I was only leaving Buenos Aires for a few days. I had been asked to land at the military aerodrome at Montevideo, over which I had flown only a few days previously.

Waving good-bye I took off, and after passing over Buenos Aires flew straight across the River Plate towards Uruguay. After my flight up the centre of the river when flying to Buenos Aires I had decided to take a slightly longer route back to Montevideo *via* Colonia, a seaside resort, as this would give me more opportunity of seeing the country. Down the River Plate many vessels were steaming, evidently bound for Europe with cargoes of chilled beef from the huge *frigorificos* (freezing works) on the river. I soon arrived over the coast of Uruguay and flew over Colonia, which reminded me of some of the towns in Spain with its flat-roofed white houses and the first bull-ring I had seen in South America. Altering course I flew on down the coast, which was really the bank of the big River Plate.

Uruguay takes its name from the great river which rises in Brazil and flows south for hundreds of miles to form the boundary between Uruguay and Argentina before joining the River Plate. The name 'Uruguay,' meaning "River of Birds," is derived from the two Indian words *uru* (" bird ") and *y* ("river "). Undulating grassy plains stretched for miles, with occasional low ridges, but the country over which I was flying was not quite so flat as Argentina. I passed over an *estancia*, as these big ranches are called, and saw many cattle grazing in the big green paddocks. Some of the white houses of the *estancias* are very Spanish-looking with their tiled roofs, and very often have lovely gardens growing oranges, peaches, and most fruits and flowers in abundance, for almost anything can be grown in the rich black soil of Uruguay with its lovely climate. As my departure had been delayed I decided not to fly over the city of Montevideo, but save time by going straight to the aerodrome. This was probably why I missed the escort of military aeroplanes, which fortunately, however, arrived over the aerodrome shortly after me.

There was a big crowd awaiting me, and as I landed and taxied through the long grass many people ran out to be the first with their greetings. As I stepped on to the wing I was welcomed to Uruguay by Señorita Olga Terra, the beautiful daughter of the President of the Republic, who presented me with a most beautiful bouquet. A reception had been arranged by the military authorities, and within the space of a few bewildering minutes I seemed to meet every one in Uruguay. The British Minister, Mr Millington-Drake, was very enthusiastic about my visit, and both he and his wife, Lady Effie, were very good friends to me. The tall, smiling Commander of the military base, Colonel Cristi, announced that I was to be made an officer of yet another air force—that of Uruguay—and pinned the lovely gold wings on my flying-suit. There were many British people present to welcome me, and I met the manager of the Central Uruguay Railways, Mr Hugh Grindley, who had very kindly asked me to be his guest during my stay.

On being escorted to the official car I was deeply moved to see that it had been draped on one side with the flag of Uruguay and on the other with the Union Jack. Stepping into the car I sat surrounded by a magnificent array of bouquets and accompanied by the President's daughter and some other charming young ladies, who were my companions during my stay.

Although it had been my intention to have a few days' rest in Montevideo I found that a number of receptions had been arranged in my honour, and I soon forgot my weariness in the company of the hospitable

BEING WELCOMED TO URUGUAY BY THE PRESIDENT'S DAUGHTER
Left to right: Señorita Olga Terra, Lady Effie, Mr H. Grindley, Mr Millington-Drake, and Colonel Cristi.

AT THE SORBONNE WITH (LEFT TO RIGHT) MM. BRÉGUET, BLÉRIOT,
LOUIS PAULHAN, DÉTROYAT, AND FONCK
[See p. 198]

people. At a big reception I met most of the British residents, who gave me a very cordial welcome.

In all the South American countries I visited I was afforded a unique opportunity of being able to study flying conditions and to learn first-hand the views not only of the British residents, but of both the civil and military aviation people and of the members of each Government as well.

At Montevideo a banquet was given in my honour by the Director of Aviation at which I met all the people connected with the air and many of the Government officials.

Before leaving Montevideo I broadcast, and, to the delight of both the British community and the Uruguayan people, I decided to give the talk in Spanish as well as English. I spoke about the vital part that aviation must play in the future of South American states. During my flight from Natal to Buenos Aires it had occurred to me that the aeroplane took a very small part in transport. True, there were the giant Clipper ships of Pan-American Airways flying regularly from New York to Buenos Aires and right round South America. There were the mail services of the Air France and Condor companies linking Europe with South America. Apart from these services and the inter-state postal services conducted by the Brazilian military aeroplanes there was at that time little flying in comparison with the size of the continent. Taking into consideration the vast distances in South America and the huge areas yet to be developed there is no doubt that aviation is not merely the most economical, but the speediest and in certain cases the only feasible way of exploiting some of the vast natural resources of the great continent. Concluding the broadcast I said, "I visualize the day in the not too far distant future when there will be as much flying here as in Europe, when the whole of the South American continent will be covered by a great network of air lines carrying passengers, mails, and freight and every city will possess an aerodrome. Because of the size of South American countries and the vast territories yet to be opened up, the great natural wealth, and the huge populations, I think that the future of the countries of South America lies in the air."

During my few days in Uruguay I had the honour of meeting the President, Dr Terra, to whom I was presented by the British Minister, Mr Millington-Drake. The President was wonderfully courteous and most hospitable, and invited me to have tea with him and his charming wife. The President's house was very lovely, with its wide staircases and panelled walls, parquet floors, and softly upholstered furniture. The British Minister spoke fluent Spanish, and came to my aid when the conversation became too deep for my Spanish vocabulary.

At the civil aerodrome I met most of the aviators of Uruguay, for the Aero Club had given a reception for me, and I was made a life member. On walking through the hangar I was shown the aeroplanes belonging to the club. I was surprised to learn that the one ground engineer with the aid of several mechanics carried out all the work on the aeroplanes, even doing the complete overhauls and renewing the Certificates of Airworthiness.

All the members of the club were very kind and friendly, and after bidding them good-bye I went on to the military aerodrome. On being shown over the base by Colonel Cristi I was very pleased to see several British aeroplanes among those I inspected.

At one end of the garden near the officers' quarters I saw a big wire cage.

" What is that? " I asked the Colonel.

" Our mascot," he replied, with a smile.

I walked up to the cage, and saw that it contained a number of large birds. " The Condor eagle," said the Colonel, pointing to a huge bird perching on a rock. Its feathers were grey, and around the pale mauve-pink of its throat was a circlet of finest white down. The great bird stood motionless, its head held high and cruel beak shut tight. He seemed quite oblivious of the presence of the smaller birds, and must have been dreaming of his home high up in the snowy Andes, where the powerful Condor eagles have been known to fly at an altitude of 20,000 feet.

My aeroplane had been refuelled for the return flight to Buenos Aires, and I greatly admired the red, white, and blue symbol of the Air Force of Uruguay which had been painted on the rudder.

It was with great reluctance that I bade farewell to the many friends who had assembled to see me take off the following day. " Good-bye! Come back again to Uruguay some day!" they cried as I waved farewell and took off. Circling the aerodrome I could see the people on the ground still waving as I set off for Buenos Aires.

Flying back along the lovely coast I thought of all the experiences that had been mine on my flight from England to South America. I felt a warm glow in my heart at the thought of palm-fringed Cape San Roque, my first sight of the great continent after crossing the Atlantic Ocean from Africa. Surely Columbus himself could not have been more pleased when in 1498 he sighted South America.

Much as I should have liked to stay longer in Argentina and see more of that delightful country, I decided to return to England by the *Asturias*, so that I could be in London for Christmas. I bade *adios* to the many friends I had made, and with the Gull snugly perched on the wide deck of the *Asturias* set sail for England on December 6. Seventeen days out from Buenos Aires the *Asturias* steamed up the Solent, and on arrival at Southampton I received a civic reception.

CHAPTER XIV: INVITATION
TO PARIS

ONE MORNING SHORTLY AFTER MY return to London I was delighted to receive a letter inviting me to visit Paris as guest of the Aéro-Club de France during the month of February 1936. This was indeed a pleasant surprise, and I wrote back immediately accepting the invitation. I had flown to the aerodrome at Le Bourget many times, but had never actually seen Paris from the ground; consequently I greatly looked forward to the visit.

My Gull was being overhauled, so for the first time in my life I travelled as a passenger in an air liner, and flew to Paris by Imperial Airways.

On my arrival I was greeted by the Baronne de Vendeuvre, who presented me with a beautiful bouquet, and among the people assembled to welcome me were the Marquise de Noailles and Lieutenant-Colonel Wateau, President of the Aéro-Club de France. The French Air Ministry was also represented.

For nearly a week I was lavishly entertained in Paris, and made many friends and met a great number of interesting people. I attended a large banquet given by the Aéro-Club de France, and the Marquise de Noailles introduced me to the former Minister of Air, General Denain, at whose home I was also entertained. Receptions were given in my honour by *Figaro* and *Le Jour*. At a luncheon arranged by the Directeur of *Paris Soir* I met many famous French aviators: Messieurs Codos and Rossi, famous for their Paris–New York return and other long-distance flights, M. Fonck, the War ace, M. Détroyat, one of the greatest aerobatic pilots, and André Japy, well known for his flights to South Africa and Japan. Madame Bastie, who later lowered my time for the Southern Atlantic Ocean section of my South American flight, was there, also Mlle Suzanne Lenglen, famous tennis player, who impressed me by her youthful appearance and vivacious manner.

I thoroughly enjoyed all the parties and receptions arranged for me. One evening at the Sorbonne I met the then Minister of Air, General Deat, and was introduced to some of the early pioneers of aviation—M. Blériot, Louis Paulhan, M. Bréguet, among others. Naturally I felt tremendously pleased to meet M. Blériot, whom I had admired all my life.

At a private dinner given by M. Blériot I heard from Mme Blériot the story of her husband's epic Channel flight, and how she had anxiously watched from the deck of a battleship the tiny monoplane linking the Continent with England by air for the first time in history.

M. Blériot was most enthusiastic about my career, and we became fast friends. He liked to trace the route of my flights on a large glass globe in his beautiful *salon*, and showed a great interest in flying in the Antipodes. In a glass case were gold, silver, and bronze medals from almost every country in the world, and many trophies adorned the rooms of the Blériots' lovely home.

I was privileged to be shown M. Blériot's own work-room, which was a revelation. Just off the exquisitely carpeted hall a door opened to reveal a small room devoid of furniture with the exception of a few chairs. A wooden bench extended the entire length of the room, and on it were various tools and lengths of spruce. On the bare walls were pinned many blue prints and faded photographs of early aeroplanes. Mme Blériot confided to me that sometimes when a brilliant reception was being held she would miss her husband, and find him working on models or designs in this little workroom.

In the majority of aviators I have noticed a deep artistic sense and love of beauty, and M. Blériot was no exception. The bare walls and ceiling of his bedroom were sky-blue. "You see," he explained, "even in mid-winter, with thick fog outside, when I wake in the morning my first impression is a happy one of clear blue skies." One of my most treasured possessions is a photo given to me by this great pioneer.

Before I left M. Blériot gave me two stamps which had been specially printed to commemorate his historic flight in 1909, and which he autographed for me. I felt deeply grieved when he died a few months later, but his cup of happiness must have been full to see aeroplanes of his design maintaining a regular air service across the South Atlantic Ocean.

During my visit to Paris I was also entertained by the Renault Caudron Company. I inspected the air cadets, and met the gallant nurses of the Aviation Sanitaire—the French Red Cross. The nurses were being trained as pilots, and quite a number already had their licences. The Marquise de Noailles is the head of the movement, and with the Baronne de Vendeuvre is doing a tremendous amount of work in connexion with it.

At a luncheon given by the Aéro-Club Roland Garros I met Mlle Suzanne Deutsch de la Meurthe, a great French patriot and sportswoman. Her father had given the prize won by Santos-Dumont for the first flight round the Eiffel Tower, which was accomplished in a balloon. She was furthering his work for aviation by sponsoring the Deutsch de la Meurthe Cup, for which all the ace French pilots compete annually, when some amazing speeds have been achieved.

Although I was only in Paris a short time and such an extensive programme had been planned, nevertheless I was able to do some sightseeing. When it became known that I had never had a previous opportunity of seeing the capital my kind French friends attempted to show it to me within the space of a few days. I would, of course, have to see the majestic Arc de Triomphe and visit the tomb of the unknown soldier. "The Eiffel Tower and Cleopatra's Obelisk," another would suggest. And no one ever visited Paris without being deeply impressed by the grandeur of Napoleon's great marble tomb. Then there was the exquisite architecture of Notre Dame and the gemlike stained-glass windows of little Saint Chapelle, some one would add. Nor could I leave Paris without a quick visit to the Louvre to see the *Winged Victory* and glimpse the smile of *Mona Lisa* as we hurried through the long galleries. It would be unthinkable to depart without viewing the wondrous splendour of Versailles and admiring the loveliness of Marie-Antoinette's Petit Trianon. Then, of course, the quaint Place Victor Hugo, the site of the Bastille, the Champs Élysées with its lovely trees and fountains, the famous bird-market, Les Invalides, to Malmaison to see the Napoleon relics, the Place de l'Opéra, Père Lachaise to see the tomb of Chopin. All these rich, beautiful scenes unfolded themselves to my eyes in those crowded hours. Sandwich in the banquets and receptions in my honour, a hurried glimpse in the fashionable shops in the Rue de la Paix, visits to Montmartre, Maxim's, Fouquet's, and drives in the Bois, and you have some idea of the kaleidoscopic whirl of my visit to Paris.

I loved Paris, and thought it must be one of the most beautiful cities in the world as I drove along the Champs Élysées and saw the lovely tree-lined avenues, the sparkling fountains and impressive monuments.

At the headquarters of the Ligue Internationale des Aviateurs at Place Normande in the Bois I saw the Harmon International Trophy, which had just been awarded to me, and was made a member of the Vieux Tigres.

While I was in Paris I had the interesting experience of broadcasting over Radio Paris.

On returning to London I felt deeply honoured to

learn that the French Government had decided to confer on me the Croix de la Légion d'Honneur. I learned that I should be one of the youngest members of this famous order and the first British airwoman to be honoured by France. It was necessary for his Majesty the King to give his permission, so while this was being granted I planned a flying holiday with my mother.

CHAPTER XV: AERIAL TOUR

THE LARGE AUXILIARY PETROL-TANK HAD been removed from the cabin of my Gull and a comfortable passenger seat fitted, complete with arm- and head-rests. As it was early April we decided to fly to North Africa in search of sunshine. Our holiday was to include a flight round Spain, with a visit to the Balearic Islands. We planned to return to England *via* Marseilles and spend a week in Paris.

On April 9, 1936, we took off from Hatfield Aerodrome, and landed at Gravesend Airport to clear customs and obtain a weather report. We had a considerable amount of luggage with us, including four suitcases, a valise, and a rug, for it was to be a leisure flight, and we expected to be away about two months.

The Gull was well loaded when we left England, and as I intended to make our first stop at Bordeaux, 560 miles away, we had a considerable amount of petrol aboard.

After we had crossed the Channel and passed over Le Touquet we flew southward. Intercepting the Seine near Rouen, passing over hundreds of miles of peaceful pasture-land, until the broad sweep of the Garonne came

into view, we glided down to a landing at the aerodrome at Bordeaux four hours out from England. News
travels fast, and as if by magic, although I had not notified any of the aero clubs at the cities we intended
visiting, wherever we landed lavish hospitality was extended to us. The fact that a daughter was flying her
mother on an aerial tour seemed to catch popular imagination. In Spain people were in turn astounded and
delighted to see the Señora and Señorita flying together,
and although I planned a quiet tour and did not seek
publicity we received an amazing Press at each place.

We met only one bad storm, and this was when
crossing the Pyrenees from Toulouse to Barcelona,
when low clouds and heavy rain obscured the pass near
Perpignan, and I had to climb the Gull to 10,000 feet
to escape the violent down-draughts from the snow-
covered peaks.

I was delighted that my mother had agreed to accompany me on this flying tour, as it showed her faith in
aerial transport and aviation in general. The weeks that
we spent on the flying holiday were among the happiest
in my life. We made many friends, and in Valencia
met Señor Ibañez, brother of the famous novelist, and
editor of a Valencia newspaper. He sent me armfuls of
the most exquisite roses. I learned afterwards that when
the war broke out he escaped to Italy by disguising
himself.

One day we drove to an orange-grove near Valencia
where the panorama which presented itself was an unforgettable one: acres of orderly trees, their green leaves
almost hidden by the gorgeous golden colouring of the

fruit, with high purple mountains forming a perfect setting for the scene, over which floated the exotic perfume
of thousands of orange blossoms.

From Valencia we planned to visit the Balearic
Islands, as I had heard and read so much about Majorca
that I wanted to see for myself if the island was as en-
chanting as it was reputed to be. There was a landing-
ground at Palma, but no hangar or any facilities. As I
was reluctant to leave the Gull exposed in the open overnight with no one to guard it we decided to leave the
machine in Valencia and travel by one of the small
boats that run between Palma and Valencia.

We spent nearly two weeks exploring the island,
which I thought was wondrously beautiful. Wild
flowers grew in abundance, and some of the giant trees
in the olive-groves were nearly a thousand years old.
We learned that at one time there was a tax on olive-
trees, and to avoid this the islanders kept the old trees
alive by grafting. The result was that some of the trees
gained enormous proportions, and many are still to be
seen with girths as big as those of the largest oak-trees.

On one occasion we drove high up into the mountains, negotiating a series of astounding hairpin bends
and passing through most beautiful scenery. At last we
arrived at the monastery at Valldemosa, where Chopin
and George Sand found short-lived happiness. It was
a wonderful experience to see the actual piano in the
small, stone-flagged room where Chopin composed
many of the preludes. I felt almost awed as I stood in
that tiny room, which was bare of furniture save for the
master's piano, a table, and a few chairs, and realized

that it was in this very room, high up in the solitude of the mountains, that Chopin composed the " Raindrop " Prelude.

Long, happy days were spent on the silvery beaches and in Palma, Formentor, Soller, Mirimar, and all the other delightful villages on the island. So enchanted was I with Majorca that I thought at one time of taking a villa there for some months, but this was not practicable in view of the big programme I had planned.

On the way back to Valencia we also visited the little island of Iviza.

On the flight to North Africa we experienced beautifully sunny weather, and sighted the rock of Gibraltar fifty miles away. Even as we crossed the Strait to Tangier we could still see the lovely white line of the snow-capped Sierra Nevada in the distance.

One of the highlights of the tour was at Seville. To fly in the comparatively calm atmosphere and escape the bumps which one usually meets when flying over such mountainous country we arrived at an early hour over the city. Imagine my consternation on finding about twenty-five bulls grazing on the aerodrome. " There doesn't seem to be anyone there!" I shouted to my mother above the roar of the engine, as I pointed to the large hangars, which were all closed. After flying over Seville several times I returned to the aerodrome, but there was no sign of anyone to move the bulls. Gliding down I flew over the herd, which scattered in all directions, until at last I managed to round them up into one corner. Landing the Gull on the cleared area, I asked my mother to watch the bulls as I taxied as fast as possible towards the hangars, silently thanking Providence that the machine was not red.

"If they start running towards us give a shout, and we will take off again and return to Africa," I told her. Fortunately this was not necessary, for the hangar doors opened and some Spanish mechanics wheeled the Gull to safety.

We had breakfast with Comandante Esteve, who was in charge of the Tablada air base, and who never ceased to chuckle about our experience, and thought it extremely funny that after flying the Atlantic I should fear *los toros*. "They are not ferocious," he explained. "*Los toros* graze quietly on the aerodrome in readiness for the bull-fight on Sunday."

The aerodrome at Seville was an excellent one. A profusion of flowers grew round the officers' quarters, or casino as they called it. This was a typically Spanish building in stucco with a cool, blue-tiled courtyard. The hospitable Comandante insisted on sending his adjutant to escort us in his car to the Hotel Christina, where we were to stay. A guard of honour was formed, and we drove in triumph from the aerodrome, crossing the Guadalquivir river to the city.

Shortly after our arrival the Aero Club of Andalusia held a *vino* in our honour, at which the British Consul was present, and we met charming little Señorita Cueva, the Spanish airwoman, whose husband was stationed at Tetuan, in Spanish Morocco. The *vino* is the Spanish equivalent of the cocktail party, and we made many friends as we sipped the excellent wine.

A banquet also was given by the Comandante of the

base and his officers, at which the charming Comandante spoke in halting English, and I had the temerity
to make a speech in my elementary Spanish.

We found Seville a most colourful city, and greatly
enjoyed the time we spent there. The Alcazar was a
revelation, and we walked through the great palace
admiring the exquisite Moorish architecture with its
gorgeous colouring, the beauty of which was almost
unbelievable. In a tiled courtyard of the palace surrounded by a profusion of beautiful flowers, orange-
trees, and palms we were shown an ingenious fountain,
evidently designed to amuse some monarch of olden
times. This consisted of a number of tiny jets con-
cealed in the pathway. When turned on, as it was for
our benefit, the jets would suddenly send forth many
fine sprays of water or, as rumour has it, scent, pre-
sumably to the astonishment of the *señoras* and
señoritas strolling in the courtyard. One could imagine
the startled cries of the ladies and the laughter of the
perpetrator of the practical joke.

We were then shown through the now deserted
palace, and were greatly impressed by the beautiful lacy
carving of the Moorish archways inlaid with gold-leaf
and coloured the most wonderful shades. There were
some lovely tapestries, and one of our friends proudly
showed us the gold telephone used by ex-King
Alphonso.

Just as we were leaving the sound of a horse's hoofs
was heard on the cobblestones, and a uniformed courier
galloped up on a jet-black steed, carrying an immense
bouquet of flowers. Reining his horse, he dismounted,

saluted, and, presenting the Comandante's compliments, handed me the flowers. Within a few seconds he was away like the wind, leaving me with a great armful of roses and an even deeper appreciation of Spanish courtesy.

There were very few, if any, taxies in Seville, but any amount of horse-drawn carriages, which seemed to be the fashion. The rate of hire was only two pesetas an hour (about one and fourpence), and we used to take a carriage and ride in the large gardens, which were filled with a profusion of gaily coloured flowers and palms. There had been an international exhibition in Seville, and many countries had built representative pavilions in the gardens, but owing to the cost they had never been dismantled. It was amazing to ride quietly along a tree-lined avenue and suddenly come upon an Indian temple, a Canadian log cabin, or a Swiss chalet. There was also a tiled Italian pavilion with two full-sized porcelain figures near by. "An adjunct to any city," a Spanish friend explained to me, when I made this international discovery in the heart of Seville.

During my stay I had the interesting experience of broadcasting for Radio Seville in Spanish.

One evening before we left we had a unique opportunity of seeing the Sevilanas and Flamencos, among other dances, performed to the exotic and colourful music of Mossorgesky and De Falla by the beautiful girls of Andalusia. It was a great sight to see these girls with their gaily coloured frilled skirts whirling to the music, to hear the click of the castanets and little crimson heels stamping the floor in rhythm with the music.

We were loath to leave Seville, and reluctantly took off one morning and flew over the city escorted by a squadron of aeroplanes from the Tablada air base and set off for Madrid. As we flew towards the Spanish capital I recalled my flight over Spain on the way to South America when we passed over the great mountain ranges and occasional villages.

Madrid lies on a high plateau about 2000 feet above sea-level, and we had a good comprehensive view of the great white city as we circled it before landing at the aerodrome of Barahas. As we drove into the city with some members of the Aero Club we passed a procession of tiny boys and girls singing. All the children were dressed in red, even to the ribbon braiding the girls' hair, and I learned that they were Communist children. There was a very fine Plaza de Toros near the city, where I later saw a bull-fight, which I failed to appreciate owing to the broiling sun, which burned down with fierce intensity while the elegant matador or toreador—I forget which—skilfully baited the bull, who on this occasion never seemed to have a chance from the commencement.

We stayed at the luxurious Palace Hotel, and I heard later that it was destroyed by an aerial bombardment, which also demolished the beautiful new University City, over which we were shown.

There were many interesting sights to be seen in Madrid, and during our stay we witnessed the May Day celebrations and met the Mayor. We spent many hours

ITH MY MOTHER AND OFFICERS OF THE SPANISH AIR FORCE AT SEVILLE

RECEIVING THE CROSS OF THE LEGION OF HONOUR FROM
LIEUTENANT-COLONEL WATEAU

Others present : *Left to right*—Mlle Deutsch de la Meurthe, the Marquise de Noailles, and Group-Captain Field.

Photo Keystone

in the famous Prado, inspecting the priceless works of Velasquez and other Spanish masters. A photographer from one of the Spanish newspapers obtained permission from the authorities to photograph me beside a lovely Goya.

The flight to Barcelona was an interesting one, and we flew over high plateaux, passing several lovely sapphire-coloured lakes, which from above looked like great jewels, before we crossed a high range of mountains to the coast. We had a wonderful view of the big city as we flew over Barcelona before landing.

I had been warned in Madrid to land only on the grass part of the aerodrome of Prat, as the large clay patches were filled-in shell-holes. The small two-way landing-ground appeared to be all clay, so, thinking it might be very soft, I landed at the equally small aerodrome of the Aero Club of Catalunya. Later I took the Gull over to Prat to clear customs for France.

The Barcelona people, we found, were most hospitable, and we had soon made many friends. Several tours were arranged so that we might see the sights of the city. Our hotel faced the Plaza de Catalunya, and the famous street Rambla was near by. At a reception I was made a member of the Aero Club of Catalunya.

During our stay in Spain we noticed that few women in the cities wore traditional Spanish dress, although many still affected the mantilla, mostly worn without the comb.

Barcelona seemed very modern, and as we strolled along the Rambla we passed a theatre advertising Charlie Chaplin in *Tiempo Moderno*, and another with

Marlene Dietrich in *Deseo*. I was sorry later that we missed seeing a film in Spanish. There were some wonderful churches in Barcelona, and we visited quite a number in the course of our sight-seeing. Several receptions were given, and I had the pleasure of broadcasting from Radio Barcelona.

It was May 1936, and I left Barcelona and flew to Paris to receive the cross of the Legion of Honour, which it had been arranged should be bestowed on me at a banquet to be held on the evening of May 7. Mother had also taken a great liking to Majorca, and she decided to return and wait in Palma for me.

I flew to Paris *via* Toulouse, where I stayed the night at the home of M. Marcel Doret, the famous French pilot, and his wife. In brilliant sunshine I landed at Buc Aerodrome, Paris, the following day, to be met by representatives of the Aéro-Club de France and greeted by my friend Mlle Suzanne Deutsch de la Meurthe. A luncheon was given at the hotel at Versailles, after which we drove to the Prince des Galles, where I stayed. That night at a banquet given by the Aéro-Club de France I was decorated with the cross of Chevalier de la Légion d'Honneur, and felt that my cup of happiness was indeed filled to the brim.

The following day the newspapers reported the fine flight of the *Graf* Zeppelin to Lakehurst, and I never fail to smile when I think of an incident that occurred that morning. When we were passing Bagatelle a friend of mine, who was driving, remarked that the roses in the garden of that little jewel of a palace were exquisite and blooming in profusion.

"What!" I replied. "Roses blooming in the open in early May! I can't believe that, even of this magic city."

"We will see them with our own eyes," my friend remarked, turning the car and driving back.

I thought the *concierge* looked slightly surprised when we asked to be directed to the Rose Garden. As we hurried along the paths my friend remarked on the myriads of the multicoloured tulips which adorned the gardens with their stately beauty.

"Yes, but I want to see those roses you were so sure about, as I don't believe there are any," I insisted as we walked on, both confident that we were right.

"There," he cried, "is the Rose Garden—beyond that hedge."

The garden was there all right, but not a rose to be seen. With a look of consternation my friend asked a gardener working near by if there were any roses out yet. The aged gardener told us that we might find a few at another part of the garden to which he directed us. With renewed confidence my companion walked quickly to the spot, while I, growing increasingly sceptical, followed him. There was a delighted shout ahead as my friend located a tiny pink bud—the only one in the whole garden that had the temerity to appear so early. "Yes, it certainly is a leader," I said. "And now that we have wasted nearly two hours searching you may as well see the name of the hardy and gallant bud that has saved your reputation for integrity." He bent and disentangled the label from the leaves, and we both read the single name—Eckener.

On flying back to London I read in the news of the riots and shipping strikes which heralded the civil war in Spain. A strike at the docks in Barcelona seemed imminent, so, fearing that my mother might be cut off on the island of Majorca, I sent an urgent telegram asking her to take the first boat and wait for me in Barcelona.

Flying to Spain from London I experienced the most atrocious weather, and landed at Toulouse in a deluge, proceeding to Barcelona the following morning. I stayed only one night in Barcelona, and next day drove to Prat with my mother, accompanied by some of our Spanish friends, including Señor Canudas, Director of Civil Aviation, and his wife. When I had cleared customs good-byes were said, the luggage carefully stowed in the machine, and Mother took her place in the cabin surrounded by bouquets of roses. I gave the Gull full throttle and took off for Marseilles.

We crossed the Spanish border to France and followed the broad sweep of the Gulf of Lions, passing over quaint little villages. In brilliant sunshine we flew over the Bouches du Rhône and landed at Marignane Airport, on the shore of Lake Berre, where we were met by my old friend M. Fournier and invited to lunch at his home with Mme Fournier and their family.

Our stay in Marseilles was a happy one. I particularly wanted to show Mother the Château d'If, from which Edmond Dantès, the Count of Monte Cristo, made his spectacular escape after long, weary years of imprisonment. The island was some miles distant from Marseilles, and we travelled in a small open boat. As the Mediterranean was in one of its boisterous moods we were drenched with spray as the tiny vessel ploughed through the white-capped waves. The Château has all the traits of a medieval fortress, with its high stone walls rising sheer from the white rocky shore, its ramparts and dungeons. It retains all the romantic atmosphere of adventure that has thrilled the youth of all countries. We climbed the many stone steps leading to the great oak door of the Château, and after seeing the tower and the view from the ramparts we groped our way through the gloom to the cells. The French guard brought an oil-lamp, which accentuated the eerie darkness and picked out the names and inscriptions which had been carved on the stone walls by prisoners in olden times. Holding the lamp above his head, the guard led the way, and in one cell showed us the exact spot where the Count of Monte Cristo spent years chipping away the stone in his endeavour to escape.

Before flying back to London we spent a few days in Paris, where we were entertained, and again experienced the most lavish hospitality. At one luncheon we met the Vicomte de Rohan, President of the Automobile Club de France, and the President of the Aéro-Club de France, Lieutenant-Colonel Wateau. Mlle Suzanne Deutsch de la Meurthe was there also. In company with the Marquise de Noailles we drove to her lovely home at Chantilly, and to see the beautiful castle where peacocks strutted on the wide lawns.

On our return to London I decided that the time had arrived for me to achieve what I considered as the ultimate of my ambition—the first solo flight to New Zealand. Consequently I commenced preparations for the flight, determined that the organization should be perfect right down to the smallest detail. Before my previous long-distance flights I had undergone a period of training, and to break the monotony of the usual skipping exercises and daily walks I planned a novel interlude. This was to be a walking tour along the South Downs, over which I had flown so many times, but had seldom had a chance to explore from the ground. I acquired large-scale Ordnance Survey maps and plotted out a daily schedule, selecting the most suitable inns at which to stay. As it was to be a walking tour we had to keep the amount of luggage we proposed taking down to a minimum. "We are not flying this time, and we won't need a wardrobe trunk," I would say, laughing heartily at the vision of myself toiling past Chanctonbury Ring in the midsummer heat bowed down with the weight of our luggage.

When Mother saw the schedule I had planned, allowing for a walk of ten to fifteen miles a day, she diplomatically reminded me that she happened to be older, not younger, than myself. "If you think you are old you will grow old," I said. "It's merely a state of the mind, and you are as fit as I am, and your spirit is just as young." Nevertheless, I thought that if the tour proved too strenuous we could always rest for a few days somewhere.

On a glorious midsummer day in July we took the train to the delightful old-world village of Amberley, which nestles snugly in a valley where the downs part to let the river Arun flow to the sea. Clad in light tweed costumes, soft felt hats, and stout walking shoes, we were untrammelled by any luggage save a small bag each with the barest necessities and two silk rainproofs. To acclimatize ourselves we stayed for two days in the peaceful village, with its thatched cottages and "jasmine-muffled lattices." We climbed the slopes of Mount Amberley and rested on the scented downland turf, drinking in the beauty of the scene as the green downs, dotted here and there with fields of golden corn studded by crimson poppies, rolled gently down to the sea.

Walking, I think, must be the greatest tonic, and it is one within the reach of all. Those who have felt the springy turf of the downs under their feet and filled their lungs with the crisp fresh air will agree with me. As you walk all the petty little worries and doubts that sometimes crowd the mind disappear, and in Nature's soothing presence new thoughts and inspirations come as if by magic.

We made good progress, and on our walk passed through Steyning, Poynings, Lewes, Newhaven, and Seaford. By the time we reached the Seven Sisters one scorching day we were able to take them in our stride, and arrived at Beachy Head well pleased with things in general.

At this stage my presence was necessary in London in connexion with the flight preparations, for I had already set the cogs of organization into motion before leaving. Mother appeared not at all disappointed at the interruption in our tour, and was, I believe, secretly grateful for a few days' respite from the rigorous walking.

When I returned to Eastbourne we continued our journey, walking on *via* Hastings and Fairlight. We left the downs at Pevensey to cross the Romney Marshes. Stopping at the quaint old towns of Winchelsea and Rye and Lydd, we went on through Dymchurch to Hythe, from where we returned to London by train, having walked approximately eighty miles on the tour.

The Gull was hangared at Hatfield, where we had taken a cottage quite near the famous old Hatfield House, home of the Earls of Salisbury, where Queen Elizabeth is reputed to have been staying when she received the news of her accession to the throne.

It was indeed gratifying to find that my name was included in the Birthday Honours of 1936, and that I was to be made a Commander of the British Empire. At the first investiture held by King Edward VIII in July I was present at Buckingham Palace, and received the decoration from the King. This decoration was an exquisitely wrought gold and ultramarine enamelled cross, topped with a tiny gold crown and worn with a royal purple bow. I placed it proudly alongside my French and Brazilian orders.

At this time I was very busy with preparations for my forthcoming flight, although, following my usual procedure, intended making no announcement until I was almost ready to depart. The Gull's Certificate of Airworthiness had been renewed, the engine overhauled, and the large eighty-gallon auxiliary tank replaced in the cockpit. I indulged in the extravagance of a self-starter, as there was usually a considerable amount of time lost starting the engine by swinging the heavy metal propeller by hand. I had completed a series of tests, and when I flew the machine to Lympne to clear customs felt quite confident of reaching my objective, Auckland, in New Zealand, 14,000 miles away. Bad weather was reported over the Continent, so I stayed a day at Lympne waiting for better conditions.

CHAPTER XVI: SOLO TO NEW ZEALAND

ON THE MORNING OF MY DEPARTURE, ON October 5, 1936, I arrived at the aerodrome at 3.30 A.M. to find quite a crowd of reporters and photographers already there, and although it was such an early hour the keen camera men placed the powerful arc lights in position to film the take-off.

"Would you say a few words, please, Miss Batten?" one of the camera men asked. I was not at all in the mood for speeches at such an early hour. However, to oblige him I stood beside the Gull staring into the blinding lights while being filmed making a speech. At last it was over, and I climbed into the cockpit. The engine sprang to life with a roar as I turned the switches on "Contact" and pressed the self-starter. Looking out the cabin window, I saw the camera man, with a look of consternation on his face, waving frantically. Leaving the engine warming up I climbed from the cockpit to say good-bye to my friends. As I left the machine the camera man grasped my arm, and with a very white face said, "Please, Miss Batten, would you repeat that speech for us?"

WITH THE GULL AT HATFIELD AERODROME

Photo Keystone

A FILM INTERVIEW BEFORE LEAVING FOR NEW ZEALAND

Photo Keystone

"No, there is no time," I replied, as I shook hands with my friends and started to climb back into the cockpit.

"Please!" he persisted. "If you don't I'll lose my job. I forgot to switch on the sound."

Leaning into the cockpit I switched off the engine. "Very well," I said, "but make sure about it this time. I want to leave England to-day, you know." I was about to remark that it was a good thing I never forgot my various switches, but thought the moment hardly appropriate for an object-lesson, so stood patiently beside my aeroplane, trying to be as tolerant as possible, and made another speech.

It was 4.20 A.M. when the gull roared along the path of the floodlight and took off on that memorable morning. It was not until I had circled the aerodrome and set off into the misty darkness over the Channel that I suddenly realized the immensity of the task I had set myself in electing to make the longest flight in the Empire. True, I had already flown to Australia and back, but on this occasion I planned to fly on from Sydney to New Zealand, a distance of 1330 miles over the Tasman Sea. Lying far south in the latitudes known to mariners as the "Roaring Forties," the sudden violent storms and icy gales from the Antarctic had earned it the title of "the most treacherous sea in the world."

My musings were cut short as I encountered a bank of cloud. Climbing above it I flew at 3000 feet, and when by my stop-watch I estimated my position was over Gris Nez I altered course for Paris. Through the mist which lay like a veil over Northern France I could see the blurred gleam of the air route beacons, and almost as soon as I distinguished the glow of the myriad lights of the capital I saw the beacon at Le Bourget.

Dawn was breaking as I crossed the Seine near Fontainebleau, and when it was light enough to distinguish the ground beneath I found the countryside wreathed in mist. Even when I arrived over Lyons there was thick fog in the Rhône valley, although this dispersed near Valence.

After flying above cloud over most of the route I arrived at Marignane Airport, Marseilles, a little over four hours after leaving England.

Only forty minutes after landing I was on my way again, and the Gull climbed swiftly over the mountains to Cap Camarat, where I left the French coast and flew over the Mediterranean on a direct course for Rome. There was a slight following wind, and I made good time, and, speeding over Corsica, reached the Italian coast in glorious sunshine. By this time I was beginning to enjoy the flight, although, according to the report from Marseilles, bad weather lay ahead over the Adriatic. I had been advised not to attempt to make Athens that afternoon, but to land at Brindisi instead.

The sky had clouded over when I sighted Naples, and I was obliged to climb through great banks of clouds to cross the Apennines. As I neared Brindisi the air became very turbulent, and the Gull was tossed about as I approached the storm area. The weather looked threatening out to sea, and banks of ominous cloud darkened the sky. At the customs aerodrome at Brindisi I heard that the storm over Greece had not abated. Heavy rain was reported at Athens, and the mountains round Tatoi were covered with low cloud. There was still sufficient daylight left to proceed to Athens, but I decided to play safe and stay the night at Brindisi, and fly straight through to Cyprus early next morning.

Before leaving London I had learned that petrol was six shillings per gallon in Italy, and it was necessary to pay cash for any supplies taken at Brindisi. If I were to make up lost time by refuelling here and going on to Cyprus without stopping in Greece payment for the petrol would constitute a serious problem. I had with me the *carnet* issued to me against a deposit, which meant that I could refuel at the towns on my schedule without paying for the petrol in local currency. The thirsty Gull would require about sixty-eight gallons on the thousand-mile flight to Cyprus in still air, and with a safety margin against head winds or having to turn back for any reason would need refuelling to approximately eighty-five gallons. This meant producing twenty-eight pounds, which would leave me about two pounds for total expenses during the rest of the flight.

Just as I was puzzling out the best plan of action two men approached and saved the situation. One of them was the representative of the Shell company, Signor Morella, and quite by coincidence he happened to be in Brindisi. As if by magic he was able to arrange for me to take fuel aboard without paying sterling.

Although I had logged 1330 miles that day I was not the slightest bit tired, and on arrival at the hotel ate a hearty dinner of macaroni, which I declared excellent, to the great delight of my two Italian friends.

When we arrived at the airport early next morning I realized that the take-off in the darkness at this aerodrome, which was not then equipped with lights, was going to be very difficult. A runway was being constructed on the landing area, leaving me with very restricted space. Signor Morella walked ahead with a torch as I taxied the Gull slowly into the wind. My kind Italian friends then drove the car to the far corner of the aerodrome, and I took off towards the headlights.

Once off the ground I climbed the machine up through the misty nimbus clouds and over a great bank of cumulus, and crossed the Adriatic Sea at an altitude of 10,000 feet. At this height the air outside was icy, but in the cabin it was warm and comfortable. There was no sign of a break in the clouds when, one hour forty-five minutes after Brindisi, I altered course for Corinth. I wanted to check up my position, but it was inadvisable to attempt to descend through the clouds at this stage on account of the high, mountainous nature of the country.

The rising sun painted the sky crimson with its rays and tinted the cloud banks a delicate pink. Snow-covered peaks reared themselves above the clouds, which lay like a mantle over Greece. Identifying some of the highest peaks I was able to approximate my position, and as I flew on glimpsed the blue waters of the Gulf of Corinth far below through a gap on the white cloud carpet beneath. Over the Gulf of Corinth

I glided down to 3000 feet, and flew out over the Ægean Sea towards the island of Paros, where I intended altering course for Rhodes.

Visibility improved as I flew over the numerous islands that dot the Ægean Sea, and passing over Rhodes I neared the Anatolian coast of Turkey. The sun shone down from a clear sky to reveal the Mediterranean at its best. As on previous occasions, the Gull was tossed about by down-draughts from the high mountains on the rugged coast even though I was flying forty miles out from the coast, and I was relieved when the island of Cyprus came into view.

I landed at Nicosia to refuel. This was done very quickly, but I had to wait nearly an hour for a weather report for the route to Baghdad. On earlier flights over this route I had experienced the fury of sand-storms, and had too much respect for the freak weather in this part of the world to set off without a weather report. It was not very detailed when it did arrive, and I took off knowing that with the head winds predicted it would not be possible to make up the time lost at Cyprus. Some of the residents had very kindly given me large bunches of grapes and some juicy oranges, and these helped to while away the time as I crossed the 150-mile stretch of sea to Beirut.

The down-draughts from the Lebanon Mountains had little effect on the powerful Gull, which climbed rapidly through the clouds to speed across the great range at 10,000 feet. Over the desert a yellow dust-haze hung like a pall, and as I flew on this became thicker, the wind wafting great clouds of sand into the sky. Two and a half hours after leaving Cyprus visibility became practically *nil*, and, flying very low, I had great difficulty in keeping the ground in view. The sun was almost blotted out, and resembled a black sphere as it sank rapidly. Would the dust be worse farther on, I asked myself, and decided not to risk flying on to Baghdad under such conditions. The nearest aerodrome was sixty miles farther on, and bore the bare title of H.3—L.G. (Landing Ground) on my map of the region.

It was now a race against darkness and the clouds of dust which swept past the Gull as I flew on. At last, just as the sun sank below the horizon, I sighted a solitary light ahead, and within a few minutes the wheels of the Gull came to rest on the sandy surface of the landing-ground. A visitor was not expected at the tiny outpost of H.3, a pumping-station on the Asiatic Petroleum Company's pipeline, along which the millions of gallons of oil flow from the Iraq oil-fields at Mosul to the ports of Beirut, on the Syrian coast, and Haifa. I was behind my schedule, and realized that I would have to hurry if I were to lower the England-to-Australia solo record as I planned to do on the way through to New Zealand. I therefore decided to omit a landing at Baghdad and refuel at Basra instead, from where I could fly non-stop to Karachi in an effort to make up time.

The manager of H.3 was most hospitable, and arranged for a supply of petrol and a guard for the Gull. The desert track would not be visible in the darkness, and it would be necessary to steer a compass course over the desert to Ramadi, where I would alter course for Basra. The position of H.3 was not accurately marked on my map, so I asked the wireless operator to get the true course for Rutbah Wells. He was able to do this, and it was a simple matter to calculate the magnetic course from that point by which I could fly direct to Ramadi.

The small band of engineers stationed at H.3 showed great interest in my flight at dinner that night as they had heard on the radio of my progress. There were only two or three buildings and a radio station on this desert outpost, and the only woman was the wife of the manager. I was impressed by the general air of comfort and cleanliness of the quarters, where in addition to the large living-room there was also a billiards-room. I promised to send a photo of the Gull for the mess-room wall.

H.3 was 2000 feet above sea-level, and it was extremely cold in the desert that night. The Gull, picketed out in the open, was exposed to the icy wind, so I let the engine warm up for some time before taking off.

Bidding the manager and his assistant good-bye I took off once again, aided only by motor-car head-lights, and steered for Rutbah. It was very dark, but I picked up the lights of Rutbah, and to the north I could see the flames from the waste-oil fire which burns day and night at H.2 pumping-station. After I passed Rutbah there was not another light to be seen, and the desert was shrouded in darkness. The moon was on the wane, but the sky above was encrusted with myriads of stars. I always noticed that the engine seemed to run exceptionally well on night flights. Although I often felt sleepy during the daytime, especially when the sun burned down and made the cabin uncomfortably hot, at night I too seemed to be at my best, and usually felt wide awake. There is no sensation quite like that which a pilot experiences on a solo night flight across the desert in clear weather especially on a moonlight night speeding through the crisp, clear air high above the shadows of the sleeping earth, with the great vault of the heavens like a vast star-spangled canopy overhead and the moon casting its pale rays on the silver wings of the aeroplane. One feels completely detached from the earth beneath, and ordinary mundane affairs dwindle into insignificance. Under the magic spell and serenity of the night the aeroplane is but a tiny atom in the vastness of the universe. On the flight to South America I had waited back for the full moon, but on this flight it would have meant delaying the start for some weeks.

One hour thirty minutes out from H.3 the lights of Ramadi slipped beneath my wings as I altered course for Basra, 300 miles on. As a grey light stole across the desert the sun rose so quickly that it looked almost comical in its hurry. At this stage I was crossing the Euphrates and over Iraq, or, as it used to be picturesquely called, Mesopotamia—the land between two rivers. After past experiences of the mirage in the desert, when I had actually seen great blue lakes ahead and searched my maps to identify them, I never believed I had sighted water until actually over it. As

I approached the Horal Hammar lake huge flocks of birds rose in thousands from the marshes bordering, disturbed by the noise of my engine. This great lake extends for over sixteen miles, and the Euphrates loses itself in the maze of swamps at the north-western end before suddenly reappearing on the other side of the lake to join the Tigris at Qurna, supposed site of the Garden of Eden. United, these rivers form the palm-fringed Shatt al Arab, and flow swiftly on through the desert past Basra to the Persian Gulf.

A surprise was in store for me: I landed at the new Margil Aerodrome, Basra, to find it a most modern one, equipped with all facilities and wide bitumen runways, each over a thousand yards in length.

It did not take long to complete customs formalities, and I had breakfast at the aerodrome hotel while the Gull was being refuelled. Karachi was 1380 miles farther on, and as I intended flying non-stop the Gull was tanked up to 130 gallons. It would be necessary to produce a bill of health on arrival in India, and a most impressive document was handed to me stating the number of cases, if any, of cholera, plague, typhus, yellow fever, etc., which had occurred at Basra during the past week. Although the Gull was well loaded with fuel and a vicious hot, variable wind had sprung up, it took off easily along the smooth bitumen surface of the long runway. Fine jets of petrol sprayed from the air-vents on the wing-tanks as the Gull met a sudden violent bump crossing the river, and righting the machine I gradually climbed to a cooler altitude.

The Shatt al Arab is very wide at Basra, and along

the banks beautiful trees, including pomegranate, apricot, banana, and date, cluster together in luxuriant profusion. There were many boats on the river, both big ships and native rafts. From Basra come the most delicious dates, which are one of the main exports of Iraq's only port. Every September on the day of full moon they work at top speed at the docks. On that important day the date crop must be in and packed aboard the boats, for then the tide will be high and deep-draught ships can slip across the bar and down the river to the Persian Gulf. There is often a race for the first ship to arrive in New York with the new crop of dates, which can practically command its own price.

I had been warned of the likelihood of sand-storms along the Persian Gulf, but the weather remained clear, and the sun burned down with increasing fierceness as the day wore on. As I crossed the Strait of Hormuz I noticed a heavy dust-haze clouding the sky, until when near Jask I encountered a dust-storm, which appeared as a wall of sand sweeping towards me. "It might be possible to land at Jask," I thought, but it was too late, for the ground was now blotted out completely, and a yellow cloud of whirring sand enveloped the Gull.

Giving the engine full throttle, I climbed up, endeavouring to rise above the storm. At 9000 feet the dust seemed lighter, and at 10,000 feet I emerged into clear atmosphere, and a remarkable sight met my eyes. Below the storm raged, and even far out to sea dust was being blown, while inland the great ranges of bare mountains lifted their rocky peaks above the wall of sand. The storm extended for many hundreds of miles, but at nightfall I flew into clear weather once more.

When nearing Karachi I saw the red beacon lights flashing from the aerodrome. I glided down to a landing on October 7, having taken only 2 days 9 hours 25 minutes for the flight from England to India.

Refuelling was carried out quite quickly, but I found there were a tremendous number of customs formalities, and an hour after landing I was still sitting in the customs office filling in various forms. It was necessary to take out an Indian firearms licence for my revolver, and the health officer insisted on spraying the cockpit of the Gull. Arrangements had to be made for lights for my take-off, and after the sand-storm I thought it necessary to have an engine schedule carried out on the Gull.

Leaving the mechanics working on the machine, I drove to Commander Watts' home on the border of the aerodrome. After a bath and an excellent dinner served by silent-footed beturbaned Indian servants I was able to enjoy two and a half hours' sleep.

Early next morning I set off for Allahabad, 932 miles distant. Crossing the river Indus, I saw the lights of Hyderabad to starboard, and was able to check up on the air beacons of Utarlai and Tilwara on my way over the Sind Desert. Dawn found me over Jodhpur, and after passing Jhansi I arrived at Allahabad six hours five minutes after leaving Karachi.

Great improvements had been made since my previous visit, and an imposing control building now stood on one side of the aerodrome. Much as I wished to take off immediately I was unable to resist the opportunity of having breakfast, so sat in the restaurant while the machine was being refuelled. The weather report, as at other places in India and Burma, was a very detailed one, giving in addition to other meteorological information the direction and velocity of winds at levels up to 12,000 feet. This enabled me to choose an altitude at which I would have the advantage of a following wind over a portion of the route to Akyab, in Burma.

At 5000 feet I was above the clouds, and only caught a glimpse of Calcutta as I flew on towards the Sundarbans and the Bay of Bengal.

The sun was setting as I landed at Akyab, having flown 1900 miles that day from Karachi. Here too vast improvements had been made since my last visit, and in addition to the all-weather runways there was a large, well-equipped hangar.

The usual work was carried out on the machine, and I arranged for a flare path to be lit for my early morning take-off. Invited to dine with Mr Price and his daughter, who had met me on my two previous visits to Akyab, I drove with them to their home.

When my alarum-clock woke me at 1 A.M. I felt reluctant to leave the comparative comfort of the resthouse, but roused myself with the thought that I had planned to fly through to Singapore before sundown. The darkness was pitch black when I taxied the Gull along the flare path and took off for Alor Star, in Malaya, a distance of 1300 miles. The lighthouses on Ramri island enabled me to check my course, and Mr

Tate, superintendent at Akyab, had very kindly arranged for flares to be lit at Sandoway so that I could land there in case of emergency.

The sky lightened with the oncoming dawn as I crossed the jungle-covered Arakan Yoma Mountains at a point 380 miles from Akyab. It was raining at Rangoon, and squalls barred my path as I flew over the Gulf of Martaban to Moulmein. Climbing to 10,000 feet to escape the mist from the steaming jungle and the great banks of cumulus that rose above it, I flew for hours without glimpsing the Burmese coastline. As I flew southward the clouds piled up ahead to immense heights, until I was unable to keep above them any longer, and glided down through the billowy carpet. At 1000 feet I was flying through a filmy curtain of nimbus cloud, and near Victoria Point the sky was an ugly grey, and banks of ominous cloud ahead heralded fierce tropical storms.

Thinking to avoid the storm area, I crossed the mountains to the eastern side of the peninsula, where I was sheltered from the full force of the storms. The elements were not to be cheated, however, and 280 miles farther on when I recrossed the mountains I was exposed to the fury of a hurricane which was raging down the west coast of Lower Siam. The Gull was wafted along like a feather, and I estimated my ground speed at approximately 225 m.p.h. Rain fell in torrents, and washed over the petrol-gauges on the wings, completely obscuring them. Trying to keep the dark blur of the coastline in view I flew very low, passing over lines of coconut-trees bent level with the beach. Water streamed into the cockpit through a small leak, and I was soon drenched through. I experienced a feeling of horror as I watched the silver dope washed off the leading edges, and wondered how long the fabric covering would last. Near Alor Star the rain became even worse, and I lost sight of the ground as the Gull plunged through low clouds and torrential rain. I realized that a landing at Alor Star was out of the question, and a group of anxious people waiting for me at the aerodrome were unable even to see the tops of the trees in the deluge, but heard the roar of my engine as the Gull flashed overhead. I had flown 1300 miles from Akyab, and had not counted on being prevented from landing at Alor Star. The nearest aerodrome was on Penang island, over sixty miles farther south, and fortunately I had enough petrol to go on.

Flying on in the hope of clearer weather at Penang I suddenly caught sight of the coastline beneath, and was able to follow it once again. It was only raining slightly when I flew over Georgetown and landed on the smooth concrete runway of the modern aerodrome.

I was surprised to see the fuel agent waiting to refuel my machine, as I had resigned myself to a wait of at least an hour for petrol, Penang not being one of my scheduled stops. "Yes, missie," the smiling little Malay agent informed me, "I expect you. I received a telephone message from Alor Star when they heard you pass over." This appeared to be a stroke of genius, and I silently blessed the faithful petrol agent at Alor Star. "Velly bad weather, yes," the little agent added, pointing to the wings of my poor Gull. I was astounded on inspecting the leading edges to find the fabric worn right through and the wood showing bare in parts.

It was imperative that I should take off again as soon as possible and try to race the storm to Singapore. We patched the leading edges as well as we could, therefore, and I used the wide bands of adhesive tape from my first-aid kit to secure the fabric.

It was still raining as I took off and continued my flight over Malaya. As I flew southward over the great coconut and rubber plantations the weather improved. I landed at the R.A.F. aerodrome, Singapore, that evening, just 4 days 17 hours out from England. As the machine was refuelled I told the astonished R.A.F. officers that I intended flying on at eleven o'clock that night.

Leaving the Gull in capable hands to have an engine schedule carried out I drove to the house of Group Captain Sidney Smith, where I had been invited to stay. On the two previous occasions I had stayed with the Group Captain and his charming wife, and once again enjoyed their hospitality. After the luxury of a bath and a good meal I lay down to rest for a while. A legion of mosquitoes, which had somehow managed to get under the net, had other views, however, and when I rose about an hour later my arms and ankles were swollen with bites.

CHAPTER XVII: SOUTHWARD FROM SINGAPORE

A LARGE CROWD OF PEOPLE HAD assembled to see the take-off that night, and the Gull, with a maximum load of petrol, speeded past the long line of flares, and was soon circling the aerodrome to gain height.

The night was pitch black but clear, and I passed over many lights marking the many islands which dot the sea just south of Singapore. Two hours after the take-off a flash of lightning illuminated the sky, and the Gull soon plunged into a fierce tropical storm. Outside the cabin was a black void, and an occasional flash of lightning showed the rain beating against the cabin windows. Would it be possible to rise above the storm, I wondered, and giving the engine full throttle put the Gull into climbing angle. I had not slept since leaving Akyab, and was in no mood to meet such weather, and my eyes were growing tired of staring at the luminous dials of the instrument panel in front of me.

The Gull roared upward through the night, and at 9000 feet I almost despaired of ever penetrating the blackness which enveloped the machine. Suddenly I saw a star like a guiding light, then another, as the Gull rose above the storm to fly in the security of a calm, clear sky.

Two hours later I glided down through a gap in the clouds to see the lighthouse at the entrance of Batavia harbour straight ahead. The city was a blaze of light, and I altered course for Soerabaya, at the eastern end of the island of Java. A steady head wind retarded my speed, and became even stronger as I left Java and flew over Bali to Lombok island, where I landed to refuel at Rambang.

That afternoon, on the way to Kupang, I should probably have dropped off to sleep had it not been for the violent bumps which shook the Gull as it battled against the strong south-easterly wind.

On arrival at Kupang I climbed stiffly from the cockpit to supervise the refuelling immediately. The fuel agent provided an amusing interlude when he wanted to take photographs. Desirous of having some local colour he mustered all the native children to form a group. I was busy checking the engine, and, hearing a lot of laughter and chattering, went round to the other side of the Gull, to find about two dozen small boys being arranged for the photograph.

"Ah, there you are," said the fuel agent. "Please stand in the centre."

"No, I shall not," I replied, "unless they are suitably clothed."

This was translated by the fuel agent's wife, who spoke English, and amid much giggling and tittering the dark-eyed little native women produced scarfs and

sarongs. There was a great deal of laughter when the
photographs were eventually taken. About twelve
natives began to push the Gull quickly over the rough
ground to the picketing area, for as yet there was no
hangar at the aerodrome.

"Don't push it backward," I cried, when I realized
what they were doing. My warning came too late, however, and there was a bang as the tail-wheel caught on
some sharp stones and the rubber tyre burst. I had no
spare inner tube in my equipment, and suddenly felt
terribly tired and disheartened as I threw myself down
on the grass to inspect the tyre. Surely the record
would not be snatched from my grasp now, when I
was only 530 miles from Australia!

The fuel agent had a brilliant idea. "You leave it to
me," he cried, "and I will fix it. We can fill the tyre
with rubber sponges, and although heavy it will serve
you for the take-off." This seemed a brilliant idea, and
we quickly drove into the village and bought up all the
rubber sponges available. I accompanied the agent's
wife to the rest-house, while her husband returned to
the aerodrome with the tail-wheel.

Next morning I bade my kind Dutch friends good-
bye and took off for Australia. Apart from a slight
head wind fine weather prevailed, and the Timor Sea
crossing took only 3 hours 55 minutes. I landed at
Darwin at 1.20 A.M., G.M.T., on October 11, just 5 days
21 hours out from England, having lowered by twenty-
four hours the solo record previously held by Mr H. F.
Broadbent.

There was a large crowd to welcome me back to

THE GULL TAKES OFF INTO THE DAWN BOUND FOR NEW ZEALAND

Associated Press Photo

[*See p. 221*]

MOUNT EGMONT, NEW ZEALAND
By permission of the High Commissioner for New Zealand

Australia. This record was, however, incidental to the flight, for I had by no means reached my goal, which was Auckland, 3700 miles farther on. There was still the overland flight of 2200 miles across the continent to Sydney, and then the final section of 1330 miles across the Tasman Sea to New Zealand, and another 150 miles on to Auckland. There were many congratulatory telegrams and cables waiting for me, and on the flight southward next morning I read them to pass away the time.

Very strong head winds persisted the following day as I continued my flight across the vast, lonely stretches of the Northern Territory and Central Queensland to land at Longreach, 1200 miles from Darwin. On the flight to Sydney the weather was so rough and boisterous that the Gull was flung about violently, and I had the utmost difficulty in keeping the machine level when crossing the Blue Mountains. It was very clear, however, and I could see Sydney fifty miles before I flew over it.

As I circled the city I saw the great harbour bridge and all the roof-tops black with waving people. I landed at Mascot Aerodrome escorted by aeroplanes of the Royal Aero Club of New South Wales, having established a record of 8 days for the flight from England to Sydney. I shall never forget the full-throated roar of welcome that greeted me from thousands of people as I taxied up to the reception daïs. There was an even bigger crowd than on my first flight to Sydney. During the official reception there were numerous speeches by Government officials and aviation representatives. After the reception I drove through streets lined with cheering people to the Hotel Australia.

After landing the Gull had been taken to the De Havilland Aircraft Company's works, where a schedule was to be carried out on the engine, as there was no time for an overhaul.

"The flight is not finished yet," I told the enthusiastic people who showered me with congratulations.

A great number of receptions were planned when it became known that I intended waiting in Sydney for conditions to improve over the Tasman Sea. I was reluctantly obliged to decline all invitations, as I felt in need of some relaxation after the strenuous flight to Australia. Instead, however, I spent many hours making final preparations for the next section, and considerable time at the observatory studying weather charts and conferring with Mr Mares, the Government meteorologist.

There was a considerable amount of opposition to my plan to continue the flight through to New Zealand. This was not to be wondered at, however, for the sudden violent storms of the Tasman were well known by all Australians and New Zealanders. No one, however, realized more deeply than I the hazards of this seldom flown sea, for I had carefully studied hydrographic charts of the South Pacific and learned of the high gale frequency and the abnormal number of cyclonic disturbances throughout each year. Several times I had crossed the Tasman by steamer, and had vivid memories of storms when I had awakened in the night and listened almost fascinated to the pounding thuds as tremendous waves shook the ship from stem to stern. Great foaming sheets of spray hurled themselves across the decks, sometimes greedily taking hatches and twisting derricks in their diabolical frenzy.

My fast flight to Australia had been acclaimed with enthusiasm by the Press, and hundreds of telegrams and cables of congratulations were arriving each hour. "Why not rest on your laurels and stay in Sydney?" a friend had suggested when I received an offer of several thousands of pounds to tour Australia right away instead of flying on. This represented a vast fortune to me, and I spent a long time trying to decide for the best.

"It's all very well for you to talk of linking England and New Zealand and all that sort of thing, but what's your reward?" asked one of the men at a discussion about the offer. "You can fly the Tasman and risk your life. Then what," he added, "are you going to benefit, and what will you gain?"

"The honour of completing the first solo flight from England to New Zealand and linking those two countries in direct flight for the first time in history," I replied quietly.

As those present looked pityingly at me for throwing away such an opportunity I thought very deeply about it. Staying in Sydney meant security and happiness. Challenging the Tasman meant what? . . . Only the next few days could decide.

Hundreds of letters and messages were coming in from all parts of the country, and some trying to dissuade me from attempting the Tasman. Some were strong, vital messages assuring me of the sender's faith in my ability to succeed on the last stage of my flight. Others again expressed premonitions of disaster, and many contained only the fears and doubts of the faint-hearted. I realized only too well, as was pointed out, that I was fairly tired and that the machine had already flown over 12,700 miles from England, but thought that if I stayed even one week in Sydney resting the continuity of the flight would be broken and the main object lost sight of. I had always thought of this as one flight, and did not consider the Tasman Sea as an additional flight after the England-to-Australia one.

It had occurred to me many times during the discussions of a proposed Tasman service that if a small subsidiary line were run to link up with the England-to-Australia air service New Zealand would be merely served by a feeder line—an afterthought, which, if unprofitable, could be discontinued without disorganizing the other schedule. I foresaw the Tasman service as a vital link in Empire air communications. A through service operated by one powerful company combining the interests of England, Australia, and New Zealand would make New Zealand not merely a terminus, but an important South Pacific junction where eventually air lines from Vancouver and San Francisco would connect up with the England-to-New Zealand service.

After two days in Sydney I received a weather report that decided me to take off on the following morning.

The engine had been carefully tested by the De Havilland mechanics, and the compass checked for magnetic deviation on all cardinal points by the veteran flyer Captain P. G. Taylor, who had accompanied Sir Charles Kingsford Smith and Charles Ulm on several of their big flights. Permission had been granted for me to use the large Air Force aerodrome at Richmond, where the Gull would have sufficient room for the full-load take-off. Every one was most helpful, and before I took off for Richmond I received word that arrangements had been made for me to be accommodated at the officers' mess overnight.

There was very little shipping on the Tasman, and it was therefore rather difficult for an accurate weather report to be compiled. During a telephone conversation with Mr Mares I learned that indications pointed to reasonably favourable weather over the first part of the sea. I intended to steer from Sydney to New Plymouth, where lovely, snow-capped Mount Egmont, a solitary mountain, reared its peak 8000 feet above the rich pasture-land. In fine weather this should be a good landmark, and when I had arrived over New Plymouth my intention was to fly to Auckland, 154 miles farther on. There was, however, a wedge of low pressure to the north that might prevent my flying right through to Auckland. My decision to take off from Richmond added forty miles on to the distance, and, as it was 1330 to New Plymouth from Sydney and another 154 miles on to Auckland, the total distance would be 1524 miles.

On arrival at Richmond Aerodrome the Gull was refuelled and wheeled into the spacious hangar in readiness for the early morning take-off. For the first time in my life I had practically no sleep that night. This was not because of any fears for what the morrow would hold for me, but because of an over-zealous sentry. Just as I was dozing off I heard a sound like thunder, and sitting up listened intently. There it was again, and I recognized the measured tread of a sentry on duty in the corridor. *Tramp, tramp, tramp,* went the heavy footsteps, and at the end of the wooden passage they would halt, right about turn, and return. I tried to shut out the noise by pulling the blanket over my ears, but the even tramp was as clear as a clarion. " I might ask him to take his boots off and put slippers on," I thought, but the idea of the sentry in stocking feet was too funny, and I wondered if he carried a bayonet or a gun. At midnight I resolved to ask him, at the risk of offending his sense of duty, to go and find another corridor to parade in. Tiptoeing across the room I cautiously opened the door and looked out. The sentry had reached one end of the long corridor, and at the other an open door revealed a large crowd of reporters and photographers smoking and talking. I had no wish to be photographed in my night attire, so I withdrew my head just as the sentry thundered past again.

At half-past two I rose, and after a light breakfast of tea and toast walked over to the hangars with Group Captain Cole, who was in charge of the base and had been most hospitable, and arranged for every possible facility to be placed at my disposal during my stay at Richmond. The Gull was wheeled on to the tarmac, and as the engine warmed up I said good-bye to the group of friends, including Mr Cyril Westcott, who had motored from Sydney to see the take-off, and Mr W. L. Clarke, of C. C. Wakefield and Co., who as on previous occasions had been of very great assistance. My small kit was placed in the locker, and the thermos and sandwiches were put in the cockpit. As I sat in the cockpit running the engine up I could see dozens of photographers and news-reel camera men silhouetted against the flares.

The previous night at dinner I happened to mention to one of the officers that before leaving England I thought of taking a lifebelt on the Tasman flight, laughingly remarking that a lifebelt in mid-Tasman would be about as effective as a black cat painted on the rudder. Great was my surprise next morning when one of the officers arrived with a life-saving jacket when I was just about to take off.

"I could never get out of the cockpit wearing this," I said, as it was slipped over my shoulders and inflated.

"You could if it were half deflated," one of the officers put in.

"All right, then, just to please you all, but I wouldn't have a chance if the engine failed," I replied, tying the jacket on securely.

Leaning forward I adjusted the compass, and placed the chart, maps, and log in the leather pockets within easy reach, and switched on the navigation lights. The long line of flares was burning brightly along the runway, and lighting a path in the darkness as I taxied out to the start.

"I want to speak to the Group Captain," I shouted above the roar of the engine, and a reporter quickly wrote down my message as he hurried forward: "If I go down in the sea no one must fly out to look for me. I have chosen to make this flight, and I am confident I can make it, but I have no wish to imperil the lives of others or cause trouble and expense to my country.

"Well, good-bye!" I shouted, smiling reassuringly at the sea of tense white faces. "I'll come back one day."

CHAPTER XVIII: ACROSS THE TASMAN SEA

RELEASING THE BRAKES, I GAVE THE engine full throttle, and the Gull roared along the flare path. The bright line of flares flashed past the left wing, and nearing the last one I gently eased the aeroplane off the ground. Swift as an arrow the Gull climbed through the darkness, circling the aerodrome to gain height, then setting off for Sydney. I flashed my torch across the instrument panel: revs., 2100; oil-pressure, 42 lbs.; altitude, 1500 feet; air speed, 140 m.p.h., etc. All was well, and I breathed a sigh of relief that at last I was on my way.

As I flew towards Sydney I felt supremely confident of success, and had I for one second doubted the reliability of my aeroplane and its faithful engine I should never have gone on. The myriad lights of Sydney were slipping beneath the wings, and I picked out the line of lights marking the harbour bridge. The Gull speeded on, and, steering a course for New Plymouth, 1330 miles distant, I left the Australian coast. I felt tremendously lonely as I looked back at Sydney and the land grew fainter, until at last it faded into the distance, and I was left alone to fly hour after hour with only the sky and the vast expanse of the ocean to look at.

The time factor had been very important on this flight, and ever since leaving England I had made all calculations in Greenwich Mean Time. There were two clocks on my dashboard, one set to Greenwich time, and the other was adjusted to the local time of each place at which I landed. I had been losing daylight at the rate of approximately an hour for every thousand miles I travelled eastward. On some sections, such as Karachi to Akyab, there had been only 10 hours 24 minutes' daylight, whereas had I been flying in the reverse direction—*i.e.*, westward—there would have been 13 hours 36 minutes' daylight for the same section. On such a long flight the time difference is considerable, Sydney time being 10 hours 2 minutes in advance of Greenwich. Auckland time is two hours ahead of that of Sydney. Consequently, although I left Richmond at 4.37 A.M., local time, on October 16, in England the time was approximately 6.35 on the evening of October 15.

I smiled as I remembered my friends in England. "They will just be dressing for dinner," I thought as I sipped a cup of coffee and took out the packet of sandwiches for my breakfast.

On leaving Australia I had encountered scattered alto-cumulus cloud and climbed to 5000 feet. Three hours out I glided down through a gap to check my drift on the white-capped waves. As I flew low over the sea I saw a silvery gleam as a shoal of flying-fish leaped from the sea to speed along, then suddenly plunge in again. I passed just south of a big storm, but dark clouds loomed ahead as storms gathered on the horizon. At this stage, just six hours out from Sydney, I noticed that the gauge on the port centre-section tank registered only four gallons. " A petrol leak," I thought immediately, as I had not used any petrol from that tank and the engine had been running on the large rear tank. The leak was not serious, however, as the tanks did not interconnect, and there was a very large petrol margin. Nevertheless I switched over to the leaking tank to use up the remaining petrol, to conserve the rest of the supply just in case I might need it all.

I made an entry in the log, and noted the time, which was now 01.00 hours, G.M.T.—just an hour past midnight in England, I thought—and made a note of the date, which was now October 16. There was an object in the sky just ahead, and the machine flashed past an albatross. I had seen no ship nor any sign of life during the seven hours since leaving land, and I was grateful for the sight of the lovely bird. I felt completely isolated from the rest of the world, and the only ties were the thoughts of my friends, who would now be wondering how I was faring over this lonely ocean.

The machine was drifting considerably, and I flew low to check up the rate of the drift. I had just decided to alter course seven degrees to port to compensate when I saw a jet of water rise from the sea just ahead. There it was again, and as I drew near I saw

the gigantic form of a whale as the great creature rose
to the surface of the sea to spout. Five minutes later I
flew over another whale as it came up to spout, then
plunged into the depths as the water rose in a spray.
The immense back of the whale looked exactly like a
reef with waves breaking over it.

Visibility had become steadily worse, and storms
were drawing in round the machine on all sides. As I
plunged into the storm area heavy rain beat down on
the Gull, which was tossed about like a feather. The
sea was whipped up into a foaming mass, and I lost
sight of it completely as I flew blind through storms of
such fierce intensity that I almost despaired of ever
reaching land. My arm ached trying to steady the
machine and steer an accurate compass course. As soon
as I would fly through one storm it was only to find
curtains of black nimbus heralding another. At times
I would fly very low, trying to keep the sea in view, and
when that was blotted out I immediately climbed to a
safe height and flew on entirely by instruments.

Tired and disheartened I watched the hours pass on
as the weather grew even worse, until it became a
supreme effort to keep my eyes on the instruments,
while sheets of rain beat against the cabin. I realized
that the slightest mistake would tip the scales against
me and the Gull would go spinning down into the sea.
The strain was terrific, and my spirits sank when nine
hours out there was no land to be seen, only an occasional glimpse of the sea beneath, when the dark rain-
clouds which pressed round the Gull parted for a few
minutes.

"If only I could see ahead," I thought desperately as I switched over to the starboard wing-tank 9 hours 20 minutes out. "If only I could see land. . . ." Suddenly a dark blur loomed ahead through the rain, and the Gull flashed past a small rocky island.

"Land!" I shouted with joy, recognizing the island as a rock just off the coast. Within a few seconds the Gull swept over New Plymouth, absolutely on its course, 9 hours 29 minutes after leaving Richmond and 10 days 23 hours 45 minutes out from England.

It was still raining heavily, and all but the base of Mount Egmont was shrouded in black cloud. My altitude was less than 500 feet as I flew over the town, and I could see people running into the streets waving a welcome.

The weather looked bad to the north, and rain was still streaming down. "Should I land at New Plymouth?" I wondered, as I flew over the large modern aerodrome and saw the big crowd waiting to see me pass. The Gull had lowered the Tasman record of 11 hours 58 minutes, previously held by Flight-Lieutenant Charles Ulm and his crew. Why not be content and land? After all, I was terribly tired, and it would require a tremendous effort to continue on to Auckland.

Throttling back I glided low over the aerodrome in salute. It would be so easy to land now and be welcomed home by my countrymen, then sleep. "No," I thought quickly, remembering my intention before leaving England—to make the first direct flight right through to Auckland, my home town. Opening up the throttle I flew on towards Auckland, 154 weary miles farther north. The weather had been too bad over the Tasman for me even to think of lunch, so I now had time to relax and eat a few sandwiches. Conditions improved, and I feasted my eyes on the mountainous coastline.

An hour later I sighted Auckland, and, escorted by a number of machines from the Aero Club, flew over the aerodrome. The ground was black with people, and hundreds of cars were parked in long lines along the boundary.

I closed the throttle and glided down to a landing, and as the wheels of the Gull came to rest felt a great glow of pleasure and pride. This was really journey's end, and I had flown 14,000 miles to link England, the heart of the Empire, with the city of Auckland, New Zealand, in 11 days 45 minutes, the fastest time in history. With this flight I had realized the ultimate of my ambition, and I fervently hoped that my flight would prove the forerunner of a speedy air service from England.

As I taxied the Gull up to the large reception daïs where civic authorities and representatives of the Government and the Services waited to welcome me I was delighted to see my father, and recognized many friends among the crowd. The machine came to rest, and I switched off the engine of my faithful Gull for the last time on that flight and entered up the time of my landing, which was 5.05 A.M., G.M.T.

I struggled out of the bulky life-saving jacket, and

FLYING OVER AUCKLAND
Photo "New Zealand Herald"

ARRIVING AT AUCKLAND
Photo "New Zealand Herald"

opening the door of the cockpit stepped on to the wing. In their enthusiasm hundreds of people had broken the barriers and were running towards the machine, and dozens of policemen were trying to hold the tremendous crowd back from the Gull, which was soon surrounded by a wildly cheering multitude. Yes, I decided, this was certainly the greatest moment of my life. The triumph of the flight had been complete, and I felt a desire to stay the hand of time and enjoy to the full this hour of success.

My father affectionately greeted me, and I went up to the daïs to receive an official welcome. I was almost completely deaf from the roar of the engine, and could scarcely hear the sound of my own voice when, following the many speeches of welcome, I was asked to broadcast. There was a gigantic traffic jam between the aerodrome and the city, thirteen miles away, and after a welcome cup of tea at the club-house I drove through lines of cheering people.

On arrival at the hotel I found hundreds of cables and telegrams of congratulations from many parts of the world. For several weeks four secretaries were kept busy acknowledging the messages, which totalled several thousands. There were congratulations from Governors-General, Prime Ministers, Ambassadors, Ministers of the Crown, High Commissioners, the Air Ministers of Britain and France, leading aero clubs, including the Royal Aero Club of Great Britain and the Aéro-Club de France, the Royal Aeronautical Society and the Society of British Aircraft Construction, the Royal Automobile Club, aviation authorities in South American countries, from different societies and institutions in many parts of the world, to mention a few of the representative messages.

At the civic reception I felt deeply honoured when the Mayor of Auckland announced that it had been decided to perpetuate my name and keep the memory of my flight to New Zealand ever green by naming an important thoroughfare in the city " Jean Batten Place."

After only a few days in my home town I left for Wellington. I had financed this venture entirely by myself, and it was imperative that the flight should pay for itself. As I was entirely dependent on myself it was of the utmost importance that I should more than clear expenses to enable me to continue my flying activities. So it was that almost immediately upon arriving in New Zealand I had to gather my remaining strength and commence a tour of the Dominion, giving talks at various cinema theatres. When I commenced the tour I knew that I was overdrawing on my reserve energy, but insisted on continuing.

Talks were given in Auckland, Hamilton, and Wellington, but after my arrival in Christchurch I was too tired to go on, and upon medical advice was reluctantly obliged to cancel the tour and take a rest. The Prime Minister of New Zealand, Mr Savage, who had sent wonderful messages of congratulation and given a reception in my honour during my visit to Wellington, very generously invited me to take a holiday for several weeks as guest of the Government. I was most grateful for this kind offer of hospitality, and enjoyed a wonderful holiday at the Franz Joseph Glacier.

Although I knew my country so well, I had not previously had an opportunity of seeing this glacier. Never shall I forget the magnificent spectacle of the great river of ice. Dark green sub-tropical vegetation and exquisite ferns covered the foothills, and grew to the very edge of the ice. To complete the matchless setting great snow-covered peaks guarded the top of the glacier as the Southern Alps towered like a chain of giants southward, and Mount Cook raised its summit to 12,349 feet.

After my stay at Franz Joseph I drove to Lake Wakatipu to do some trout-fishing, and spent happy days amid most glorious scenery.

On my return to Auckland it was announced that the fund raised for me now totalled almost £2000, and I felt deeply grateful to my countrymen for their help. Whereas on my first flight round New Zealand there were no regular air services then in operation, I now found a network of airways extending over the entire length of the Dominion, and speedy services linked the North Island and the South, enabling people to travel in speed and comfort. For the comparatively small population of less than 2,000,000 people I considered this network of airways a great achievement. Within the space of a few years aviation has made tremendous strides, and the majority of the people are very air-minded.

During the Christmas season I enjoyed a holiday with my mother and father, and we drove to Rotorua, my birthplace, where a reception was to be held by the Maori tribes. At this reception many spirited *hakas* were danced by the Maori men, and the pretty raven-haired native girls performed skilful *poi* dances, in which they twirl tiny balls on the ends of strings, keeping perfect time, and the beat of the *pois* on their flaxen skirts forms a soft accompaniment to their singing. I was presented with a valuable kiwi feather mat which had once belonged to a chieftain and given the picturesque name of Hine-o-te-Rangi—"Daughter of the Sky."

Great was my joy when I received news of three important trophies that had been awarded to me for my New Zealand flight. For the second year in succession the Royal Aero Club had awarded me the Britannia Trophy for the most meritorious flight of the year by a British subject. The Segrave Trophy for the most outstanding demonstration of the possibilities of transport on land, sea, or in the air had also been awarded to me by unanimous vote of a committee representative of aviation, motoring, and the Press. This was a very great honour, and I felt that my dearest wish would be realized when a speedy air service was inaugurated between England and New Zealand. It was announced shortly afterwards that I had won the Harmon International Trophy for the greatest flight of the year by an airwoman, and that the trophy for airmen was awarded to Howard Hughes the American flyer. This was the second time I had won the Harmon Trophy, for the previous year I had held it jointly with the great American airwoman Amelia Earhart, whom I had always wanted to meet, and who only a few months later lost her life so tragically.

I stayed some time in Auckland renewing old friendships, and felt that it was indeed good to be home again. Lazing away the hours sunbathing on the golden sands of wide beaches and swimming in the clear blue waters, I let the world roll by for a little and felt utter contentment. It had been my intention to settle in New Zealand after my flight, but sometimes I found myself gazing out over the blue Tasman, as I had so often done as a child, and longing to go forth again. " Why not rest on your laurels and settle down? " many of my friends suggested. " After all, you have had more than your share of success. Apart from your records remember you are the first woman to fly from England to Australia and back, to fly from England to South America, to cross the South Atlantic Ocean, and the first airwoman to fly from England to New Zealand and conquer the Tasman. No one can ever take these distinctions from you, so what is the use of going on and on until eventually your luck deserts you and disaster overtakes you? "

" Yes, yes, I know," I would say, determined to take the wise advice, and, putting all ideas of further flights from my mind, would thereupon make preparations to settle down. It seemed that all through my life I had been forced to make these big decisions and usually alone. I wanted very much to settle down in my own country and lead a calm, peaceful life, but in my heart I knew only too well that I was destined to be a wanderer. I seemed born to travel, and in flying I found the combination of the two things which meant everything to me : the intoxicating drug of speed and freedom to roam the earth. In my innermost thoughts I knew the fire of adventure that burned within me was not yet quenched, and that urge was drawing me on—to what?

CHAPTER XIX: AUSTRALIA

ONE DAY THE GULL WAS LIFTED ON TO the deck of the s.s. *Awatea*, and, accompanied by my mother, I sailed for Sydney. Even when I waved good-bye to the vast crowd that came to say farewell I intended only to take a holiday in Australia, then return to my native land. Fate had other plans in store for me, however. On February 19, 1937, I arrived in Australia, and that very evening news was flashed through that an air liner bound for Sydney from Brisbane was missing with seven passengers and two pilots aboard. One of the pilots was a great friend of mine. He was a very skilful airman, and I thought highly of him. A cyclonic storm was raging to the south when the machine had left Brisbane.

My aeroplane was taken to Mascot Aerodrome, and mechanics worked all night to assemble the machine so that I could join the search that was being organized. The distance between Brisbane and Sydney is 500 miles; I felt confident that the machine was down in some clearing and would be found at any moment. Although the greater part of the route was mountain-ous and heavily timbered, it seemed incredible that such a big machine could disappear so completely.

There were many aeroplanes taking part in the search, and as the days passed the number increased. Every morning I would take off at about five o'clock and fly for hours, passing over rough, mountainous country, searching ravines and thickly timbered areas, hoping to glimpse a sight of the big machine among the trees, and at other times searching the coast for some trace.

A strange feature was that hundreds of reports came in from different parts of the country, and the times when the machine was alleged to have been seen coincided with the regular scheduled times for it to pass over those places. People of undoubted integrity were positive that they had seen the air liner, and the search was narrowed down to the country between Newcastle and Sydney. I had a feeling that the machine was farther north, so made Newcastle my base and continued the search from there.

The quest seemed fruitless, and sometimes I would glimpse a wisp of smoke in the distance, perhaps fifty miles away, rising from inaccessible country, and would fly hopefully towards it, thinking it might be a signal, only to find an isolated bush fire.

Reports were most confusing. Some people were positive that the machine had come down in the sea: they had seen the wreckage—which on investigation proved to be great branches of seaweed. Some declared that they had observed signals coming from the mountains, and others were equally sure that they had heard the air liner crash in the bush.

TROUT-FISHING AT LAKE WAKATIPU

SEARCHING FOR THE MISSING AIR LINER
Photo "The Sydney Morning Herald"

Flying on to Brisbane I vainly continued my search. By this time I had spent approximately thirty-eight hours in the air and flown 5000 miles altogether. Tired and disappointed I flew back to Sydney. The day after my return the air liner was found high up in the ranges, on the border of Queensland and New South Wales, a charred, burned-out wreckage hidden in the dense bush. A young bushman made the discovery and heroically rescued two passengers, who were the only survivors.

At Mascot Aerodrome, where I kept my aeroplane, I used frequently to meet the famous Australian airman H. F. Broadbent. He was making final preparations for a flight to England to lower the existing solo record of over seven days. Frequently he would laughingly suggest that we should have a race back to London, and add that in any case I should probably set out to break his record immediately he established it. "The race is a good idea," I would reply, "but I could never be mean enough to try and take your record immediately. You can keep it for six months, anyway."

Although the summer was on the wane, the wonderful ocean beaches round Sydney were always crowded with a happy throng of bathers. Swimming had been my favourite sport from childhood, and Mother and I decided to take a flat at one of the beaches for the remainder of the summer. Sometimes I would go into the foamy surf two or three times a day, and lie for hours basking in the sun, listening to the long Pacific rollers thundering on to the beach. We explored nearly all the lovely drives near Sydney, and would often take my car high up into the Blue Mountains and picnic amid the glorious scenery. This to my mind was an ideal existence, and I often lazily thought of seeking out some Pacific island where I could spend the rest of my life in perpetual sunshine and contentment.

One day I had just returned home from my morning swim, when I noticed a large crowd of people on the promenade excitedly pointing out to sea. On looking over the bay I beheld an awe-inspiring sight, and one which I shall never forget. Black dorsal fins cut through the water, and the sea was lashed into a foam as three monster whales plunged again and again to escape a school of vicious thresher sharks. A fierce fight ensued, the sharks trying to force the whales into shallow water in an effort to beach them. When it was estimated that the whales were within only two hundred yards of the beach they turned about and headed out to sea. They were again attacked by the sharks, who followed them to the entrance of Sydney Harbour, where another fierce fight took place watched by hundreds of people.

To commemorate the landing of the Australian and New Zealand troops at Gallipoli during the World War an Anzac Day was established, and is observed annually on April 25 with ceremony which compares with that of Armistice Day in England. That year I was asked by Canon Howard Lea to give an address during the Anzac Service at St Mark's Church, Sydney. This was an entirely new experience for me, as I had not previously been asked to speak in a church. I decided to give my address on "Faith and the Elimination of Fear." That memorable autumn evening when I stood at the lectern in the beautiful little church and delivered my address will always remain vividly in my memory. All my life I had believed in faith as indispensable if one were to achieve success in any undertaking.

My return to New Zealand had been postponed several times, and now I found myself longing to see England once again. From my point of view the most logical way of making the journey was to fly, so I decided to make preparations for a flight back.

The solo record of 6 days 9 hours had been established by Mr H. F. Broadbent during a wonderful flight, and I knew it would be extremely difficult to reduce this time. Although I intended to use the same aeroplane, there was a considerable amount of work necessary, and the Certificate of Airworthiness needed renewing. The engine was given a complete overhaul by the De Havilland Aircraft Company, who also completed the other work required.

In order to make myself specially fit for the flight I trained systematically. The training took the form of physical exercises, skipping, running, swimming, walking, and horse-riding. My mother had never been present to see me land at the conclusion of any of my flights, so we arranged that she should travel by steamer to England and meet me when I arrived at Croydon.

The flight preparations went very smoothly, and I spent a considerable amount of time working out various schedules which I hoped would gain me the

record. When work on the Gull was finished I flew the
machine, and made exhaustive tests to check the
efficiency of the various component parts, petrol-
consumption, etc. By October arrangements were completed. The authorities were most helpful, and the
Director of Civil Aviation in India cabled offering to
waive all customs formalities during my flight across
India.

On October 15 I left Sydney for Darwin, where I
planned to spend two days waiting for the full moon,
and also for good weather in which to start the record
bid.

After taking off from Richmond I circled the aerodrome, climbing steadily to gain height to cross the
Blue Mountains. Dark rain-clouds shrouded the mountains, and I climbed through a cloud layer to 8000 feet.
At this height I was above the mist and rain and flying
in sunshine. The shadow of the aeroplane speeded
along on the silvery cloud carpet beneath. The light
was reflected on to the clouds in such a way that the
shadow of the Gull was encircled by a miniature rainbow of lovely colours. Once across the mountains I
flew into fine weather and brilliant sunshine. North-
westerly winds prevailed, however, and the whole way
to Darwin I had to fly against strong head winds. After
landing to refuel at Charleville I flew on to Winton,
where I stayed for the night. It is infinitely more difficult to fly from Australia to England than in the
opposite direction. The main reason is that the prevailing winds are westerly, and therefore over a greater
part of the route there are following winds. From

England one can await suitable weather, and set off on the first stage of the flight fresh from a good night's sleep. Flying from Australia means a long and arduous trip of 2200 miles across the continent to Darwin, the starting-point. Head winds retard progress on the route to England, and in October there is always the possibility of encountering bad weather or fog over Europe.

Leaving Winton at dawn I flew on across the vast tracts of Central Queensland. To minimize the effect of the head winds I sometimes flew only 100 feet above the ground. Herds of kangaroos hopped away across country at the noise of my engine, and great flocks of brightly coloured parakeets and galahs rose in alarm as I crossed the dried-up-looking Diamantina river.

Passing Cloncurry I flew over very rough, mountainous country. At Mount Isa, the zinc-mining centre, the wind changed to southerly, and visibility became steadily worse. A heavy red dust-haze covered the country, and nearing Camooweal I encountered a bad dust-storm. Trying to keep the ground in sight I gradually lost altitude, until the machine was just clearing the tree-tops. The heat was terrific, and the Gull dropped suddenly in some violent bumps. The gusty southerly wind swept the machine along at a much higher speed than I cared to achieve at such a low altitude. As clouds of dust enveloped the Gull I lost sight of the ground, but a few minutes later managed to pick up the stock route leading to Camooweal.

The machine suddenly flashed over a great herd of cattle, which promptly stampeded, and I hoped the drover would be tolerant in his thoughts of me. It was imperative that I should not lose sight of the track, for visibility was becoming even worse, and if I missed the isolated township of Camooweal my predicament would be serious.

Visibility was less than 400 yards when the Gull swept over Camooweal, and I realized that landing in the thick dust-haze was going to be a difficult manœuvre. Although my altitude was only seventy feet and people could hear the engine, it was not possible to distinguish my silver aeroplane from the ground. As I knew there were radio masts 120 feet high I kept near the outskirts of the township and flew over the aerodrome. When I turned to fly back I lost sight of the ground completely. Shutting off the engine I glided down, straining my eyes to distinguish the ground through the clouds of red dust.

Suddenly the boundary fence appeared, then the aerodrome immediately beneath me, and levelling back I landed the Gull. As the machine ran along the runway I saw the blur of a motor-car ahead and followed it to the aerodrome entrance. The car proved to belong to the sheriff, who was accompanied by the matron of the hospital. They were very much surprised that I had found Camooweal in the dust and had managed to land.

Everything in the aeroplane was coated with a film of red dust, which had even permeated into my kit. It was impossible to refuel the Gull in the choking dust, and all we could do was to arrange for a guard. The sheriff produced a tarpaulin, with which we covered the engine. Groping around in the dust, I was able to plug the air-intake, Pitot tube, and all the oil and petrol air-vents with waste cloth.

When we took my kit from the machine I suddenly remembered the two boxes of orchids which friends had given me just before I had left Sydney. " Flowers! " echoed the matron when I took them from the cockpit. " Why," she added, " I haven't seen a flower for two years! " She was delighted when I gave her some of the lovely blooms, and took them forthwith to show the patients in the hospital, where the orchids no doubt underwent rejuvenation treatment.

Although it was not yet noon there was no possibility of flying on to Darwin that day. There was no hangar, so I had no alternative but to leave the Gull exposed to the Bedourie, as they call this particular type of dust-storm which blows up from the moving sandhills near the town of that name.

When we drove to the tiny hotel it was impossible to see the blue gum-trees at the end of the main street, but the wind changed in the evening, and the air became clearer.

Next morning I said good-bye to the little community of Camooweal and took off for Darwin. Crossing the vast grassy plains of the Barclay Tablelands, I flew over some of the largest cattle stations in Australia, among them Brunette Downs, with an area of 5500 square miles, and carrying about 40,000 head of cattle. This great station adjoins the even larger one of

Alexandria, covering 10,700 square miles. On previous flights I had landed at Brunette, but on this occasion I flew on to refuel at Daly Waters.

Apart from the head winds and the Bedourie the weather had been fairly good on the flight from Sydney. Approaching Darwin, however, I met a thunderstorm of tropical intensity accompanied by torrential rain. When I crossed the bay to Darwin the sun was shining brightly, and the Japanese pearl-luggers looked like luxury yachts as they gleamed white against the deep blue waters of the harbour.

On reaching Darwin I felt more as if I were arriving at the conclusion of a record flight than just about to set off on one. A large crowd had assembled to see me land, and I was handed a great sheaf of telegrams and messages from well-wishers. After arranging for an engine schedule and for special weather forecasts I drove into the town.

The Administrator of the Northern Territory, Mr Abbot, had sent a representative to welcome me, and I was invited to stay at Government House while in Darwin. Mr and Mrs Abbot were most charming and hospitable, and I felt greatly refreshed after tea on the veranda of their home. Government House is built on a rise overlooking the bay. Wide terraces slope down from the cool veranda to the sea, and in the garden grow tall palms and lovely tropical flowers, including hibiscus and bougainvillæa.

With the Administrator and his wife were their two daughters, who contributed to make my stay in Darwin a very happy one. During dinner on the evening of my

MAGNETIC ANTHILLS NEAR DARWIN

Form 41.

COMMONWEALTH OF AUSTRALIA.

CUSTOMS CLEARANCE.

State of ~~Queensland~~ *Northern Territory*.   Port of *Darwin*

These are to certify, to whom it doth concern, that *Miss J. Batten*

(British)/(~~Foreign~~) man Master of the ~~Ship~~ *Aircraft GADPR 1610* registered ~~tons~~ *tns* (net) navigated with a

crew of *one* British ~~and~~ *ui* Foreign men, *British* built and bound

for *London* , having on board cargo and stores as per statements attached, hath

here entered and cleared his said ship according to law.

Given under my hand, at the Customs House at the Port of *Darwin*, in the

State of ~~Queensland~~ *Northern Territory*, this *Nineteenth* day of *October* One thousand nine

hundred and *Thirtyseven*   *Brennon*

Collector.

555/37.   Govt. Printer, Brisbane.

CUSTOMS CLEARANCE DOCUMENT FROM PORT DARWIN

arrival I mentioned flying over hundreds of giant ant-hills on the way from Daly Waters. On all my flights over the Northern Territory the sight of these anthills dotted among the trees had never failed to fascinate me. When Mrs Abbot offered to drive me into the bush so that I could see some of them at close quarters I was delighted.

Next morning we drove many miles along tracks in the bush, until we finally arrived at a clearing which bore the name of Cemetery Plain. This name, although gruesome, was appropriate, for ranged round this open space were large grey mounds looking exactly like tombstones. These were all magnetic anthills, so called because, strangely enough, they all face magnetic north —in whatever part of the country they happen to be built. This uncanny fact has never been explained. Two or three feet thick at the base, they tapered very finely at the top, which in most cases was rounded and about fifteen feet high. If a portion of the hard, cement-like structure was broken away the ants imme-diately set to work to repair the damage. The sickly-looking little white ants do not apparently like the sun, and work always in the dark, as there was no sign of them until we broke off a piece of the structure and found thousands in their tiny cells.

We drove farther into the bush in search of a giant red anthill, and eventually came upon one almost thirty feet in height. Although not quite as interesting as the magnetic ones, it looked most imposing towering among the gum-trees. The sergeant who accompanied us went ahead, beating the undergrowth in case there were any snakes about, and we followed him through the tall grass to inspect the giant at close quarters. It was thick through from base to summit, composed entirely of red earth, and looked almost as if it had been made by human hands, for it seemed incredible that such an imposing structure could have been built by tiny ants.

On the drive back I kept a look out for little native koala bears, but there was none to be seen, nor did I glimpse a crocodile during my stay in Darwin.

A native meeting, or corroboree as the aborigines call it, was to be held in Darwin, and arrangements were made for me to watch the dances. The corroboree took place in the native compound, and when we arrived there was a great deal of excited chattering coming from the trees where the aborigines were making preparations. We had to wait a considerable time before the native musicians appeared and, squatting on the ground, commenced playing their weird instruments. There was a bloodcurdling shout as the aborigines rushed forth from the trees on to the clearing and commenced the dances. On their dark bodies were painted most elaborate designs in white, and they were clad in loincloths of bright colours, and many wore feather headdresses. Only the men took part in the dances; the womenfolk were seated at a respectful distance. Two of the natives were painted from head to foot with a dull pink shade of paint, and I learned that this signified that the corroboree was a peaceful one. The dances were different from anything I had ever seen. They were really action dances, and the mimicry was amazingly clever. There was none of the precision of the Maori dancing; instead each dancer played a part, and the result was really a native ballet. Although the aborigines are mostly tall and thin all the movements were very graceful. Each dance seemed to finish with the same tremendous stamping in which all took part, jumping harder and harder, until the ground shook and clouds of dust rose into the air. One dance portrayed catching the turtle, another spearing the crocodile, and perhaps the most spectacular was the pelican dance.

The afternoon before leaving Darwin I spent some time at the aerodrome checking the compass for magnetic deviations, studying weather charts, and making final preparations for the flight. My stay in Darwin had been a pleasant one, and it was with reluctance that I said good-bye to all my new friends. The Administrator and Mrs Abbot with their two daughters accompanied me to the aerodrome to bid me farewell and God-speed.

CHAPTER XX: FLIGHT TO
ENGLAND

DAWN WAS JUST BREAKING AS I TOOK OFF from Darwin on October 19 at 6 A.M., L.T., and set a course across the Timor Sea for Kupang. The aeroplane rose easily despite its heavy load of petrol, and I left the coast feeling glad that I had waited for reasonable weather. Rambang, on Lombok island, 1100 miles away, was to be my first stop, and after refuelling I intended to leave immediately for Batavia.

Although this was my fourth flight across the Timor Sea I felt just as lonely as on other occasions. There was a slight following wind, and I sighted land just three hours fifteen minutes after leaving Australia. After passing Kupang I flew on over another 150 miles of sea to Flores island. The weather was good, although I encountered some violent bumps as I flew along the islands of the Dutch East Indies before landing for fuel at Rambang. The Administrator of Lombok was waiting to welcome me. After a cool drink and some biscuits I said good-bye to the kind Dutchmen, who insisted on giving me some sandwiches, oranges, and a bunch of bananas which nearly filled the cockpit.

The refuelling had not taken long, and I was in the air again only thirty-five minutes after landing. As I flew over Bali I met more terrific bumps, and low clouds made visibility poor. Nearing Batavia I ran into a violent thunderstorm, but was soon through it, and on arriving at the aerodrome found a large crowd waiting for me. Everything had gone to schedule, and although the day's run had been nearly 1800 miles I did not feel the slightest bit tired. Every one was most hospitable, and I was invited to stay at the home of a director of the Shell company and his charming wife.

My next landing was to be at Alor Star, 1000 miles from Batavia, and I intended flying on another 900 miles to Rangoon the same day. When I left Batavia it was a clear, moonlight night. Flying over the brightly lighted city I left Java and steered for Muntok island, off the coast of Sumatra. Although the night seemed so clear, I was not at all happy about the weather ahead. On this section I would make my fifth flight across the equator, and on all previous occasions violent rain-storms had tossed the machine about. To increase my uneasiness I had that day received a letter and meteorological report from the pilot of the mail 'plane bound from Singapore to Darwin. He had left the message at Rambang so that I should receive it and know what weather lay ahead. Part of the letter read: " I should think that you will encounter monsoon conditions with S.W.–N.W. winds, low clouds and rain between Batavia and Singapore over the last 300 miles judging by our experience to-day, as we had to sit in it for nearly three hours, about 75 per cent. instrument flying."

One hour out from Batavia clouds began banking up, and I climbed to 9000 feet to try to keep above them. Wispy clouds drifted across the moon, which was soon completely obscured. The two layers of cloud between which the machine was flying gradually closed together, and I decided to go down to a lower altitude and fly beneath them. Throttling back the engine, I glided down, gradually losing height, until at 2000 feet the blackness outside was still just as dense. Giving the engine a little throttle, I groped cautiously down through the cloud, trying to find the base. At 1000 feet a flash of lightning illuminated the cabin, and I saw sheets of rain sweeping over the machine. I watched the needle on the dial of the altimeter drop lower and lower, and at 500 feet I glanced at my air-log and saw that I was two hours out from Batavia, and must be nearing Muntok island. Giving the engine full throttle, I climbed upward again. There was no alternative but to climb to a safe height and settle down to instrument flying until dawn, when I could see where I was going. It was too risky to fly low at this stage, for some of the peaks on Muntok were over 2000 feet, and only 140 miles farther on lay Linnga island, with its 4000-feet cone, invisible in the rain and darkness. The air was very turbulent, and heavy rain beat against the windows as the Gull rocked about in the darkness. It was extremely difficult at times to control the machine, and blind flying under these conditions was terribly difficult.

After an eternity the darkness outside faded and dawn broke. The machine was flying between two layers of cloud. Above were dark, ominous clouds that threatened at any moment to descend in torrents on the Gull. There were only scattered clouds beneath. It was imperative that I should check up my position on some landmark, so I glided down through a gap. A thick mist covered the sea, but above it rose the peaks of hundreds of tiny islands which lie just south of Singapore. Identifying one of the islands by my chart I flew on and passed over Singapore as heavy rain commenced to fall. I saw the magnificent new civil aerodrome, and felt tempted to land and have breakfast. There had evidently been a tremendous amount of rain, for as I flew on again over Malaya I noticed that nearly all the cleared patches were under water. The head wind increased, until my ground speed was only 110 m.p.h., and over Lower Malaya the wind reached gale force.

More rain-storms swept across my path, and my spirits sank lower as I neared Alor Star and thought of the long flight ahead to Rangoon. From above, the aerodrome at Alor Star looked as if it was under water, so I was obliged to land cross-wind on the long runway. The sun came out and shone down fiercely, and I learned from the white residents who had assembled to greet me that on the previous day even the runway had been under water. The British Administrator who welcomed me to Malaya insisted on my accompanying him to the rest-house, where I enjoyed a light meal.

The weather improved after I left Alor Star, and

apart from the head wind the flight to the Burmese capital was a pleasant one. I felt very sad flying over this section, because it was somewhere along this lonely Burmese coast that Sir Charles Kingsford Smith lost his life. It is doubtful if anyone will ever know exactly what happened at that zero hour when the accident occurred. After the sea had jealously guarded its secret for over a year wreckage definitely identified as part of Kingsford Smith's aeroplane was found near the island of Aye, just south of Moulmein. A relative of Kingsford Smith had written asking me to ascertain whether the island was marked on my map of this territory—a map similar to the one used by Sir Charles. It is now thought that in the darkness his machine struck this island, which rises sheer from the sea to a height of some hundreds of feet. The maps of this part of the world are of a very small scale and not very detailed. The island of Aye is not marked on either the 40-miles-to-the-inch-scale map of this territory or the larger 15.75-miles-to-the-inch-scale map. I discount this new theory of the accident (unless there was a mechanical or structural failure at this point) because of Kingsford Smith's superb knowledge of the England-to-Australia air route, which was impressed on me during the many talks we had together.

When I arrived at Rangoon it was raining heavily, and from the air the aerodrome appeared to be partially under water. I flew round to select a dry patch on which to alight. On landing, however, I found the red gravel surface excellent and quite firm. As I taxied towards the hangars I saw a group of English and

Burmese people waiting to greet me, and recognized several friends whom I had met on previous flights to Rangoon. The Gull was refuelled and wheeled into the hangar while I cleared customs and arranged for flares for the take-off. On the drive into Rangoon I entered up my log-books, and saw that I was already well ahead of the record. It was just exactly 1 day 12 hours 40 minutes since I had left Darwin, 3700 miles away. By arriving in Rangoon in this time I was many hours ahead of the record. To maintain this lead over the rest of the route I should have to fly night and day, and probably through weather which would ordinarily keep an aeroplane on the ground. On the following day I planned to make the longest day's journey of the flight. This was to be from Rangoon right across Burma and Bengal, to refuel at Allahabad, 1200 miles from the Burmese capital, then fly on nearly another thousand miles to Karachi. The distance was 2150 miles, and as the weather forecast predicted head winds it would probably mean a night landing at Karachi.

There were many people at the aerodrome to watch the take-off from Rangoon, and just as I was climbing into the cockpit a woman hurried forward and thrust a package into my hand, saying that she hoped I would accept it, as she and her friends all prayed for my safety and success. On opening the package I felt deeply moved to find a beautiful rosary.

The flares were lit, and the Gull took off, eager to be on the wing again. Climbing to 10,000 feet I crossed the jungle-clad Arakan Yoma Mountains in bright moonlight. As dawn broke a strong north-westerly wind sprang up, and as I altered course at Chittagong to cross the Bay of Bengal it swung round to westerly, retarding my progress to the extent of 30 m.p.h. Nearing Calcutta I encountered thick mist, and had to waste time climbing above it, where the wind was even stronger. At last Allahabad appeared ahead, and I landed, having taken almost nine hours thirty-five minutes to complete the 1200 miles from Rangoon. This was fairly slow progress for the Gull, and I learned from the weather report that the head winds were even stronger farther on, and between Jodhpur and Karachi were over 40 m.p.h. It was impossible to arrive at Karachi before dark, so I telegraphed my E.T.A. (estimated time of arrival), and also a request for the floodlights.

After only thirty minutes on the ground to refuel I took off and continued my flight across India. The sun burned down fiercely, and at times the heat was almost unbearable. The air coming into the cockpit through the ventilators was like the blast from a furnace, and the crêpe soles of my shoes melted and stuck to the rudder-bars. It would have been cooler at a higher altitude, but I flew very low, sometimes only 500 feet above the ground, in an effort to minimize the effect of the head wind. Strong vertical currents rose from the hot, parched earth, and at times the machine would be carried up several hundreds of feet, only to drop suddenly immediately afterwards. Some of the bumps were particularly fierce, and my shoulder ached righting the machine after them.

As time wore on I grew increasingly tired, and not

far from Jodhpur a terrible desire for sleep nearly overcame me. All day I had been flying into the sun, and the terrific glare was very trying. The sun, beating down on to the huge steel auxiliary tank in the cabin, made it so hot that it was impossible to touch, and the air in the confined space of the cockpit was pervaded with the odour of petrol fumes. There had been little opportunity for rest since I had left Australia, and my eyes, swollen from the glare, felt like red-hot coals. All these factors were conducive to sleep, and it was only sheer will-power and the fact that I was so superbly fit that kept me awake.

At Jodhpur I felt tempted to land while it was still light, for I was in no mood to risk a night landing at Karachi, and in any case I doubted if I could keep my eyes open much longer. Taking out a bottle of eau de Cologne I soaked my handkerchief and bathed my burning head, and, cupping my hand just outside the cabin window, managed to direct some fresh air on to my face. After an orange and some black coffee I felt considerably better, and decided to continue to Karachi and draw even farther ahead of the record.

The heat across the Sind Desert was scorching, and I was relieved when the sun finally set and the air became cooler. The stars came out and the wind dropped a little as I neared the edge of the desert, but by this time I was so sleepy that I leaned my head against the side of the cockpit, and held one eye open at a time. This terrible longing for sleep might not have been accentuated if it had been possible to communicate with the outside world, for a radio would have kept my interest up. I felt so completely shut off, and would often long to hear the sound of a human voice or see some sign of life on the territory over which I was passing. A co-pilot would have been a tremendous help, and I often thought how wonderful it would be to have some one to take over the controls occasionally and share the responsibility of the navigating.

At last the lights of Karachi appeared ahead, and the air beacon was a welcome sight. On landing I was greeted by a group of enthusiastic people, who congratulated me on the flight from Burma, and I learned that this was the first time the Rangoon–Karachi flight had been accomplished during one day by a solo pilot. Every one was most helpful, the machine was refuelled, formalities speedily completed, and the precious bill of health supplied within a short space of time. When arrangements had been made for an engine schedule and lights for the take-off I decided there would be time for about four hours' sleep before flying on. Once again I was the guest of Commander and Mrs Watt, and surprised every one that evening by falling asleep at dinner.

Four hours' sleep refreshed me, and when the alarum-clock rang I quickly dressed, and after a cup of tea and some biscuits hurried across to the hangar. Despite the big load of petrol for the next section of 1350 miles to Basra, the Gull was soon off. As usual the additional weight of the additional fuel decreased my speed to 140 m.p.h. for the first few hours until some of the petrol in the rear tank was used. It was just 9.45 P.M., G.M.T., when I left Karachi. Flying along the Persian

Gulf I landed at Basra nearly ten hours later, after flying against head winds all the way.

My log-book was stamped, and on receiving the meteorological report I saw that head winds and sand-storms were predicted on the desert crossing to Damascus. There was no time to lunch at Basra if I was to arrive at Cyprus, 1000 miles farther on, before sundown, so when the refuelling was completed I climbed into the cockpit to fly on immediately. My throat felt parched after the hot, tiring flight from India, and I longed for a large glass of iced soda-water. There was none to be had at the aerodrome hotel, however, and kind English people who had come to welcome me telephoned the town for some, but I could not spare the time to wait for it. Just as I was about to take off a taxi arrived, and a native servant ran out to the aero-plane with a huge glass of iced soda-water on a tray. Throttling back the engine as the glass was handed to me, I drained it, to the astonishment of all present, and felt as refreshed as a parched flower after rain.

Over Iraq a strong westerly wind whipped the sand up into high columns which whirled across the desert, and visibility became less as I neared Ramadi. Altering course at Lake Habbaniya, which I could only dimly distinguish through the dust, I steered for Rutbah Wells. Head winds still retarded my progress, and when I reached the Lebanon Mountains they were covered with rain-clouds. The sky was leaden, and heavy rain fell as I crossed the mountains. There was just sufficient daylight left to make Cyprus, but as I flew on the weather became worse, and half-way across the mountains I wheeled the machine round and started back towards Damascus.

Even to this day I cannot say what finally decided me to turn back, and it seems almost uncanny in view of what transpired. At Basra I had been unable to obtain a report farther than Rutbah, and I had no idea what weather lay ahead, as the Gull was not fitted with wireless. The first person to greet me at Damascus when I landed was the President of the Aéro-Club de Damas, who handed me a telegram from Cyprus. The telegram read: " Urgent advise Jean Batten not to land here aerodrome temporarily unserviceable." It appeared that there had been a cloudburst that afternoon, completely flooding the aerodrome at Nicosia. A terrible storm was raging over the Mediterranean, and waterspouts were reported off the Syrian coast. When it was learned that I had passed Damascus heading for Cyprus many of the kind Cypriotes had gone to the aerodrome with picks and shovels to try to drain some of the water off. Photographs I later received show that my decision to turn back was a wise one, for had I landed at Cyprus it would not have been possible to take off again.

The people at Damascus were very hospitable, and I decided to stay for twelve hours in the hope that conditions over the Mediterranean might moderate, although meteorological reports were not promising—low cloud, rain, and the possibility of further cloudbursts were forecast. The Mezze Aerodrome, where I had previously landed twice, had been improved immensely, and was now an excellent modern airport with lighting

RAMBANG WITH THE DUTCH ADMINISTRATOR, M. BAKKER, AND HIS PART
[See p. 272]

THE AERODROME AT NICOSIA AFTER THE CLOUDBURST

equipment. A good sleep refreshed me, but as I taxied out to take off I felt uneasy about the weather ahead, which was reported as very bad between Beirut and Athens. The kind French authorities offered to keep the aerodrome lighted until dawn in case I was forced to return.

The Mezze Aerodrome is 2000 feet above sea-level, and it was frightfully cold as I took off and climbed to 10,000 feet before setting off across the mountains. The weather was clear as I passed over Beirut and steered over the Mediterranean for Nicosia, Cyprus, 150 miles distant. The air became very turbulent as I left the coast, and twenty-five miles out I encountered a storm of such intensity that to this day I wonder how the Gull weathered it. A fierce rain-squall tossed the machine about so violently that it was almost impossible to control it, and flying entirely by instruments was a terrific strain under such conditions.

A flash of lightning suddenly penetrated the blackness, and I was horrified to see a thin blue circle of light round the metal hub of the propeller. This recurred at short intervals, and the Gull was thrown about like a tiny boat in a rough sea. Water was pouring through a leak in the roof of the cabin, and the flashes of lightning temporarily blinded me, so that I could not see the instruments on the panel in front. It became impossible to fly on, and I managed to turn the machine round and plough back through the storm. Suddenly through the sheets of rain I saw a lighthouse on the Syrian coast piercing the darkness with its friendly beam, and it was almost as though an unseen hand had guided the machine back to safety. "Should I return to Damascus?" I wondered, but the thought of losing the record was too terrible, and instead I decided to fly north in an attempt to avoid the worst of the storm area, which appeared to lie between Beirut and Cyprus.

When dawn broke it was still raining, but the air was calm, and as I flew northward up the Syrian coast I wondered if after all it would be possible to make Athens. Once more I turned the nose of the machine seaward, and the Gull speeded towards the storm like a charger going to battle. Until nearing Rhodes I flew through some of the most atrocious weather I have ever experienced, and at one stage I saw the black, sinuous column of a water-spout ahead. This was a new experience, for I had never seen a water-spout from the air before, although a big one had appeared in the Darwin harbour the day before my departure. It was a weird though fascinating sight to see the great column of hundreds of tons of water revolving between sea and cloud. I was glad when the machine had passed the vicinity.

Towards Athens the weather cleared, and I arrived in sunshine. On hearing of my experience the people at the Tatoi Aerodrome told me that the worst storm for many years had raged over the Mediterranean the previous night, and I had been exceedingly fortunate to make Athens.

That afternoon I crossed the Adriatic Sea to Italy, and flew on over the Apennines in more bad weather. At Naples the weather was fine, although the sky was leaden and rain seemed imminent. As I flew on to

Rome rain fell heavily and visibility became very bad. Flying low along the coast, I made good progress, but twenty-five miles from Rome at a height of less than fifty feet the Gull plunged into low cloud and misty rain. It was too dangerous to continue in such conditions, and so I reluctantly turned the machine round and flew another hundred miles back to Naples. This again proved a wise decision, for on landing at Naples I heard that visibility at Rome was less than 500 yards. Strangely enough I did not feel very tired, and as I taxied up to the tarmac was delighted to see several people waiting to greet me.

"How did you know I would land here?" I asked Mr Meuser, the representative of K.L.M.

"We didn't," he replied. "We came here to meet the mail 'plane, but the weather is very bad over Europe, and it has turned back to Paris. Never mind," he added, laughing, "you have arrived instead."

The President of the Aero Club of Naples arrived to welcome me, and with charming hospitality which I have always experienced in Italy invited me to be the guest of the Aero Club during my stay. My new friends stayed up till late that night getting weather reports and taking telephone calls for me from England and the Continent, answering eighteen calls after I had retired. Very bad weather was reported over Europe, and from the meteorological reports it seemed rather doubtful if I should be able to fly through to England on the following day.

Rain fell steadily in the night, but as we drove to the aerodrome in the morning the weather had improved.

Everything depended on this last 1100-mile section to England, and yet as I studied the meteorological reports it seemed that I was not to achieve the record without a final battle with the elements. The weather was bad in the Mediterranean, with low cloud and rain over Corsica, but, apart from head winds, fairly good between Marseilles and London. The best plan, we agreed, was for me to fly round the Gulf of Genoa *via* Pisa, and thus skirt the low-pressure area. There appeared to be a bad patch between Spezia and Genoa, but from there on it was fair. This long *détour* would add about sixty miles on to my journey, but I did not mind as long as it was possible for me to fly through to England. It was just 4 days 18 hours since I had left Darwin, and my new friends were most enthusiastic and anxious that I should gain the record, which was now almost within my grasp.

Leaving Naples, I set off for Marseilles, but northward the weather became steadily worse. Rain fell heavily as I neared Pisa, and visibility was so poor that I had the utmost difficulty in keeping the coastline in sight. Flying very low, the Gull suddenly plunged into low cloud, and I completely lost sight of the coast. It was too dangerous to fly on in the vicinity of such mountainous country with visibility practically *nil*, so I swung the machine seaward and flew back until I located the coast again. " Should I land at Pisa in the hope that the weather would improve? " I wondered. The thought of losing the record was not to be tolerated, so I decided to fly direct across the gulf to St Raphael.

Leaving the Italian coast at Livorno I climbed to 3000 feet, and flew entirely by instruments for over an hour through cloud. When the weather cleared and I emerged from the clouds it was just like flying from night into day. St Raphael was bathed in sunshine, but a strong westerly wind caused violent down-draughts from the Alps, and when I crossed the mountains to Marseilles at times the Gull seemed to be making no progress at all against the head winds.

At Marseilles there was quite a large crowd to welcome me, and I was presented with a lovely bouquet and a large box of sweets, which were put in the already crowded locker.

After the extremely bad weather I had experienced that morning it was like a tonic to hear that, apart from slight head winds, the weather to London was favourable. A cup of coffee and all the good wishes of the kind French people dispelled my tiredness, and with renewed enthusiasm I wearily climbed back into the cockpit and set off for England. France certainly had put on her best weather for me, and I flew up the Rhône valley and over Lyons in brilliant sunshine. The continual bad weather during the flight and the lack of sleep had made me dreadfully tired—much more so than I cared to admit. It seemed centuries since I had taken off from Darwin, and I had practically lost count of time. When I left Australia it was spring-time, and the trees were in blossom; now, as I looked down on woods, I saw that the trees were tinted with the gorgeous reds, orange, and golden brown shades of autumn. It was forcibly brought to my mind that I had flown from spring into autumn in the space of five days.

As I passed Paris and drew nearer my goal my feelings were indescribable. When at last I sighted the English Channel and then the white cliffs of Dover it seemed almost too good to be true that the record was actually within my grasp.

Circling Lympne Aerodrome to land, I saw that a great crowd of people had assembled to greet me. On the smooth green surface the wheels of the Gull came to rest on English soil on October 24, exactly 5 days 18 hours 15 minutes after leaving Australia, and I realized that I had lowered the existing solo record by more than fourteen hours.

As I taxied towards the hangars a great crowd of cheering people surrounded the Gull. On climbing from the cockpit I was carried triumphantly to the customs office, where my precious journey log-book was officially stamped.

Only twenty minutes after landing I taxied out again, and took off for Croydon with an aerial escort. My mother, who had always been my inspiration and the guiding light of my whole life, would be there to welcome me, and probably a few friends, I thought. Not for one moment did I expect the tremendous welcome which awaited me. When I flew over Croydon the most amazing sight met my eyes. The boundaries of the aerodrome were black with people and a huge crowd had assembled to greet me. As I glided down to a landing, then taxied up to the tarmac, I felt deeply moved by the spontaneity of the welcome, which far outshone

THE WELCOME AT CROYDON
Photo Keystone

AT THE ROYAL AERO CLUB RECEPTION

Left to right: The Marquess of Londonderry, Commander Perrin, Lord Gorell, Mr Lindsay Everard

Photo Keystone

anything I had ever before experienced. It seemed more like a homecoming than just the final landing of a record flight.

When the Gull paused on the tarmac and I switched the engine off for the last time and stepped out on to the wing a great roar of welcome greeted me. I saw my mother smiling up at me from the sea of faces round the machine, and Mr Jordan, the High Commissioner of New Zealand, standing beside her. Thousands of cheering people were surging across to the Gull, which was soon surrounded. A huge bouquet of flowers was thrust into my hands, and I found myself being carried on the shoulders of two stalwart policemen. Remarkable scenes of enthusiasm were enacted, and I felt that it had been worth while flying all the way from Australia to receive such a royal welcome from my warm-hearted English friends.

CHAPTER XXI: GUEST OF HONOUR

FOR MANY WEEKS AFTER I LANDED THE MOST wonderful hospitality was showered on me: banquets, luncheons, and receptions were arranged, and I was entertained by many clubs and societies.

One evening a banquet was given in my honour by the Royal Aero Club. When I rose to make my speech I felt that it was indeed a difficult task—not merely because I was the only woman present, but the distinguished gathering included many of the pioneers of flying and some of the most brilliant men in aviation. Among the guests was the Marquess of Londonderry, at whose lovely home I had been entertained several times and experienced the lavish hospitality for which the Marchioness of Londonderry is famous. After my flight back from Australia in 1935 I had been invited to the Air Ministry and congratulated by Lord Londonderry, who was then Minister for Air. He had demonstrated his faith in aviation in a most practical manner by becoming a pilot and flying his own aeroplane extensively.

At the Aero Club banquet speeches were made by

the Marquess of Londonderry; Lord Gorell, a former Secretary of State for Air; Mr Lindsay Everard, Chairman of the Aero Club; Mr Handley Page; Commander Perrin; and Captain Percival. On the table in front of me I was delighted to see the lovely silver Britannia Trophy, which had been awarded to me by the Royal Aero Club for two years in succession for my South American and New Zealand flights. It was announced by Mr Lindsay Everard that the coveted gold medal of the Royal Aero Club was to be presented to me for my flights. The evening was a most memorable one, and I felt deeply honoured.

Another function which I greatly enjoyed was a dinner given for me by the Forum, one of the most exclusive women's clubs in London. Once before I had attended a dinner at the Forum Club to commemorate the proposed Atlantic air service, and several famous Atlantic flyers had been present. On this occasion my toast was very ably proposed by Miss Amy Johnson, the famous airwoman. Not long afterwards I was made an honorary member of the Forum Club, a gesture which I greatly appreciated.

One of the most interesting of the dinners at which I was guest of honour was that of the Women's Automobile and Sports Association. Some years previously honorary membership of this club had been extended to me, and I had often experienced the charming hospitality of the President, Viscountess Elibank. At this dinner I had the unique experience of having my toast proposed by Lord Sempill, and supported by Sir Malcolm Campbell. I had already met Lord Sempill on several occasions. He had once gallantly descended from the sky in Australia when I had made a forced landing and was struggling to mend a leaking petrol-union. This incident occurred when I was on my way to attend the inaugural ceremony of the Australia–England air mail at Brisbane. After helping consider-ably Lord Sempill resumed his journey, and when the trouble was rectified I flew on to Brisbane.

I had looked forward to meeting Sir Malcolm Camp-bell at the Royal Yacht Club dinner, where I had been asked to present the trophies, but he was unable to attend on that occasion. There were many distinguished people present, including Colonel Moore-Brabazon, the first Englishman to gain a pilot's licence. When he and Claude Grahame-White, whom I met at another dinner, used to fly 'way back in 1908 or thereabouts aviation was a real adventure. In those days it was often necessary to lie on the aerodrome to see if the aeroplane actually left the ground even for a few inches, in which case it was called a flight.

It was expected that Captain Eyston, who had just lowered the land-speed record by attaining 312 m.p.h., would be present. He had not returned from America in time, however, but I had the pleasure of meeting him at a private luncheon shortly afterwards at the Countess of Gainsborough's home. At the same time I met Admiral Evans, "Evans of the *Broke*," who among his many achievements accompanied Captain Scott to the South Pole on his epic journey.

At the various functions I met many people famous in different walks of life. At the Savoy one night at a

BEING TELEVISED AT THE B.B.C. STUDIOS, ALEXANDRA PALACE

B.B.C. copyright photograph

TEA AT THE MANSION HOUSE WITH THE LORD MAYOR AND LADY TWYFORD
AND VISCOUNT WAKEFIELD

Photo Wide World Photos

charity dinner I had the pleasure of proposing the toast of Miss Gracie Fields, whose personality seemed just as strong and her humour equally infectious off the stage as on.

Shortly after my arrival at Croydon I had given two broadcasts, one to the Empire and the other on the famous "In Town To-night" programme, on which I had also broadcast after my flight back from Australia in 1935. A new experience for me was to be invited by the B.B.C. to take part in the television programme. Years before I had sat enthralled in a London theatre watching the Grand National being televised for the first time. Great strides have been made since those days, and when I visited the television studios at Alexandra Palace I was able to watch the film of my landing at Croydon being re-transmitted. Hearing that pastel shades are most suitable for television, I decided to wear my flying-coat, and before I went into the studio my face was made up with special preparation to eliminate all shadows. During the time I was being televised it was necessary for me to stand in front of a blinding light, which was so bright that it was not possible even to see the many technicians standing near the set. Every one at the studio was most helpful, and I thoroughly enjoyed the experience. Some time later I had the pleasure of being televised a second time.

One day I received an invitation from the Lord Mayor of London and Lady Twyford to tea at the Mansion House. Viscount Wakefield escorted me, and the afternoon proved to be a most enjoyable one. After

tea I was shown over the beautiful Mansion House by
the Lady Mayoress, who also took me to the giant
strong-room to see the wondrous array of gold plate. I
had already met the Lord Mayor and Lady Mayoress
at the City Livery Club banquet at the Guildhall,
where I also had the pleasure of meeting many of the
sheriffs and their ladies. It was at this dinner that I
first witnessed the ancient ceremony of passing round
the loving-cup.

Among the first telegrams of congratulation which
I had received on the completion of my flight was one
from Viscount Swinton, Minister for Air. Shortly after
my arrival I was invited to lunch at his home, where I
had on previous occasions enjoyed the charming hospitality of Viscountess Swinton.

A luncheon, which I greatly enjoyed, was given in
my honour by the British Sportsman's Club at the
Savoy. Lord Decies, whom I had met at several other
functions, presided, and many people famous in the
sporting world were present.

At a luncheon given by the Holborn Chamber of
Commerce I had the pleasure of renewing the acquaint-
ance of Sir Alan Cobham, whom I had met several
years previously, and on this occasion he proposed my
toast.

In the beautiful and ancient hall of the Merchant
Taylors a luncheon was given for me by the City
Livery Club. It was a great honour to be en-
tertained by the Livery Club, representative of all
the historic companies of London. The President,
Sir John Laurie, I had met at the Guildhall ban-

quet, and sitting at table near me were the High Commissioners of Australia and New Zealand, Mr Stanley Bruce and Mr Jordan. There were 350 people present at the luncheon, and when I responded to my toast I felt inspired by the beauty of the ancient hall, with its tall Gothic arches and great stone-flagged floor and high stained-glass windows. It was difficult to believe that we were in the heart of the City of London, and that just outside in Threadneedle Street the great business wheel of the Metropolis speeded on unceasingly.

One of the most interesting of all the functions was a reception given by the Parliamentary Air Committee in the House of Commons. This was a wonderful gesture, for it can surely fall to the lot of few women to attend a reception held in their honour amid such historic surroundings. At this reception I was received by Admiral Sueter, and the same evening was presented with the Gold Medal of the Royal Aero Club by Mr Lindsay Everard, M.P. After dinner I was shown round the building, and heard the discussion of proposed amendments to the Air Raid Precautions Bill.

I was invited by Air Vice-Marshal Baldwin to visit the Royal Air Force College at Cranwell and address the cadets. I looked forward to this visit and drove my car to Cranwell, where I was deeply impressed by the prevailing air of efficiency. My lecture was received with enthusiasm by the cadets, who crowded the great hall where I spoke. It was another memorable experience, and I regret that time did not permit me to see more of the college, but I enjoyed my brief visit and the hospitality I received as guest of Air Vice-Marshal Baldwin at his home.

My aeroplane, now veteran of three great flights, was exhibited in London and also in Liverpool. Arrangements were made for me to visit many towns in England and give short lectures on my various flights. I visited the majority of the large towns, and the tour proved most enjoyable and a great success. At each place I was greeted with tremendous enthusiasm, and so warm-hearted was each welcome that it was almost like a homecoming.

From my earliest childhood I had heard of Madame Tussaud's famous exhibition of historical wax models. Several times after my first year in England I had visited the exhibition and been intrigued to see the figures. Great was my delight when after my flight back to England in October 1937 I was asked by the directors to sit for a portrait model which they intended to place in the exhibition. Mr Bernard Tussaud himself made the model, and it was a relaxation for me to sit for it. In my home there was great interest when the figure was completed, for I happened to be the first New Zealand-born person to be included in Tussaud's collection. I received quite a shock when the model, dressed in my flying-kit, was placed in position. It looked so lifelike, waving from amid a most distinguished gathering including M. Blériot, Sir John Alcock and Sir Arthur Whitten Brown, Colonel Lindbergh, Squadron-Leader Hinkler, Sir Charles Kingsford Smith, Mr and Mrs

WITH "JEAN BATTEN" AT MADAME TUSSAUD'S
Photo Keystone

ARRIVAL AT STOCKHOLM
Photo Wide World Photos

Mollison, Miss Amelia Earhart, Sir Henry Segrave, and Sir Malcolm Campbell.

At this time Leopold, King of the Belgians, was paying a state visit to London. The day before he returned I received word that he wished to meet me, and was commanded to Buckingham Palace that afternoon. This was indeed an unexpected honour, and I looked forward to meeting King Leopold with the greatest pleasure.

After a reception given in my honour by the New Zealand Society I drove to Buckingham Palace. King Leopold was very much interested in aviation, and I was extremely surprised that he knew so much about my various flights and the countries over which I had flown. This was explained by the fact that he is himself a great traveller and deeply interested in aviation.

While I was at the palace I was overjoyed to receive an invitation to visit her Majesty Queen Elizabeth in her private apartment. The Queen was wonderfully charming, and with her sweet smile and gracious manner immediately put me at my ease when I was presented to her. Her Majesty was wearing a delphinium-blue gown and a magnificent necklace of pearls. I thought she looked very beautiful with her exquisite colouring and flawless complexion.

During the happy time I spent in her presence I met little Princess Elizabeth. She has a charm of her own, and with a delightful gesture brought her pet terrier into the room to show me.

As the door opened the Queen, who was sitting alongside me on the blue brocade settee, rose, and the next moment I was being presented to his Majesty King George VI. The King said that he had heard I was at the palace and wished to meet me. I was deeply impressed by his extensive knowledge of aviation and the interest he showed in my flights and the equipment used. Both the King and the Queen spoke with pleasure of their visit to New Zealand in 1926, when as the Duke and Duchess of York they endeared themselves to all New Zealanders during their tour of the Dominion.

In January 1938 I learned with great pleasure that the coveted Gold Medal of the Fédération Aéronautique Internationale had been awarded to me. This medal is perhaps the highest international award in the aviation world. I felt deeply honoured, especially so in view of the fact that representatives of twenty-two different nations had participated in the voting. Only eleven other aviators have received this gold medal. They are: General Pinedo, Sir Alan Cobham, Colonel Lindbergh, Squadron-Leader Hinkler, M. Dieudonné Costes, General Balbo, Dr. Eckener, Señor Juan de la Cierva, Mr Wiley Post, Mr C. W. A. Scott, and M. Jean Mermoz. This was the first time, therefore, that it had ever been awarded to an airwoman.

Shortly afterwards I received a letter from the British Council conveying an invitation for me to visit Stockholm and address a combined meeting of the Swedish-British Society and the Royal Aero Club of Sweden. The British Council were to make all arrangements for the visit, which was extended to enable me to visit

Gothenburg and Copenhagen as well. I was very pleased to have this opportunity of visiting Scandinavia, for in the summer I intended flying to some of the European countries which I had not before visited, and I looked forward to seeing the Scandinavian countries. I wished also to revisit Paris and see my many friends there. Being intensely patriotic I welcomed the opportunity of associating myself with the British Council, who, under the patronage of his Majesty the King, are doing great work in making the life, thought, and achievements of British people better known abroad, and thus strengthening international friendship and goodwill.

My visit to Sweden and Denmark proved a tremendous success, and I was accorded a wonderful welcome by the warm-hearted Scandinavian people. H.R.H. Prince Gustaf Adolf presided at my lecture in Stockholm, which was held in the large concert hall and received with great enthusiasm. At the conclusion I had the great honour of receiving from Prince Gustaf Adolf the Gold Medal of the Royal Swedish Aero Club.

Many functions were arranged in my honour, and a reception was held by the British Minister, Sir Edmund Monson. At a dance I had the pleasure of dancing with H.R.H. Prince Carl Juan, and greatly enjoyed all the functions which I attended. My visit to Scandinavia was really a revelation to me. I had always imagined that the countryside would be mantled in white and that the people would be reserved and phlegmatic. There was very little snow in Sweden, and the brilliant

sunshine which heralded my arrival continued throughout my stay.

The people proved to be wonderfully warm-hearted,
and I experienced the most lavish hospitality. It was
deeply gratifying to find that my lectures were so keenly
appreciated, and that nearly every one I met spoke
excellent English. As on my first visit to Paris, an
attempt was made to show me the sights of each
city within the space of a few days, and which to see
thoroughly would take some weeks. A welcome was
extended to me in the town hall in Stockholm, which
deeply impressed me with its dignity and majestic
beauty. At a luncheon at Skansen I was able to taste
the famous *smörgåsbord* and to learn to give the customary toast or skoal, which is performed with as much
seriousness as the loving-cup ceremony in England.

A new experience for me was ice yachting, and one
which I thoroughly enjoyed as the wind filled the sail
and the yacht, balanced on skids, speeded across the
frozen lake at great pace.

At the three towns which I visited, Stockholm, Gothenburg, and Copenhagen, I found fine aerodromes
equipped with every modern facility. In both Gothenburg, where I gave my lecture in the university hall,
and in Copenhagen I also experienced wonderful hospitality.

During my stay in Denmark I had the opportunity
of attending a performance of the Royal Danish Ballet,
about which I had heard so much. My lecture in Copenhagen was attended by H.R.H. Prince Axel, himself a
keen airman, whom I had the pleasure of meeting at

several other functions arranged in my honour, and also by Sir Patrick Ramsay, the British Minister. The Royal Danish Aeronautical Society presented me with their gold medal at the conclusion of my lecture.

Sightseeing tours were arranged in each place, and while in Denmark I was taken to Elsinore to see the castle where Hamlet is reputed to have lived, and on another occasion to see the lovely bronze statue of Hans Andersen's little mermaid. A photograph reproduced in the Press at the time bore the title of " The Airmaid and the Mermaid." I was very sorry that time did not permit me to visit Norway, but I decided to fly to Oslo at a later date, when I would also be able to pay a return visit to Sweden and Denmark.

During my various flights I have visited many different countries, and have had a unique opportunity of meeting peoples of a great many nationalities. My flights have taken me from the calm serenity of the English countryside over the pasture-lands of France, the mountains of Italy, the great snow-covered ranges of Greece, the length of the Mediterranean, over the mighty Lebanon Mountains and the Holy Land, the burning deserts of Syria and Iraq, the barren, rocky mountains of Persia, the deserts and rice-fields of India, the dense jungles of Bengal, Burma, and Siam, the great rubber plantations of Malaya, and along the island chain of the Dutch East Indies to Australia, and on across the big cattle stations of that vast continent, and still farther south across the icy wastes of the Tasman Sea, 1300 miles, to my own country, New Zealand. They have also taken me over sunny Spain and Morocco, the deserts of Mauritania and Senegal, to the scorching heat of West Africa, and across the immensity of the South Atlantic Ocean to the orchid-scented jungles of Brazil, and on again to the vast, rolling plains of Uruguay and Argentina. There have been times when vital decisions have had to be made in the fraction of a second—decisions that meant life or death, and that depended on a clear brain working in perfect co-ordination with a steady hand. There have been other times when the loneliness has been so intense that I have longed for the sound of a human voice or the sight of a ship, or even a tiny native village, to dispel the feeling of complete isolation that one feels when flying alone over the sparsely inhabited tracts that comprise such a great area of the earth's surface.

Every flyer who ventures across oceans to distant lands is a potential explorer; in his or her breast burns the same fire that urged the adventurers of old to set forth in their sailing-ships for foreign lands. Riding through the air on silver wings instead of sailing the seas with white wings, he must steer his own course, for the air is uncharted, and he must therefore explore for himself the strange eddies and currents of the ever-changing sky in its many moods.

PRINCIPAL FLIGHTS

1934. England–Australia solo flight (women's record): 10,500 miles in 14 days 22 hours 30 minutes.

1935. Australia–England solo flight: 17 days 15 hours. First woman to make return flight.

England–Brazil solo flight (world record): 5000 miles in 2 days 13 hours 15 minutes.

First woman to fly solo across South Atlantic Ocean and make England–South America flight.

1936. England–New Zealand solo flight (world record): 14,000 miles in 11 days 45 minutes.

First direct flight between England and New Zealand.

England–Australia solo flight (world record, established on same flight): 5 days 21 hours.

1937. Australia–England solo flight (world record): 5 days 18 hours 15 minutes.

First person to hold both England–Australia and Australia–England solo records at the same time.

HONOURS

1935. *Brazil:* Officer of the Order of the Southern Cross.

1936. *France:* Chevalier of the Legion of Honour.

Great Britain: Commander of the British Empire.

PRINCIPAL TROPHIES

1934. Challenge Trophy, awarded by Women's International Association of Aeronautics, U.S.A.

1935. Britannia Trophy, awarded by the Royal Aero Club for the most meritorious flight of the year by a British subject.

1935. Harmon International Trophy.

Johnston Memorial Air Navigation Trophy.

Challenge Trophy (U.S.A.).

1936. Britannia Trophy.

Segrave Trophy, awarded for the most outstanding demonstration of the possibilities of transport on land, sea, or in the air.

Harmon International Trophy.

Challenge Trophy (U.S.A.).

1937. Harmon International Trophy.

Coupe de Sibour.

GOLD MEDALS

Fédération Aéronautique Internationale.

Royal Aero Club of Great Britain.

Aéro-Club de France.

Royal Swedish Aero Club.

Académie des Sports.

Royal Danish Aeronautical Society.

Ligue Internationale des Aviateurs.